W9-ADN-799

Marvell's Pastoral Art

MARVELL'S
PASTORAL ART

Donald M. Friedman

UNIVERSITY OF CALIFORNIA PRESS
BERKELEY AND LOS ANGELES · 1970

UNIVERSITY OF CALIFORNIA PRESS
Berkeley and Los Angeles, California

Standard Book Number 520 01631 9
Library of Congress Catalog Card Number: 74–97356

Printed in Great Britain

Contents

Abbreviations of Full Titles of Periodicals

EC	Essays in Criticism
ELH	English Literary History
JHI	Journal of the History of Ideas
JWCI	Journal of the Warburg and Courtauld Institute
MLQ	Modern Language Quarterly
MP	Modern Philology
NQ	Notes and Queries
PMLA	Publications of the Modern Language Association
PQ	Philological Quarterly
RES	Review of English Studies
SP	Studies in Philology

Acknowledgements

Marvell's poetry, like Donne's, has attracted some of the most acute, learned, and sensitive critics of our century; and any writer who attempts yet once more to offer a reading of that poetry is bound most willingly to acknowledge, as I do now, his debt to the work of his predecessors. Some part of that debt is recorded in the citations, notes, and in comments in the text of this book. But such references are inadequate to express the value of suggestions that stimulate further thinking or listening, or of the internal dialogue one carries on with Marvell's commentators and explicators. The only appropriate way to express one's gratitude, however unsuccessfully, is to add to the continuing conversation.

The early stages of my work were overseen by Douglas Bush and Reuben Brower; I want here to thank them, as so many others have done, for providing models of what scholarship and the art of literary criticism can be. If I could have profited more from their examples, this would be a better book.

My friends and colleagues at Berkeley have continued my education; and for advice, criticism, and encouragement I thank Paul J. Alpers, Jonas A. Barish, Josephine Miles, Leonard Nathan, and Stephen K. Orgel. Theodore Guberman and Irene Smookler helped prepare the book for the press.

The Regents of the University of California provided a Summer Faculty Fellowship which enabled me to complete the manuscript. The staffs of the Harvard College Library, the Library of the University of California at Berkeley, the New York Public Library, and the Huntington Library deserve my thanks for their help.

I

An Idea of Pastoral

When T. S. Eliot first proposed 'a tough reasonableness beneath the slight lyric grace'[1] as the identifying characteristic of metaphysical wit, he probably did not intend his tentative and evocative phrase to be received as critical dogma. Indeed, the very attempt to describe an elusive quality of mind by pointing to the uneasy union between two dissimilar qualities of style does not promise very much in the way of useful definition. But the phrase held Eliot's familiar power to illuminate by suggestion, and it was grasped at as an aid to evaluation and analysis. Even F. R. Leavis commented approvingly on its 'pregnancy' and 'compression'.[2] Leavis noted, too, that although the phrase appeared initially in an essay on Andrew Marvell, its application was more properly to an entire body of poetry—what he called 'the line of wit'. Eliot's remarks on Marvell, in point of fact, are much less precise, much less confident in their identification of the components of his witty style. They speak of 'an equipoise, a balance and proportion of tones'; or, in a sentence whose involution barely hides the lack of a central, positive statement, wit is said to involve 'probably, a recognition, implicit in the expression of every experience, of other kinds of experience which are possible'.[3] Finally, with mild and honest diffidence, Eliot admits that 'the quality which Marvell had, this modest and certainly impersonal virtue—whether we call it wit or reason, or even urbanity—we have patently failed to define'.[4]

Curiously enough, this graceful admission of failure—almost like the Renaissance paradoxes on 'nothing' discussed by Rosalie Colie[5]—has generated the terms and the assumptions that have governed most Marvell criticism written in the last forty years. A recent and popular assessment of Marvell by A. Alvarez, for example, holds that the main element in his poetry is 'its balance, its pervading sense of intelligent proportion', and that its dominant impression is that of 'the mind detachedly at play over a number of possible choices'.[6] And no matter how widely we range through the critical spectrum we find that Marvell is 'the most coolly elusive of poets'[7] or that the 'unharmonized attitudes' of his poems are an index of his 'balanced, impersonal complexity of mind'.[8] It is inevitable, I suppose, that the language in which these critics try to praise a quality so difficult to single out and describe must suggest, if only faintly, some disapproval, some discontent, growing from their understandable bafflement. It is painful to frustrate the mind's drive toward certainty; and if the task of criticism is to describe comprehensibly and to evaluate, that task can be made maddeningly burdensome by confronting a poet whose distinctive trait is to elude description and evaluation.

The critical situation is complicated further by facts of history: the times Marvell lived through, and the course of his poetic career. For, as if to add another stage to this ziggurat of confusion, his poems move from the apparent Royalism of the complimentary verses to Lovelace and the elegy to Hastings,[9] through the moral and political complexities of the 'Horatian Ode' on Cromwell, to the unqualified admiration of the lines commemorating the first anniversary of the Protectorate and Cromwell's death. Not that this pattern was unusual in mid-seventeenth-century poetry; the winds of political doctrine blew strong, and no one has shown much concern with the weathervane tactics of Dryden's public poems, or of Waller's. Rather, it is precisely Marvell's obvious intelligence, the fine moral discrimination he exhibits in 'An Horatian Ode', pre-eminently, that has embarrassed his interpreters when trying to explain the alterations in his political allegiance.[10]

The puzzle finds yet another dimension in the analogous change in Marvell's poetic practice. It is well known that for most of his lyrics it is impossible to assign a date of composition;[11] it is equally well known that from the Restoration until his death in 1678, during the years of his service in Parliament as M.P. for Hull, Marvell wrote only social and political satires in rhymed couplets. In the main, they are as different from the lyrics in manner, subject, diction, and poetic technique as two groups of poems can conceivably be. Attempts to explain or to find a formula that will describe the change have been, in general, as unsuccessful as similar

2

attempts to rationalize his political career. Perhaps as a consequence Marvell has as often been called 'a poet of transition', as he has been labelled a poet of judgment, poise, or whatever term will suggest an uncommitted analytic mind. It is as if, even in the matter of poetic style, he had been unable or unwilling to mediate—in this case, between the conceited verse of the 1640s and the Augustan manner which, in some measure, he heralded in his satires. A fairly representative example of the kind of estimate of Marvell still commonly found is the following, by F. L. Lucas:

> Andrew Marvell stands on the frontier of two sharply severed periods, between the lyric dream that was dying and the common sense that was coming to birth, between John Donne and John Dryden, between the kingdom of poetry and the kingdom of prose.[12]

But in recent years this sort of 'neither one thing nor the other, but . . .' placing of Marvell has given place to the recognition that his relations to literary tradition are of a much more subtle kind. Rather than dwell on aspects of his verse which, in isolation, may seem to link it with one of the canonical 'styles' of the seventeenth century, or with the 'school' of Jonson, Donne, or even Pope,[13] criticism has turned to the examination of Marvell's remarkable responsiveness to poetic genres. George Williamson may have hinted at the possible fruitfulness of such an approach when he noted, in 1930, that:

> There are times when Marvell's poems seem distilled from the very air about him. This does not mean that he has not a distinctive talent of his own . . . but it does mean that his verse makes us conscious of the penetrating influence of a literary inheritance.[14]

And certainly the pervasive influence of Rosemond Tuve's *Elizabethan and Metaphysical Imagery*, while it revised our notions of the structure of metaphoric language in the Renaissance, did as much to restore the doctrine of literary 'kinds' to a prominent place in the critic's consideration of any seventeenth-century poem.[15] But it remained for Ruth Wallerstein to bring the relevance of these perceptions home to Marvell. In *Studies in Seventeenth-Century Poetic* she pointed out that he was 'highly conscious of form and genre in the design of his poems', and that his poetry 'gives clear evidence that he conceived his craft in terms of types in which each poem treatment of subject, mode of development, and expression have a common traditional character'.[16] Since the publication of Miss Wallerstein's book almost every critic writing on Marvell has paid attention to his treatment of genres; some, like Lawrence Hyman, Dennis Davison, and John Press,[17] have organized their essays primarily on this principle. Even so, the application of the principle to certain poems has given rise to debate over the genre to which they properly refer. Dennis Davison and Rosemond Tuve think of 'The Definition of Love' as belonging to a particular set of seventeenth-century poems that pretend to be 'definitions' of hopelessly abstract or complicated terms, while Frank Kermode denies not only that Marvell's poem belongs to the set, but also that the set exists.[18] 'Upon Appleton House' has been categorized as a 'country-house poem', a miniature epic, and as a vast Hermetic allegory of the history of mankind.[19] Professor Kermode has gone so far as to insist, in another essay, that 'The Garden' can be understood only as a conscious parody and criticism of contemporary *libertin* 'garden poems'; he calls Marvell's, thus, an 'anti-genre' poem.[20]

It appears, then, that to insist too closely on the detailed similarities between a poem by Marvell and its contemporary or traditional analogues is to court the same indecision from which the theories based on historical comparisons have suffered. But another appeal to the principle of genre is open, if we can broaden our notion of what is meant by a genre. Although it is no novelty to remark on the importance of pastoral poems and motifs in Marvell's *corpus*, the consideration of that importance has frequently been limited to formal and unmistakable instances, such as the pastoral *débat*, the pastoral love elegy, perhaps even the pastoral of the mental or Edenic garden. But it seems to me that all of Marvell's good poetry responds in some degree to the demands of the pastoral vision, considered as one of the major ways of literary thinking that the European mind has found and followed.[21] A brief way to make the point, one which will be pursued at length in this essay, is to point out that from Marvell's earliest known poems, through the achievements of the Nunappleton period until the assured political poems on Cromwell and the later, sardonic political satires, he draws on the vocabularies of natural description or natural mythology—the twin storehouses of pastoral diction—and almost always when he is seeking figures or metaphors to express

4

the values a particular poem is concerned to defend. That is, when he wants to suggest the graces of civilization that have been tarnished or lost through the violence of the Civil War, when he wants to embody poetically the beauties of innocence, of contemplative clarity, of the orderliness of the created world which both serves as a model for, and succumbs to, the power of human rationality, when he wishes, above all, to pay homage to the deep-rooted creativity of traditions and institutions which link man and the outside world in a fruitful harmony—whenever, in short, Marvell confronts one of the many themes in his poetry that require the just weighing of different but desirable forms of action or thought, his mind turns to the paradigm of such evaluative experience, the pastoral mode.

For example, the first English poem Marvell published, 'To his Noble Friend Mr Richard Lovelace, upon his Poems',[22] begins with a sketch of 'That candid Age' which preceded the embroilments of the 1640s, and the description conforms not only to a nostalgic Royalist's idea of Charles's reign but also to the innumerable classical pictures of the delights of the Golden Age, here conceived as a time of primitive social virtue.[23] About the same time Marvell contributed an elegy on the death of Lord Hastings to the volume, *Lachrymae Musarum*. Even at this early stage of his career his poem is clearly superior to the others in the collection (with the possible exception of Dryden's, which was *his* first published poem). But, more to the point, the best lines in the poem are those which differ from all the standard tropes and conceits that run through the mass of seventeenth-century elegies. Like the other poems in the Hastings volume they focus on the untimeliness of the young man's death at eighteen, on the eve of his marriage, but they find a source for grief in natural figures, in the sad destruction consequent upon interrupting the ordered processes of growth:

Go, intercept some Fountain in the Vein,
Whose Virgin-Source yet never steept the Plain. . . .
Go, stand betwixt the *Morning* and the *Flowers*;
And, ere they fall, arrest the early *Showers*.
Hastings is dead; and we, disconsolate,
With early *Tears* must mourn his early *Fate*.

(ll. 1–2 & 5–8)[24]

The use of pastoral figures in 'Clorinda and Damon', 'A Dialogue between Thyrsis and Dorinda', 'The Picture of little T. C. in a Prospect of Flowers', 'The Gallery', the 'Mower' poems, 'The Garden', and 'Upon Appleton House' hardly needs surveying; but I am concerned to show that not only the opening lines of 'An Horatian Ode', but the metaphor of the circling years in 'The First Anniversary of the Government under O. C.', and the description of the heroic death of young Douglas in 'The last Instructions to a Painter'[25] are equally dependent upon the pastoral mode of analogy and emblem, and on Marvell's particular interpretation of the potential uses of that mode.

It should be clear that I am not limiting the meaning of 'pastoral' to the received definitions, and some explanation is needed at this point. Pastoral is one of the literary genres or kinds recognized by Western critical theory since its beginnings. Although its place in the hierarchy of poetic forms never entitled it to the profound and comprehensive theoretic consideration given to epic and tragedy, it earned a paradoxical sort of eminence as the decreed starting-place for the aspiring poet. It found no place in Aristotle, was barely touched on by Horace and Quintilian, and, in brief, was defined in classical antiquity primarily by being written rather than by being theorized about. Nevertheless, the example of Virgil's career and his scrupulous adherence to the principles of stylistic decorum acted so compellingly on medieval and Renaissance critics that what had once been *praxis* changed slowly into dogma, so that the *rota Virgilii* established clearly and definitively not only the diction appropriate to the pastoral poem, but the time of life when it was best written, and also its precise emblematic settings and subjects, down to the level of a tree, an instrument, a place.[26] At all times during its varied and perdurable career pastoral was associated with the low or mean style, presumably because it was thought to maintain a decorous relationship with its rustic speakers and scenes. But from the time of the *Idylls* of Theocritus the allegorical potentialities in the pastoral manner were apparent; his successors, Bion and Moschus, developed this strain, but were surpassed by Virgil in his subtle and wide-ranging exploration of the uses of Arcadian backgrounds and literate swains to speak to the questions of political excellence, of the nature and value of poetry, of the realities of love.[27] For Renaissance theorists the work of Mantuan was of almost equal importance in revealing the power of indirect pastoral allegory to criticize and comment on matters of ecclesiastical polity

6

and the abuses of the pastorate. All of these are in the mind of Spenser's commentator 'E.K.' when he says, in the *Epistle* to Harvey that introduces the 'new poet' of *The Shepheardes Calender*, that the pastoral disguise is meant to 'unfold great matter of argument covertly';[28] and Puttenham makes the same point in *The Arte of English Poesie* when he denies that pastoral was the earliest form of poetry because

> ... the Poet devised the *Eglogue* long after the other *drammatick* poems, not of purpose to counterfait or represent the rusticall manner of loves and communication, but under the vaile of homely persons and in rude speeches to insinuate and glaunce at greater matters. . . .[29]

Pastoral, then, was understood and discussed almost from its putative beginnings in two major ways: it was thought of as a device to allow the poet to speak about political or literary problems from within a conventional disguise; and it was described as a literary form with particularized qualities of style, diction, and subject. It was rarely limited to specific verse forms—the origins of the eclogue were debated, but received Renaissance theory held that the name signified merely a rough collection of the genre itself. Nor was it limited or prescribed as to its subjects; shepherds talked about the pains of fruitless love, and their talk could also 'glaunce' at weightier concerns; but no critic would have thought to speculate on what pastorals should be about, as he thought about the nature of a tragic action or the proper didactic purpose of an epic poem. Nor is this surprising; English Renaissance criticism, as it learned from and developed out of the sixteenth-century Italian schools, was predominantly rhetorical, concerned with stylistic classification and the outlining of governing principles of decorum. But modern criticism, particularly under the impetus of Empson's pioneering work, *Some Versions of Pastoral*,[30] has done much to illuminate the developing tradition of pastoral,[31] as well as to open up the possibilities of its relevance to major intellectual, theological, and literary themes. If we understand pastoral as a mode, literally as a way of interpreting experience, a measure of ordering that experience and giving it conspicuous artistic form, then the limitations of the genre viewed narrowly as a rhetorical specimen fall away, and lead us to a position from which Marvell's uses of pastoral can be seen in their full richness of implication.

To begin with, Marvell's poems rarely sound like the 'decorated' pastoral lyrics epitomized by the collection in *England's Helicon* of 1600. With their detailed descriptions of natural pleasances, their iterated love-plaints, their endlessly articulate swains and coyly fleeing nymphs and shepherdesses, these constitute the type of the artificial 'Elizabethan' pastoral whose unaccountable popularity at the end of the sixteenth century dwindled rapidly into cliché and parody. Marvell may make use of some of the familiar stage properties, like the cave and the fountain in 'Clorinda and Damon'; but he forces them to serve as symbols, often by placing them in a spare context, isolating and highlighting them. In the same manner, the speeches of his shepherds and shepherdesses do not so much imitate conventional accents as 'refer' to them, questioning and exploring the assumptions that underlie standard phrases and tropes. Marvell's relation to the Spenserian tradition would seem to be of the same character. Whether we consider the Eclogues of *The Shepheardes Calender*, or the pastoral interlude in Book VI of *The Faerie Queene*, we cannot mistake Spenser's profound appreciation of Virgil's sense of pastoral allegory. Indeed, *The Shepheardes Calender* touches many of the issues raised in the *Bucolica*, particularly the place of poetry in civilization and the state, the disrupting consequences of passionate love, and the responsibilities and peculiar talents of the poet. It cannot be fortuitous that Spenser chose a pastoral *persona* through which to utter the first poems of his public career, that the *persona* speaks for him in a major poem of social and cultural criticism, *Colin Clouts Come Home Againe*, or that he makes his last appearance in that unfathomable scene on Mount Acidale, piping to the dancing Graces, a scene that intimates the perfection of artistic stasis and creative movement, a scene that is destroyed by the intrusion of Spenser's own creation, his knight of courtesy, Calidore. Although Marvell, I think, learned much from Spenser[32] (especially in the matter of shaping an expressive emblem whose surface was as smooth and engaging as its meaning was complex), nevertheless, he did not follow him in the traditional identification of shepherd and poet; not, at least, to the extent of speaking through the pastoral mask for himself or about the art of poetry. Marvell is unique among the major lyric poets of the English Renaissance in referring very infrequently to his own art, its problems, rewards, and purposes; and this is conspicuously true in his pastoral poems, where the tradition invited, almost required, this specific allegorical dimension to be added to every mention of the shepherd. In rejecting the freely available symbol of shepherd as poet, he also denied himself another level of resonance in the figure, that of the shepherd as pastor of the Christian flock. The two interpretations had been so completely interfused by centuries of allegorical readings of Scripture that it took more effort for a Renaissance poet to separate them in his reader's mind than it did to impress his reader with the double significance of the role of his pastoral protagonist.[33] Much of the brilliance and power of the design of 'Lycidas' is Milton's response to the need to explore both kinds of pastorate fully before they are allowed to come together in the poem's final passage.[34] That Marvell is not, finally, interested in renovating either part of this joint tradition is suggested in another way by his turning to the figure of the Mower in a group of four poems which are fully involved in pastoral subject and diction.

We have seen that Marvell exhibits throughout his career a careful, almost professional, interest in the characteristics and potentialities of verse forms and poetic genres. Yet, if 'The Match', 'Mourning', 'Daphnis and Chloe', and 'The unfortunate Lover' are all comments on modish *vers de société*;[35] and if 'Upon Appleton House', by the same token, is at the same time both an example and a critique of the 'country house poem',[36] it seems all the more remarkable that Marvell's pastoral poems diverge with such apparent deliberateness from their inherited models. Furthermore, the recurrence of pastoral motifs in poems clearly allied to other genres—the shepherdess's 'towers' in the devotional poem, 'The Coronet'; the figure of the shepherdess at the centre of that ironic courtly compliment, 'The Gallery'; the analogies drawn from the image of Eden and the primitive world scattered through 'The First Anniversary of the Government under O.C.'—all these suggest that Marvell thought of the possible subjects for pastoral as encompassing much more of human experience than prior examples of the genre allowed for. Any assessment of the scope of his idea of pastoral must begin with the recognition that, for the Renaissance, the involvement of the classical pastoral with theories, historical or mythical, about a Golden Age was coloured by the belief in the typological coincidence of that primitive era of natural harmony with the Christian notions of prelapsarian life in Eden, of the nature of man as first created, and of the consequences for both man and nature of sin and the Fall.[37] Centuries of allegorical interpretation of Genesis and Canticles had dwelt on these problems, and the syncretistic impulse of both Hellenistic and Florentine neoplatonism had reinforced the notion that pagan poets and philosophers had been granted a sight of the one truth that reveals itself fitfully through moments of human history. The example of Virgil's Fourth, or 'Messianic', Eclogue sanctioned the belief that poetic inspiration could forecast the truths of Revelation; and the medieval *Ovide moralisé* showed, again, how the most unlikely material, if properly interpreted, could be absorbed into the current of the providential theory of history. St Jerome's famous rereading of the passionate eroticism of The Song of Songs as an allegory of the love of Christ and His Church demonstrated the technique that was to dominate medieval and Renaissance explications of both Scripture and secular literature; and by this token the visions of a primitive perfection found in the works of Hesiod, Homer and Ovid were viewed as intimations, blurred but essentially correct, of the state of man and the created universe at the end of the six days of Creation.

The terms of the two descriptions, classical and biblical, differed, to be sure, in details and in emphasis. Classical literary accounts of the Golden Age focused on the concept of *otium*, the ease and peacefulness of the era when man and the natural world existed in undisturbed sympathy. This ease was made possible by the spontaneous bounty of fertile nature, which fed and nurtured its human denizens out of a flowing spring of creativity. Nature took no thought, and man was not distinguished from other forms of life that fed and rested on the earth. But the state of symbiosis depended on man's passive acceptance of his undifferentiated existence. The quality of life in the Golden Age is most often characterized by the absence of law, coercion, ambition, external restrictions, or appetitive acts that take from one man to enrich another—in other words, the absence of all those activities that comprise *negotium*, business, the denial of ease and placidity. In Ovid's retelling of the myth, the falling away from perfection proceeded as a natural development, as the Silver and Bronze Ages followed the Golden. The seasons appeared, became harsher, and man began to sail the oceans in pursuit of commerce and to violate the earth by digging for gold.[38] In Hesiod and in Virgil's 'Messianic' Eclogue the advent of human ambition and the lust for wealth is responsible for moral and physical decay, and for the disappearance of the harmonious Age of Gold. Clearly, the Christian equivalent of the pagan sin of greed is Adam's disobedience; whether it is attributed to *libido sciendi*, or to the same restless discontent that overwhelmed Satan and the rebel angels, or to the submission of natural reason to the demands of erotic passion, it corresponds to the classical story in that it marks the dawn of human consciousness. That is, in each case man chooses to act in a way that destroys a preordained harmony, and in each case the myth accounts for the origin of human experience as we know it in the fallen, or iron world.

The major difference, of course, between the two accounts of lost perfection lies in the understanding of man's nature and his position in the created universe. The classical poets write of man as a part of *natura naturans*, as simply another creature, albeit a creature with the latent power to disrupt the orderly processes of nature. But Christian doctrine holds that man is a unique creation, mediating between angelic intelligence and the level of sensitive intelligence appropriate to other animals.[39] Furthermore, his position makes him not only subordinate to God but superior to the natural creation below him, and therefore responsible for it.[40] The nature of that responsibility raised difficult questions for the commentators on Genesis, since they had to decide whether the world, and particularly the earthly Paradise, was made for man's enjoyment, or whether it had been given to him to command and protect, as an earnest of his role as God's vice-regent within the created order. Tangential problems vexed the Fathers and the scholiasts as well, such as the precise location of Adam's creation. The texts of Genesis 1 and 2 are ambiguous; they give two accounts of the forming of Adam, and the second says that God 'put' man in the garden He had made. The point of debate was whether Adam had been formed within Paradise, and therefore shared its perfection, or whether he had been placed in it after his creation, as a sign that he was made of the same dust as the world outside Eden, and so was merely a guest whose tenancy was contingent upon his behaviour and conformity to the divine will.

But within the tradition of hexæmeral commentaries there was almost complete agreement in interpreting Genesis 2: 19–20; Adam's naming of the animals was taken as a sign not only of his delegated sovereignty over the creatures of Paradise, but also as the outward symbol of the intuitive wisdom with which he had been endowed. The power of 'naming' was equivalent to the ability to perceive essences without resorting to rational inquiry or experiment;[41] and the 'name' itself was invested, by both medieval and Renaissance thinkers, with a quasi-mystical significance. Thus the very existence of the sciences of logic and natural philosophy was understood as evidence of the decline of man's intellectual powers after the Fall. What classical antiquity had pictured as man's violation of the nurturing sanctity of his relations with surrounding nature in the Golden Age, Christianity interpreted as the rupture of a covenant of responsibility and obedience to God, and a loss of intuitive knowledge of the order of creation.

The general correspondence we have noted between the literary myth of a primitive Golden Age and the Christian vision of pre-lapsarian Eden can be documented more precisely with regard to their component elements. The most important of these is probably the figure of the garden, the setting that lies at the heart of the myth, the scene in which takes place the drama of the birth of the mind. The list of classical gardens that represented a place of natural perfection long lost or long sought-after includes the Garden of the Hesperides, the garden of the palace of King Alcinous in Homer's *Odyssey*, and others catalogued in Book IV of *Paradise Lost*; and Milton's purpose in comparing them to Eden is to show how the primal Christian garden surpasses them all in beauty, and provides an archetypal model for all subsequent literary and spiritual gardens. The traditional interpretations of Canticles, again, created a store-house of emblems and metaphors which could be applied to real and imaginary gardens; each was to be seen as a version, however inadequate, of the protected and ultimately beautiful *locus amoenus* in which Christ woos the beloved spirit.[42] And within this large metaphoric identification of the garden of Canticles with the devout spirit there developed the narrower, but widely influential, tradition of the *hortus conclusus*, the enclosed garden as a symbol of the Virgin, the contemplative retreat wherein was fostered the quest for spiritual purity and the wisdom lost through Adam's sin. D. C. Allen, speaking of 'The Nymph complaining for the death of her Faun', but referring as well to 'The Garden', says succinctly that 'the garden is a classical equivalent of the mind', and cites passages from Plato, Pindar, Epicurus, Cicero, and Seneca in substantiation.[43] And the continuity of the classical *figura mentis* with the Christian interpretation is suggested by G. H. Williams in a recent work on the history of the concepts of the wilderness and the Garden of Eden:

> . . . the pleasance (*locus amoenus*) with its background in pagan literature supplemented by the image of the nuptial garden enclosed in Canticles played itself out over against and intermingled with the more strictly religious garden (*hortus caelestium deliciarum*).[44]

Nor was the symbolic power of the garden limited to the mind itself; scriptural allegorists, pre-eminently Gregory of Nyssa and Origen, devote much ingenuity to establishing the correspondence between the meaning of the Garden of Eden and the description of man's complex nature.[45]

As part of the Book of Nature, then, the garden was variously interpreted as an emblem of a legendary time when man and the created world existed in unexamined harmony, or as a figure for the spiritual perfection to be sought for in the contemplative life, and to be found in a reunion with Christ that would erase the marks of mental decay that resulted from the Fall. It is my contention that this multiplex garden figure is the generative source of Marvell's idea of pastoral, that its implications govern the many poems that drew their unique richness from pastoral conventions, no matter what these poems may seem to owe to different or more easily available genres. Further, although Marvell is as concerned as Milton is, as concerned as any Christian must be, 'to repair the ruins of our first parents by regaining to know God aright',[46] he does not have Milton's faith in the power of education (that is, the power of man's instructed will) to achieve once more Adam's prelapsarian wisdom. Marvell has no programme that promises such results. Rather, his lyrics are scrupulous contemplations of the relationships between man and nature, between soul and body, between mind and matter, between the knower and the known—relationships that have been altered from their once perfectly harmonious state, and which we now experience as fallen men, encumbered by fallible senses, a scarred and crippled rationality, and, most poignantly, by a dim spiritual insight, a lingering memory or a faint intimation of the harmonious knowledge now lost. Edward Tayler puts the point well when he says that: 'Marvell sees the Fall primarily as a change that occurred in the mind of man, as a change in the way man looks at or thinks about Nature . . . .'[47]

Just as Milton, in *Paradise Lost*, confronts the problem of speaking of ultimate Christian truths in a language made necessary solely by man's fallen state, so Marvell confronts the world of his poems from within the poet's mind. His pastoral poems trace the difficulties encountered by that mind in trying to cross the barriers set up by consciousness between it and the world it would be united with. Sometimes, as in 'The Garden', the poem itself acts out the struggle of the mind to cross or erase that barrier. But for the most part Marvell conforms to the kind of description of him we discussed earlier; the poems examine without judging, weigh without deciding; above all, they *present* the consequences of the Fall through tropes and subjects that embody those consequences in the most expressive and compelling way—through pastoral.

II

The inherent figural capacity of the pastoral mode to encompass the great question of man's relation to the created order is not strictly the result of literary genetics. What Tayler calls 'the central tenet of pastoral verse, the idyllic correspondence between man and Nature known as the pathetic fallacy',[48] is clearly one expressive form of the cosmology that dominated Western thought until Marvell's time, the cosmology which, in various versions and subject to innumerable qualifications and adjustments, helped to establish a firm continuity between classical antiquity and Christian philosophy;[49] perhaps more accurately, it is an expression of that part of the cosmology which focused on man as a microcosmic model of the macrocosmic universe. The metaphysics of correspondence[50] drew sustenance from sources as diverse as the theory of physical elements;[51] the parallel theory of humours, in matter and in man; astrological influences and their role in determining personality;[52] and even the analogy between the creative imagination and the divine act of creation itself.[53] This 'idyllic correspondence', then, was not simply a cry of nostalgia or a sentimental defence against harsh and chaotic reality; it represented a vision of basic and underlying harmony, made discordant by man's sinfulness, but open to rediscovery and re-establishment. The theological debate centred on the need for intervening grace to accomplish the re-establishment; Catholic doctrine held that man's faculties could not succeed unaided, while the distinctive note of Protestant thinking on this subject was a measured confidence in the ability of corrupt

human reason to reconquer a considerable extent of the lost realm.[54]
But among theologians of all persuasions the disagreement seemed
to focus on the degree of difficulty to be expected, not on the
inevitability of success or failure. No one suggested that reason
alone could attain the certitude or insight granted to the spirit
inspired by faith and illuminated by grace. Moreover, many felt
that to ask it to do so would be to ask the human intellect to
transcend itself. It was by no means certain that prelapsarian man
had been endowed with knowledge beyond the grasp of senses
functioning perfectly and a clear and healthy reason; if he had
not, then it was conceivable that by education, in Milton's sense,
and by the effort of his regenerate will, that state of knowledge
could once again be approached. Within the Protestant community there was substantial agreement on this point. John Salkeld,
an alleged Roman Catholic converted to the Anglican communion under James I, says in his *A Treatise of Paradise*, that man
'may ascend unto God' by studying the creation and by 'reflecting
upon himselfe'.[55] At the other end of the doctrinal spectrum, the
Puritan William Perkins, in trying to account for the decline of
human rationality without denying the possibility of its restoration,
explains that 'sinne is not a corruption of mans substance, but onely
of faculties; otherwise neither could mens soules bee immortall,
nor Christ take upon him mans nature'.[56] But the voice of the firm
centre of Anglican thought can be heard in the works of Edward
Reynolds who, at the end of his lengthy *A Treatise of the Passions
and Faculties of the Soule of Man*,[57] turns from the familiar anatomy
of mental faculties and the sources and effects of 'perturbations'
to a consideration of the present state, the past history and the
probable future of the rational faculty in man. At first he is
concerned to read the signs of our past dignities.

The top and highest pitch of Nature toucheth the hemme
and lowest of Grace. We have in us the Testimonies, though
not the Goodnesse of our first estate; the Ruines of a Temple
to be lamented, though not the holy Places thereof to be
Inhabited. It is true indeed those great endowments of the
most severe and illightned Heathen, were indeed but glorious
miseries and withered Vertues, in that they proceeded from
a depraved Nature, and aymed at sinister and false ends: yet
withall both the corruption of them proves their praecedent

losse (which also the Heathen themselves spied in their distinction of Ages into Golden and Iron times:) And likewise the pursuit and practice of them (though weak, imperfect, corrupt) imply manifestly that there was much more an Originall Aspiring of Nature in her perfection to be like her Maker in an absolute and universall Purity. Now in this Rectitude and Perfect Regularity of the Soule in the divine Habit of Originall Justice did man most eminently beare the Image and Signature of God on him. And therefore notwithstanding we continue still Immortall, Spirituall, Reasonable; yet we are said to have defaced that Image in us by our hereditary Pollution. And hee always recovereth most thereof, who in the greatest measure repaireth the ruines, and vindicateth the Lapses of his decayed estate, unto that prime Originall Purity, wherein he was Created. (pp. 441–442)

Reynolds, a little further on in this discussion, attempts to justify both his suggestion that the reality of the prelapsarian state is hinted at even in the corruption of pagan tales, and his confidence in man's ability to restore that state, by sketching the body of knowledge from which we have fallen.

God made all things *exceeding Good*, and Perfect; and therefore the perfection naturally belonging unto the Soule of Man, was doubtlesse given unto it, in its first Creation. Hee made Man *right* and straight; and the Rectitude of the Minde is in *Knowledge* and light. . . . Without Knowledge hee could not have given fit Names, and suteable to the Natures of all the Creatures which for that purpose were brought unto him. Hee could not have awed and governed so various, and so strong Creatures, to preserve Peace, Order, and Beauty amonst them. . . . *Experimentall Knowledge* hee had not but by the Exercise of his Originall light upon particular Objects, as they should occurre. Knowledge of *future Events* hee had not, it being not Naturall, nor Investigatable by imbred light, but Propheticall, and therefore not seene till Revealed. *Secret Knowledge* of the Thoughts of Men, or of the Counsells of God hee could not have, because *secret things belong unto the Lord*. But so much light of *Divine Knowledge* as should fit him to have Communion with *God*, and to serve him, and obtaine a blessed life; so much of *Morall Knowledge* as should

16

fit him to converse in Love as a Neighbour, in Wisedome as a Father, with other men; so much of *Naturall Knowledge* as should dispose him for the Admiring of Gods Glory, and for the Governing of other Creatures over which hee had received Dominion; so much wee may not without notable injurie to the perfection of Gods Workmanship, and to the Beauty and rectitude of our first Parent, deny to have beene conferred upon our Nature in him. (pp. 457–458)

The kinds of knowledge attributable to Adam are carefully listed; but Reynolds' point is rather to show the inborn purpose of each kind, the moral and devotional end implicit for him in all knowing. In Book VIII of *Paradise Lost* Raphael warns Adam against unrestrained speculation particularly in astronomical matters, but Milton's attitude toward the proper limits of intellectual inquiry can be paralleled in any number of mid-century writings: in some it appears as a kind of anti-intellectual fideism; in *Paradise Lost* itself it serves as a guide to the basic forms of moral behaviour required to preserve natural order; in Bacon, for another example, it allows the experimental natural philosopher to hurry off eagerly to observe phenomena, content to leave questions of value and of eschatology to the mystical realms of faith.

But such solutions left untouched problems which came increasingly to absorb seventeenth–century thinkers, problems concerned not only with the composition of the physical universe and the movements of the heavenly bodies, but more intimately with the precise nature of the act of knowing, with that seemingly impenetrable barrier that divided the material thing known (the object) from the incorporeal, perhaps spiritual, knower (the subject) —the mind of man. Not a small part of the intensity with which this question was pursued derived from its relevance to the doctrine of Christian incarnation; what can be seen as the informing miracle of the Christian faith is endlessly repeated, *in petto*, whenever the mind commands the responses of the body, whenever the pains of the flesh blur the clarity of the intellect, whenever the line is crossed between flesh and spirit, matter and mind. But even if it had not been infused with this powerful symbolic influence the problem of how the mind knows anything would have drawn the attention of poets and philosophers; for as the traditional analogical systems were challenged, and as each, in some measure, was found to be faulty as an explanation of the architectonics of the universe, the thoughtful man was impelled to devise more refined explanations. The result was not always, or even frequently, giddy despair nor wholesale dismissal of the system whose inadequacy had just been discovered. The passage in 'An Anatomy of the World: The first Anniversary', in which Donne speaks of 'new Philosophy' which 'calls all in doubt', is most often cited to illustrate his alleged belief that the recent astronomical theories of Copernicus, Kepler, and Galileo had destroyed the orderly patterns of the Ptolemaic universe, and (as if one touch of experimental science were sufficient to dissolve the conceptual ties of the Christian cosmos), had shattered the delicate web of human social structures, and emptied all symbols of their meaning. Such an interpretation makes of Donne a slightly hysterical version of Godfrey Goodman, whose apocalyptic vision of the decay of the world is so grimly celebrated in *The Fall of Man* (1616). It also contradicts much of what we know of Donne's thinking on the question of whether the visible universe is gradually declining in vigour; and, perhaps more important, the interpretation falsifies the major strategy of the poem and the local importance of the mention of 'new Philosophy'. In brief, Donne uses the new astronomy as an example, a symptom, of the decay of the entire created universe which he attributes to the loss of Elizabeth Drury, whom the poet feigns as the informing spirit of the world during her short lifetime. Thus contemporary natural philosophy is typical of the disorder, the random, meaningless activity, that characterizes the twitching corpse of the world since Elizabeth's death. These are the same astronomers of whom Donne says, within a few lines:

For of Meridians, and Parallels,
Man hath weav'd out a net, and this net throwne
Upon the Heavens, and now they are his owne.
Loth to goe up the hill, or labour thus
To goe to heaven, we make heaven come to us.

(ll. 278–282)

There is neither admiration for the new science here, nor fear of its conquests; Donne's position is consistent throughout the two 'Anniversaries'; the world is moribund, and all man's pride in his intellectual achievements is utterly vain; true knowledge is gained only by the soul's flight to its heavenly home. There is nothing

surprising in Donne's composing a major poem on the theme of
contemptus mundi; what is surprising and revealing about the
preoccupations of the early seventeenth century, is that a great
part of the poems' illustrative material is drawn from learned and
popular science, and that the poems as wholes are so thoroughly
concerned with the nature of truth and the problems of knowing.[58]

The profound paradoxes at the heart of any Christian epistemology had been operative since Adam was first commanded not to
eat of the fruit of the Tree of the Knowledge of Good and Evil; if
man's distinctive faculty is a rational power only slightly inferior
to the pure angelic intelligence, how then is it to be limited in
scope, and how is it to perform its operations when hindered by
the bonds of the flesh? Within the comparatively brief span of the
English Renaissance, attitudes toward the desire to know changed
radically, and not always because of theological strictures. The aura
of the *libido sciendi* in Marlowe's Faustus burns through the damnation of his inflexible will; but as the century turns we find that
the sheer appetite to know is tempered by a restless desire to understand what 'knowing' is. The process itself becomes for a period
more interesting than its products, and the moral and religious
dimensions of human knowledge are resolved into the purely
epistemological. Once again Reynolds can help us to understand
the viewpoint of the informed centre, from which the genius of
Marlowe or Bacon, or even Milton, can be seen only as aberrant:

> ... for albeit, the fall and corruption of Nature hath darkned his
> eyes, so that hee is enclined to worke Confusedly, or to walk as
> in a Maze, without Method or Order (as in a Storme the Guide
> of a Vessell is oftentimes to seek of his Art, and forced to yeeld
> to the windes and waves) yet certaine it is that in the minde of
> Man there still remaines a Pilot, or Light of Nature; many
> Principles of Practicall prudence, whereby (though for their
> faintings a man do's often miscarry and walke awry) the course
> of our Actions may be directed with successe and issue unto
> Civill and Honest ends. And this is evident, not only by the
> continuall practise of Grave and Wise men, in all States, Times,
> and Nations; but also by those sundry learned and judicious
> Precepts, which Historians, Politicians, and Philosophers have
> by their naturall Reason and Observation framed for the
> compassing of a Mans just ends, and also for Prevention and

disappointment of such inconveniences as may hinder them.

Lastly, for the Attribute of Knowledge, It was doubtlesse after a most eminent manner at first infused into the Heart of Man, when hee was able by Intuition of the Creatures to give unto them all Names, according to their severall Properties and Natures; and in them to shew himselfe, as well a Philosopher, as a Lord. *Hee filled them*, sayth *Siracides*, *with the Knowledge of Understanding*. And herein, if wee will beleeve *Aristotle*, the Soule is most neerely like unto *God*, whose infinite Delight is the Eternall Knowledge and Contemplation of himselfe, and his Works. Hereby, saith hee, the Soule of man is made most Beloved of God, and his minde, which is Allied unto God, is it selfe Divine, and, of all other parts of Man, most Divine, And this made the Serpent use that Insinuation only, as most likely to prevaile, for compassing that Cursed and miserable project of Mans ruine. By meanes of which Fall, though Man blinded his understanding and robd himselfe of this, as of all other blessed habits, I meane of those excellent Degrees thereof, which he then enjoyed: yet still the Desire remains Vast and impatient, and the pursuit so violent, that it proves often praejudiciall to the estate both of the Body and Minde. So that it is as true now, as ever, that Man is by Nature a Curious and inquiring Creature, of an Active and restlesse Spirit, which is never quiet, except in Motion, winding it selfe into all the Pathes of Nature; and continually traversing the World of Knowledge.[59]

Thus, just as the Fall has left man with some faint signs of his original moral excellence—what Donne called 'a glimmering light, A faint weake love of vertue';[60] what the Cambridge Platonists called 'the candle of the Lord'—so has his original intellectual preeminence left its lingering mark on his present powers of mind. And the use of those powers is enjoined upon man by God; Henry Reynolds, in *Mythomystes* (1632), refers to a familiar Pauline text, and explains the two-fold necessity for unremitting exercise of man's faculties.

Wee live in a myste, blind and benighted; and since our first fathers disobedience poysoned himselfe and his posterity, Man is become the imperfectest and most deficient Animall of all the field; for then he lost that Instinct that the Beast retaines;

though with him the beast, and with it the whole vegetable and generall Terrene nature also suffered, and still groanes under the losse of their first purity, occasioned by his fall. What concernes him now so neerely as to attend to the cultivating or refining, and thereby advancing of his rationall part, to the purchase and regaining of his first lost felicity? And what meanes to conduce to this purchase can there bee, but the knowledge first, and love next (for none can love but what hee first knowes) of his Maker, for whose love and service he was only made? . . . by two meanes only: the one, by laying his burden on him that on his Crosse bore the burthen of all our defectes, and interpositions betweene us and the hope of the vision of his blessed Essence face to face heereafter; and the other, by carefull search of him here in this life (according to Saint *Paules* instruction) in his works [Romans, I, 20]; who telles us, *those invisible things of God are cleerely seene, being understood by the things that are made*, or by the workes of his blessed hands?[61]

Reynolds does not point out that St Paul is inveighing against the 'unrighteous' who have failed to heed the lesson of 'the things that are made', and who have sinned most grievously because they 'worshipped and served the creature more than the Creator' (Romans, I, 25). But the great danger in the Book of Nature has always been its power to attract admiration for its beauties, admiration that should flow properly toward the Book's author.[62] Nor was the danger much modified by the ambivalence within Christianity's attitude toward created nature. In one sense the world was celebrated as God's handiwork, one form of revealing Scripture, the bounteous creation given to man to enjoy and rule; in another view it was man's earthy prison, clog to his soul and deceptive, alluring temptress of his fallible senses, corrupted judgment, and weakened will.

Nor was this inner contradiction eased by the intermingling of Renaissance neoplatonic doctrines with orthodox Christianity. Plato's division between the realm of the Ideas and the world was drawn according to a scale of metaphysical reality; but in the thought of Plotinus and his followers—Porphyry, Iamblichus, Proclus—the dichotomy was made to bear moral weight, and the world of matter was defined not as a shadowy imitation of ultimate reality but as base, passive, inert, evil—as actively opposed to, not simply lesser than, intellectual good. Nevertheless, even Plotinian cosmology provided a theory of redemption; in this case, matter was rendered intelligible by its relation to mind, its passivity serving as a field of contemplation and offering a reflective image to the emanations of Intelligence.

> ... the soul cannot be entirely dragged down ... she administers the universe by the contemplation of the intelligible world .... What she receives from above she communicates to the sense world as she herself is always illuminated from above.[63]

And in the Hermetic philosophy received by Italian and English neoplatonists of the sixteenth and seventeenth centuries the account of the creation of the physical universe not only depended heavily on this notion of matter's subjection to mind, but it also introduced the erotic note that was to dominate so much of the work of Ficino's Florentine Academy.

> During the first stage in his development man was mind only, like God. However, soon after his creation man penetrated downwards through the seven planetary spheres until he reached the earth. There he sees reflected 'the fair and beautiful Shape or Form of God' and falls in love with it. This reflection is that of his own mind, which is immortal and divine and part of God. On seeing 'a shape like unto himself' reflected in the watery element, man 'loved it, and would cohabit with it; and immediately upon the resolution, ensued the Operation'. As a result of this union was created man's 'unreasonable Image or Shape,' that is an image devoid of reason because composed of matter only.[64]

Whatever mistakes Ficino and Pico della Mirandola may have made about the antiquity and authenticity of the Hermetic texts, they recognized their usefulness as a foundation for their philosophic attempt to synthesize intellectual truth with the spiritual insights of the love of God. Ernst Cassirer has shown, in *The Individual and the Cosmos in Renaissance Philosophy*, how in Patrizzi

> the act of knowledge and the act of love have one and the same goal, for both strive to overcome the separation in the elements of being and return to the point of their original unity.... The highest intellect became an itellect, a thinking consciousness, only when it was moved by love to divide

itself in two, and to confront itself with a world of objects of knowledge as objects of contemplation;[65]

and has gone on to assert that Italian neoplatonism, as a school, held that,

to 'know' a thing means to become one with it. But this unity is only possible if the subject and object, the knower and the known, are of the same nature; they must be members and parts of one and the same vital complex.[66]

Now Professor Kermode has warned us against the critical excesses that tempt those who would read Plotinus to understand Marvell;[67] but one does not have to believe that he had read the *Enneads*, or the Victorines, or even the *Pymander* of 'Hermes Trismegistus'[68] to believe that the theories and doctrines peculiar to these and other similar works, as mediated through the writings of the Florentine neoplatonists, must certainly have reached Marvell in a fairly compelling form in the sermons, treatises, discourses, and perhaps even the private and pedagogic conversations of the group of men known as the Cambridge Platonists.[69] Cassirer has elsewhere pointed out the importance of Plotinus and the Florentines in the minds of the Cambridge men;[70] and the most cursory inspection of Cudworth's *The True Intellectual System of the Universe*, Smith's *Discourses*, or any of More's works in prose or verse, will reveal the justice of his remarks. Although there is considerable diversity within the 'school', and although the work of its members covers a span of sixty years or more, they share almost uniformly the view that the structure of the universe is intelligible, that it is available to the enlightened reason of man, that man carries within him a microcosmic example of divine spirit, and that the spiritual and the rational are best united in the inquiry after truth and spiritual good, a unity recognized by the God-given faculty of 'right reason'.

There is very little in the way of printed evidence to demonstrate Marvell's connections with the philosophers and theologians of the Cambridge school. But we can say that they were the most famous and influential Anglican theorists of the period, and that during Marvell's years at Cambridge (he matriculated in 1633, graduated B.A. in 1638, and left some time before 1641): Benjamin Whichcote was at Emmanuel, and preached at Trinity Church from 1636 on; Joseph Mede, Milton's mentor and *doyen* of the group, was at Christ's until 1638; John Worthington was at Emmanuel; John Smith entered Emmanuel and took his B.A.; Nathaniel Culverwell matriculated at Emmanuel the same year in which Marvell came to Trinity, taking his M.A. in 1640; Peter Sterry, later Cromwell's chaplain, attended Emmanuel between 1629 and 1637; Ralph Cudworth was at Emmanuel from before Marvell's arrival until after his departure; and Henry More entered Christ's College in 1631, and remained there until after the Restoration. In short, every major figure of the Cambridge school of Platonism or Latitudinarianism was either writing, preaching, tutoring, studying or lecturing during the entire time of Marvell's stay at Trinity College. It is hard to believe that a man of Marvell's intellectual alertness could have remained uninformed of or unaffected by their activities, even if we ignore the obvious sympathy between some of his pronounced religious and political views[71] and the mediated Anglicanism preached by Whichcote, Smith, and the rest.

What remains to be demonstrated is not the coincidence of religious beliefs between the poet and the philosophers, but the relevance of their epistemological doctrines to the model of mind I believe to underlie Marvell's pastoral poems. These doctrines were shaped, in part, as weapons in the mortal combat against the materialistic atomism of Hobbes; but they were also sharpened by the more subtle, and unexpected, controversies with Cartesian metaphysics and epistemology. More and Cudworth, in particular, began by finding support for their doctrines of right reason and intelligible forms in the early writings of Descartes; but they both grew to see that Descartes' categories of thought and extension contained a disguised threat to the intelligible unity of the universe that the Platonists hoped to demonstrate. A modern historian of science characterizes the Cartesian attack on the traditional analogical cosmology thus:

Now Descartes' God, in contradistinction to most previous Gods, is not symbolized by the things He created; He does not express Himself in them. There is no analogy between God and the world; no *imagines* and *vestigia Dei in mundo*; the only exception is our soul, that is, a pure mind, a being, a substance of which all essence consists in thought, a mind endowed with an intelligence able to grasp the idea of God, that is, of the infinite (which is even innate to it), and with will, that is, with infinite freedom.[72]

To an historian of psychology the change from the old emblematic universe of macrocosmic correspondence can be seen as the transition from Augustine to Descartes.

Augustine brought to an end the effective philosophy of the ancient world by retiring into the sanctuary of the heart. Descartes inaugurated the effective reunion of the inner and the outer worlds, the world of introspection and the world of scientific prediction, by going forth from the inmost chambers of the intellect to the boundaries of its new domains.[73]

In less heroic terms, Brett describes the epistemological problem to which Descartes addressed himself.

The current theory of perception postulated three terms, an object, an image of the object, and an idea or mental grasp of the image. This scheme implies a universe of objects reproduced in a universe of thought; Descartes rejects that scheme and is then driven back on the problem of the ideas as effects of some agency. If the idea is not an effect of the object it must be an effect of the subject, a product of subjective activity.[74]

It will be convenient to examine Cudworth's theory of knowledge as representative of the Cambridge school because he wrote more on the subject than any of the others, was more consistently and profoundly interested in the problem of knowing, and was more articulate about his beliefs than any of his colleagues, with the possible exception of Henry More. And Cudworth begins by confronting the same problem that inspired Descartes to search for a way of arriving at his 'clear and distinct ideas'; if the mind participates in divine mind, and if intellection is a model of God's understanding, how can mental activity be determined by the nature of the material world? The inherited faculty psychology described the mind as essentially an agent of abstraction, creating general ideas and formulae out of the discrete images formed by the imagination or the *sensus communis* from the physical impressions transmitted by the outward senses. To Cudworth this rendered the mind, however intricate and incredibly rapid its operations, essentially passive, and required that it submit to the material flux in order to create the forms of intelligibility. Descartes was bemused by the metaphysical difficulty of matter acting on mind; Cudworth and the Platonists were more immediately concerned to defend and illustrate the active power of reason to give shape to physical nature. Thus Cudworth chooses to go somewhat further than even earlier proponents of 'innate ideas' had done, on the basis of Plato's original assertion of the reality of Ideas; he goes so far as to suggest that the intelligible ideas are not merely shadows of a higher metaphysical order, but products of the mind itself:

> . . . sensible things themselves (as for example light and colours) are not known or understood either by the passion or the fancy of sense, nor by any thing merely foreign and adventitious, but by intelligible ideas exerted from the mind itself, that is, by something native and domestic to it.[75]

John Smith, in a more purely theological vein, made much the same point about the relation of the created world to the model of divine intelligence which had been implanted in the human mind.

> 'The heavens', indeed, 'declare the glory of God, and the firmament sheweth His handywork,' and 'that which may be known of God'—even 'His eternal power and Godhead,' as St Paul tells us, is to be seen in these external appearances: yet it must be something within that must instruct us in all these mysteries, and we shall then best understand them, when we compare that copy which we find of them within ourselves, with that which we see without us.[76]

This is, of course, the end toward which Cudworth is driving too, the re-establishment of the mind's sovereignty over created nature, the repairing of the defects of the Fall; but he is trying as well to accomplish this task by an analysis of the relations between mind and matter that will need no inexplicable help from the fountain of grace. He wants to win the victory of intelligibility with nothing but the weapons of the creative reason and, further, to win it without sacrificing external nature or condemning it to a metaphysical limbo or to a Manichean realm of inert evil. He does this not only by distinguishing between the *actions* of the senses and of the mind, but also by particularizing the objects of both kinds of actions:

. . . whereas the only objects of sense are individual corporeal things existing without the mind, which the soul perceives by looking out from itself upon that from which it suffers, not actively comprehended within itself; the primary and immediate objects of intellection and knowledge, are not things existing without the mind, but the ideas of the mind itself actively exerted, that is, the intelligible rationes, 'reasons,' of things.[77]

M. H. Abrams has written definitively on the later history of the implicit concept of the mind as a fountain or source of light shedding influence on the world of objective reality;[78] but even though he mentions the Cambridge Platonists as precursors of Coleridge's doctrine of the creative imagination, we must note that Cudworth's theory is not at the service of an ideal portrait of the poet, or of any other specifically creative artist. Cudworth and the rest are concerned with a universal process of knowing, and their overriding aim is to reconcile the powers of the mind with its destined field of activity, not to create a new reality nor to clothe nature in a garment embroidered by the imagination. Cudworth is uncompromising in his assertion that nature holds no truths necessary for the proper exercise of the mind's functions.

The essence of nothing is reached unto not by the senses looking outward, but by the mind's looking inward into itself.[79]

And he goes even further in exploring the potencies of mind, as if to redefine the ancient principle of plenitude, which held that the universe must be filled by all possible beings, hierarchically arranged.[80] Rather, Cudworth invokes the equally venerable idea that the microcosm contains examples of all created things to be found in the macrocosm; but he reinterprets the doctrine in the light of his idea of intellect.

For as the mind of God, which is the archetypal intellect, is that whereby he always actually comprehends himself, and his own fecundity, or the extent of his own infinite goodness and power; that is, the possibility of all things; so all created intellects being certain ectypal models, or derivative compendiums of the same; although they have not the actual ideas of all things, much less are the images or sculptures of all the several species of existent things fixed and engraven in a dead

27

manner upon them; yet they have them all virtually and potentially comprehended in that one vis cognitrix, 'cognoscitive
power,' of the soul, which is a potential omniformity, whereby
it is enabled as occasion serves and outward objects invite,
gradually and successively to unfold and display itself in a vital
manner, by framing intelligible ideas or conceptions within
itself of whatsoever hath any entity or cogitability. As the
spermatic or plastic power doth virtually contain within itself
the forms of all the several organical parts of animals. . . .[81]

The relevance of this notion to the description of the mind containing 'all that's made' in 'The Garden' is obvious, but Cudworth
is pursuing an idea of mental creativity that goes beyond the mind's
reproduction in conceptual form of the species it discovers in the
external world. He is finally concerned with the mind's power to
create its own objects of contemplation, which he calls

. . . that strange parturiency that is often observed in the mind,
when it is solicitously set upon the investigation of some truth,
whereby it doth endeavour, by ruminating and revolving
within itself, as it were to conceive it within itself, parturire, 'to
bring it forth out of its own womb;' by which it is evident,
that the mind is naturally conscious of its own active fecundity,
and also that it hath a criterion within itself, which will enable
it to know when it hath found that which it sought.[82]

This would seem to derive from the vision of the soul's 'separation'
from the body which was so attractive to the Florentine neoplatonists, Ficino in particular. This separation, this 'turning away of
consciousness from external impressions',[83] is understood as the
only avenue toward the discovery of truth.

[When the function of sense perception is interrupted,] then the
Soul collects itself in some way and is not occupied either in
perceiving corporeal qualities or in governing and moving the
members of its own body or in treating external affairs, which
easily happens in sleep. Yet the more the external act is lessened,
the more the inner act is increased. Inner acts are the visions of
imagination and the discursive procedures of reason.[84]

Indeed, as in the Plotinian raptus, this state of spiritual self-absorption, 'Casting the Bodies Vest aside',[85] is ultimately desirable; and the soul's hunger for it is mediated only by the knowledge that

> . . . outward functions are necessary for the preservation of the body and for the continuation of empirical life. Hence, we can understand why the Soul cannot continue long in pure contemplation during its earthly existence and, consequently, why it cannot attain its highest goal, the direct intuition of God, before death.[86]

With the best will in the world, the neoplatonists cannot be said to view the world of phenomena as anything more than an ever-present annoyance, able on occasion to interrupt the proper inward meditations of the soul.

There is an important distinction to be made here between the thinking of Ficino and Cudworth's speculations on the interdependence of mind and body. Whether he felt the need to 'save the appearances' of the traditional scheme of epistemology, or whether the metaphoric power of nature as God's second Book was still active, nevertheless, Cudworth, like the rest of the Cambridge group, does not view the material creation as simply an obstacle in man's quest for intuitive knowledge. In conspicuous ways Cudworth's theories are more pragmatic, certainly more responsive to the realities of experience, in that he begins by recognizing the yoking of mind and body as the *donnée* of man's postlapsarian condition. A recent interpreter of Cudworth's philosophy gives some sense of the complexity of his position by pointing out the way in which Cudworth reinterprets the Christian-Platonic doctrine of the conflict between the spirit and the flesh.

> 'The soul', he says, 'might be considered as double or as having two theories of life'; 'the flesh' is not merely an urgent passion but a theory of life, 'spirit' is not merely a theory of life but also an urgent passion. Two distinct systems of passion constitute the human soul; on the one side 'animal appetite', on the other side 'love' or 'charity' or 'the instinct of honesty' or simply 'spirit'. In some human beings, spirit may exist only as a 'glimmering,' but no soul is ever *simply* animal or *simply* spiritual.[87]

Even this is only to insist that man cannot function as a rational creature if he attempts to deny or circumvent the conditions of his nature. But Cudworth goes further in defining the nature of 'that subtile knot, which makes us man'.[88] Cudworth's appreciation of the eternal yoking of matter and spirit tends neither toward the neoplatonist's grief at the imprisonment of spirit within flesh, nor toward Donne's wry, grim amusement at the 'witty' ruin of man's divided estate, nor yet toward the sacramental view that saw that estate as a living symbol of the Incarnation. Rather, Cudworth tries to report the predominant conditions under which the mind knows and the soul suffers passion; for prior to ethical or religious exhortation lies the necessity to understand.

> For the soul and body by reason of that vital union which is betwixt them, making up one compositum, 'compound' or 'animal', do of necessity mutually suffer from each other, the body being variously moved by the soul, and the soul again variously affected from the body, or the motions which are made upon it. Neither doth the soul suffer indifferently from any body, but all sense arises from that natural sympathy or compassion which the soul hath with that individual body with which it is vitally united. And had not the soul such a passive principle in it, it could not possibly be vitally united to any body, neither could there be any such thing as an animal or living creature.[89]

It would be difficult to find a more useful gloss to 'A Dialogue between the Soul and Body', in which Marvell's interest in the oft-neglected claims of the body in this abrasive partnership is clearly demonstrated, if only by the fact that the body is allowed the last speech in the debate. But perhaps the quality of mind that Marvell shares with Cudworth and his colleagues can be suggested by comparing both Marvell's poem and Cudworth's treatise on morality with Donne's conjectures on the links between matter and spirit. 'The Extasie' and 'An Anatomy of the World' are, of course, deeply concerned with the problem of knowledge and its sources in the relations between mind and body; but the problem is made the point of a variety of conceits throughout Donne's secular and devotional poetry, and he is clearly conscious of it in many different regards. But Donne is committed to the inherited faculty psychology, and is less interested in the precise nature of the mind's operations than he is in the paradoxes of existence that well endlessly from the metaphysical dichotomy that is their source. Donne sees the problem of knowledge, in short, as one of the many riddling enigmas that God has seeded in the Christian universe, as a sign of the limitations of speculative reason, and as an implicit exhortation to seek philosophical as well as religious truth in contemplation of the miraculous nature of Christ, in whom all such riddles are explained and resolved. Put another way, Donne approaches the paradoxes of knower and known, incorporeal spirit moving and being moved by mindless matter, as a connoisseur of paradox, as a mind observing and characterizing the consequences of the paradox, as, essentially, an outsider, an intelligence not itself engaged in trying to understand from *within* the paradox.

And I think it is just here that Marvell distinguishes himself from all the seventeenth-century poets who wrote, at some length and with some seriousness of intent, about the mystery of the soul's life within the flesh (to be sure, such a category must include almost every poet we read today). For Marvell does not so much describe or ramify through conceits or philosophical discourse the mystery itself, as a problem in epistemology; he rather writes poems about the difficulties of both flesh and spirit as they exist within their impossible union, poems about the mind as it tries to comprehend its limitations, transcend them, and possibly to return to its forfeited state of harmony with a material creation it now experiences primarily as hostile, burdensome, or simply recalcitrant. When Marvell uses pastoral figures to shape a poem, then, he is often employing them as metaphors for faculties and processes of the mind.[90] And when he writes explicitly about the debate between the divided principles within man, he is often trying to draw an analogy between the mind's own problematic state and the moral dichotomies in the world of men and institutions, dichotomies that may be, ultimately, reflections of the primal one in the mind of man.

Marvell's poetry has often been interpreted as a collection of unrelated exercises which have in common only the poet's obvious predilection for states of opposition (presumably they allow him to exhibit his famous poise and balance). 'An Horatian Ode' oscillates between respect for 'the antient Rights' and admiration for 'The force of angry Heavens flame'; 'The Garden' and 'Upon Appleton House' carry on, among other things, the argument about the relative merits of the active and contemplative life; and Marvell's recurrent choice of the *débat* form for pastoral poems, both plain and philosophical, needs no comment. There can be no doubt that his genius was stirred more immediately by complex choices than by the passion of certainty, nor that his talent is best employed in dramatizing those precariously balanced states of mind that Donne saw as invitations to witty expatiation, and which Milton felt as challenges. But Marvell is not chosen by his subjects; his preferences among possible poetic forms, genres, and themes are determined by an antecedent interest in the kind of experience his poetry can properly embody. It seems to me that the model of mental and spiritual activity Marvell must have studied under the tutelage of the Cambridge Platonists, and which had descended to them through the intertwined lineages of neoplatonism and Christianity, is the generative source of his poetry; further, the model's inherent concern with the problem of knowing, of reconciling the operations of the mind with the external world it must know, seems also to demand its expression within the pastoral mode, the mode sanctioned by decorum and rendered appropriate by philosophical necessity.

Notes

1 T. S. Eliot, 'Andrew Marvell', in *Selected Essays*, 3rd edn (Faber & Faber, 1951), p. 293.

2 F. R. Leavis, *Revaluation* (London, 1949), p. 24.

3 T. S. Eliot, op. cit., p. 303.

4 T. S. Eliot, op. cit., p. 304.

5 Rosalie Colie, *Paradoxia Epidemica* (Oxford University Press, 1966). See particularly Chapters 7 & 8.

6 A. Alvarez, *School of Donne* (London, 1961), pp. 105–107.

7 Hugh Kenner, *Seventeenth Century Poetry* (New York, 1964), p. 443.

8 Douglas Bush, *English Literature in the Earlier Seventeenth Century 1600–1660*, 2nd edn rev. (Clarendon Press, 1962), p. 168.

9 H. M. Margoliouth offers evidence to support Marvell's authorship of 'An Elegy upon the Death of my Lord Francis Villiers', a poem much more uncompromising in its Royalism than those to Lovelace and Hastings. See *The Poems and Letters of Andrew Marvell*, 2 vols., ed. H. M. Margoliouth, 2nd edn (Clarendon Press, 1952), I, pp. 332–334. All quotations from Marvell's poems are taken from this edition. Throughout the text the first citation of a poet indicates the edition to which it and all subsequent citations will be made.

10 The *locus classicus* for this Marvellian controversy is the exchange between Douglas Bush and Cleanth Brooks, which began as an attempt to determine the extent of Marvell's sympathy for Charles, and the nature of his reaction to Cromwell's successes. The discussion branched

out toward the larger, supposed, debate between interpretive and historical criticism; but it never reached any useful conclusions. See Cleanth Brooks, 'Criticism and Literary History: Marvell's Horatian Ode', *Sewanee Review*, LV, 2 (1947), pp. 199–222; Douglas Bush, 'Marvell's "Horatian Ode" ', *Sewanee Review*, LX, 3 (1952), pp. 363–376; Brooks, 'A Note on the Limits of "History" and the Limits of "Criticism" ', *Sewanee Review*, LXI, 1 (1953), pp. 129–135. A different sort of debate arose over the view of history implicit in the 'Ode' and the degree to which Marvell had been influenced by Machiavelli: see J. A. Mazzeo, 'Cromwell as Machiavellian Prince in Marvell's "An Horatian Ode" ', *JHI*, XXI, 1 (1960), pp. 1–17; Hans Baron, 'Marvell's "An Horatian Ode" and Machiavelli', *JHI*, XXI, 3 (1960), pp. 450–451. For interpretations based on Marvell's use of Roman history and on his involvement in contemporary political thinking, see R. H. Syfret, 'Marvell's "Horatian Ode" ', *RES*, N.S. XII, 46 (1961), pp. 160–172, and J. M. Wallace, 'Marvell's Horatian Ode', *PMLA*, LXXVII, 1 (1962), pp. 33–45. Wallace's *Destiny His Choice: The Loyalism of Andrew Marvell* (Cambridge University Press, 1968) argues for the lifelong consistency of Marvell's political allegiance.

11 There is, nevertheless, good reason to think that many of the most important ones were written during his stay in Lord Fairfax's household at Nunappleton between 1651 and 1653. See M. C. Bradbrook and M. G. Lloyd Thomas, *Andrew Marvell* (Cambridge University Press, 1940), pp. 2 & 23–25 hereinafter cited as 'Bradbrook'; and Pierre Legouis, *Andrew Marvell* (Oxford University Press, 1965), pp. 17–20 & 27–29.

12 F. L. Lucas, *Authors Dead and Living* (Chatto & Windus, 1926), p. 16.

13 Geoffrey Walton's remark, in *Metaphysical to Augustan: Studies in Tone and Sensibility in the Seventeenth Century* (Bowes & Bowes, 1955), is typical: 'He gives us a perfect fusion of the wit of Donne and the wit of Jonson; his urbanity far surpasses Dryden's and . . . one is tempted to see a poetic strain running through him from Jonson to Pope', p. 20.

14 George Williamson, *The Donne Tradition* (Oxford University Press, 1930), p. 151.

15 Rosemond Tuve, *Elizabethan and Metaphysical Imagery* (Cambridge University Press, 1947), pp. 237–247.

16 Ruth Wallerstein, *Studies in Seventeenth-Century Poetic* (Madison, 1951), p. 155.

17 Dennis Davison, *The Poetry of Andrew Marvell* (E. Arnold, 1964); Lawrence Hyman, *Andrew Marvell* (New York, 1964); John Press, *Andrew Marvell*, Writers and their Work: No. 98 (London, 1958). J. B. Leishman's uncompleted *The Art of Marvell's Poetry* (Hutchinson,

1966), published posthumously, comments extensively on Marvell's sensitivity to genre and provides a wealth of comparisons to earlier, and contemporary, poets.

18 Dennis Davison, 'Marvell's "The Definition of Love" ', *RES*, N.S. VI, 22 (1955), pp. 141–146; Rosemond Tuve, op. cit., p. 302; Frank Kermode, 'Definitions of Love', *RES*, N.S. VII, 26 (1956), pp. 183–185.

19 G. R. Hibbard, 'The Country House Poem of the Seventeenth Century', *JWCI*, XIX (1956), pp. 159–174; Maren-Sofie Røstvig, ' "Upon Appleton House" and the Universal History of Man', *English Studies*, XLII (1961), pp. 337–351.

20 Frank Kermode, 'The Argument of Marvell's "Garden" ', *EC*, II, 3 (1952), pp. 225–241.

21 In 'Marvell's "Songs of Innocence and Experience" ', *Studies in English Literature*, V, 4 (1965), Ruth Nevo says that 'Marvell's versions of pastoral . . . provide the essential bearings for an account of Marvell's imagination', p. 4.

22 Margoliouth, op. cit., I, pp. 3–4.

23 Notice the similarity between Marvell's description and Spenser's sketch of an unspecified 'antique world' in the proem to Book V of *The Faerie Queene*.

24 Margoliouth, op. cit., I, pp. 4–5. The lines, particularly in the matters of emphasis and imagery, seem to be indebted to the opening of 'Lycidas'.

25 Cf. Harold E. Toliver, *Marvell's Ironic Vision* (Yale University Press, 1965), pp. 206–209.

26 See E. Faral, *Les Arts Poétiques du XIIe et XIIIe Siècle* (Paris, 1924), p. 87.

27 See the excellent discussion in Bruno Snell, *The Discovery of the Mind* (Blackwell, 1953), pp. 281–309; also Erwin Panofsky, *Et in Arcadia Ego*, reprinted in *Meaning and the Visual Arts* (Garden City Press, 1955).

28 *The Poetical Works of Edmund Spenser*, 3 vols., eds. J. C. Smith and E. de Sélincourt (Oxford University Press, 1909–1910), I, p. 7.

29 George Puttenham (?), *The Arte of English Poesie*, in *Elizabethan Critical Essays*, 2 vols., ed. G. G. Smith (Oxford University Press, 1904), II, p. 40.

30 William Empson, *Some Versions of Pastoral* (Chatto & Windus, 1935); also published under the title, *English Pastoral Poetry*.

31 W. W. Greg's *Pastoral Poetry and Pastoral Drama* (London, 1906), remains the fullest historical survey; Frank Kermode's Introduction to *English Pastoral Poetry* (Harrap, 1952), is original and illuminating.

32 The relation between the two poets invites extended investigation; Douglas Bush touches on it in *English Literature in the Earlier Seventeenth Century*, p. 168. Marvell pays specific homage to Spenser in 'Clorinda and Damon', where the final Chorus echoes the refrain of *Epithalamion*.

33 We can judge the familiarity of the figure by the ease with which 'E.K.' identifies 'Great Pan' with 'Christ, the very God of all shepheards', in the Gloss to the May Eclogue.

34 John Milton, 'Lycidas', ll. 165–193; *John Milton: Complete Poems and Major Prose*, ed. M. Y. Hughes (New York, 1957), pp. 120–125.

35 Bradbrook, *Andrew Marvell*, pp. 28–29.

36 Hibbard, 'The Country House Poem', p. 159.

37 A. Bartlett Giamatti, in *The Earthly Paradise and the Renaissance Epic* (Oxford University Press, 1966), pp. 11–86, surveys the most important Greek and Latin versions of the earthly paradise, or Fortunate Isles, and traces similarities between some of them and Christian images of Eden. The indispensable guide to the literary history of the concept of the Golden Age is *A Documentary History of Primitivism and Related Ideas*. Only volume I of this projected series, *Primitivism and Related Ideas in Antiquity*, A. O. Lovejoy and G. Boas, was published (Oxford University Press, 1935).

38 Ovid, *Metamorphoses*, I, ll. 76–215. All quotations from classical poets are drawn from the Loeb editions of their works.

39 See, for example, St Thomas Aquinas, *Summa Theologica*, Part I, QQ LXXV–LXXXIX; and Aristotle, *De anima*. The fullest and most discursive historical treatment is A. O. Lovejoy, *The Great Chain of Being* (Oxford University Press, 1936).

40 See Raphael's discourse in Book V of Milton, *Paradise Lost*, and the description of man's creation in Book VII, ll. 519–550.

41 See St Thomas Aquinas, *Summa Theologica*, Part I, Q. CII, Fourth Article.

42 See Stanley Stewart, *The Enclosed Garden: The Tradition and the Image in Seventeenth Century Poetry* (Wisconsin University Press, 1966), especially Chapters I–III.

43 D. C. Allen, *Image and Meaning. Metaphoric Traditions in Renaissance Poetry* (Baltimore, 1960), p. 108.

44 G. H. Williams, *Wilderness and Paradise in Christian Thought* (New York, 1962), p. 49.

45 Williams, op. cit., p. 40.

46 John Milton, *Of Education*, in *Complete Prose Works of John Milton*, II, ed. E. Sirluck (Oxford University Press, 1959), pp. 366–367.

47 Edward Tayler, *Nature and Art in Renaissance Literature* (Columbia University Press, 1964), p. 159.

48 Edward Tayler, op. cit., p. 154.

49 J. H. Muirhead, in *The Platonic Tradition in Anglo-Saxon Philosophy* (Allen & Unwin, 1931), observes that both Christian and Platonic thought 'start from the assumption of the affinity between the structure of the world and the mind of man. To Plato it was the same principle

that was the source both of the being and the knowledge of the world', p. 26.

50 See J. A. Mazzeo, 'Metaphysical Poetry and the Poetic of Correspondence', *JHI*, XIV (April 1953), pp. 221–234.

51 See the standard account in E.M.W. Tillyard, *The Elizabethan World Picture* (Chatto and Windus, 1943), pp. 55–73; and the much fuller exposition in R. Klibansky, E. Panofsky, and F. Saxl, *Saturn and Melancholy* (Nelson, 1964).

52 See H. Craig, *The Enchanted Glass* (Blackwell, 1950), Chapters I–V.

53 See Sir Philip Sidney, *An Apologie for Poetrie*, in *Elizabethan Critical Essays*, I, p. 156.

54 See Sister M. I. Corcoran, *Milton's Paradise with Reference to the Hexameral Background* (Washington, 1945), p. 119.

55 John Salkeld, *A Treatise of Paradise* (London, 1617), Sig. 14ᵛ.

56 William Perkins, *A Golden Chaine* (London, 1597), Sig. B6r.

57 Edward Reynolds, *A Treatise of the Passions and Faculties of the Soule of Man* (London, 1640).

58 See the Introduction and Commentary in F. Manley, ed. *John Donne: The Anniversaries* (Baltimore, 1963).

59 Edward Reynolds, op. cit., pp. 438–439.

60 John Donne, 'An Anatomy of the World', ll. 70–71, in *The Poems of John Donne*, 2 vols., ed. H. J. C. Grierson (Oxford University Press, 1912), I, p. 233.

61 *Critical Essays of the Seventeenth Century*, 3 vols., ed. J. E. Spingarn (Clarendon Press, 1908), I, pp. 163–164.

62 See E. R. Curtius, *European Literature and the Latin Middle Ages*, trans. W. R. Trask (London, 1953), pp. 319–326.

63 In *The Philosophy of Plotinus*, ed. J. Katz (New York, 1950), p. 73.

64 See Maren-Sofie Røstvig, 'Andrew Marvell's "The Garden": A Hermetic Poem', *English Studies*, XL, 2 (April 1959), p. 70. She is quoting Everard's translation of Hermes, published in 1650.

65 Ernst Cassirer, *The Individual and the Cosmos in Renaissance Philosophy*, trans. M. Domandi (Blackwell, 1964), p. 134.

66 Cassirer, op. cit., p. 148.

67 F. Kermode, 'The Argument of Marvell's "Garden" ', pp. 225–241.

68 See the article by Røstvig cited above, n. 64, and also her ' "Upon Appleton House" and the Universal History of Man'.

69 See the discussion in Pierre Legouis, *Andrew Marvell*, pp. 3–8; and in H. E. Toliver, *Marvell's Ironic Vision*, pp. 14–32.

70 Ernst Cassirer, *The Platonic Renaissance in England*, trans. J. P. Pettegrove (Nelson, 1953), p. 8.

71 See *The Rehearsal Transpros'd* and *An Account of the Growth of Popery*,

and Arbitrary Government in England in the four-volume edition of
A. B. Grosart (n.p., 1872–1875).

72 Alexandre Koyré, *From the Closed World to the Infinite Universe* (Oxford
University Press, 1957), p. 100.

73 G. S. Brett, *A History of Psychology*, 3 vols. (Allen & Unwin, 1912–1921),
II, p. 198.

74 Brett, op. cit., II, pp. 206–207.

75 Ralph Cudworth, *The True Intellectual System of the Universe*, 3 vols.
(Tegg, 1845), III, p. 62.

76 John Smith, *Select Discourses*, ed. H. G. Williams (Cambridge University
Press, 1859), p. 130.

77 Cudworth, *A Treatise Concerning Eternal and Immutable Morality*,
reprinted in the edition of the *True Intellectual System* cited above, III,
pp. 579–580.

78 M. H. Abrams, *The Mirror and the Lamp* (Oxford University Press,
1953), *passim*, but especially pp. 57–69.

79 Cudworth, op. cit., III, p. 566.

80 A. O. Lovejoy, *The Great Chain of Being*, *passim*.

81 Cudworth, op. cit., III, pp. 580–581.

82 Cudworth, op. cit., III, p. 582.

83 P. O. Kristeller, *The Philosophy of Marsilio Ficino* trans. Virginia
Conant, (New York, 1943), p. 215.

84 Kristeller, op. cit., p. 365.

85 Andrew Marvell, 'The Garden', l. 51.

86 Kristeller, op. cit., p. 365.

87 J. A. Passmore, *Ralph Cudworth: An Interpretation* (Cambridge University
Press, 1951), pp. 55–56.

88 John Donne, 'The Extasie', l. 64, *Poems*, I, pp. 51–53.

89 Cudworth, op. cit., III, p. 559.

90 In *Paradoxia Epidemica* (p. 283) Rosalie Colie suggests that the frequent
appearance of images of reflection and reduction 'in Marvell's work is
related to his complicated personal view of the nature and functions of
mind', and mentions that Geoffrey Hartman is presently at work on
this idea in connection with 'The Nymph'. Hartman's ' "The Nymph
Complaining for the Death of Her Fawn": A Brief Allegory' has
since appeared, *EC*, XVIII (1968), pp. 113–135. Miss Colie also promises
a paper on the microcosmic mind in 'The Garden'.

2

Forms of Debate

Marvell learned the skills of the lyric poet, and found his congenial subjects and attitudes, fairly swiftly. From the schoolboy Latin verses of 1637, *Ad Regem Carolum Parodia*, to the assured achievements of the Nunappleton years, the development took little over a decade; and if we take the poem to Lovelace as the first announcement of serious poetic intention, then the speed of Marvell's maturing can be compared to the miraculous last years of Keats: he moved from the laboured compliments of the first public poems to the mordant precision of 'The Definition of Love' and 'To his Coy Mistress', we may assume, within five years. Even so, there was a time for preparation, for brief and selective experimentation with contemporary forms and styles—a period which preceded Marvell's settling on pastoral modes and motifs as his major resources. The experiments consisted largely in the public poems to Lovelace, the memory of Hastings, and (possibly) to Villiers, and verses described by M. C. Bradbrook as 'poems of the fashionable world, the compliments or scandal of a coterie'.[1] They deserve our attention, albeit briefly, not only as examples of Marvell's attention to the stylistic demands of various genres, but also because they reveal the beginnings of his lifelong attraction to pastoral.

As I have suggested already, 'To his Noble Friend Mr Richard Lovelace, upon his Poems', opens the way to literary compliment by glancing at the civilization adumbrated in the elegies, pastorals, and love lyrics of *Lucasta*. Marvell speaks of it as if it had already vanished, its memory set against a bitter vision of the English world of letters in the 1640s. In so far as Lovelace's imaginary world has become an anachronism, then, it becomes in Marvell's poem a version of the Golden Age. The poet's emphasis falls not on the usual theme of *otium*, but on the vanished correspondence between

38

moral integrity and artistic genius. To make the point he does not turn, however, to the easily available *topos* of the decay of the physical world, but tries to explain the debasement of the arts by a variation on mimetic theory.

> And as complexions alter with the Climes,
> Our wits have drawne th' infection of our times.

> (ll. 3–4)

The complication of the word-play is an index of the kind of social theory Marvell is setting forth: there is deliberate confusion between 'our' minds and the practising 'wits' of poetry; and in drawing the speaking picture of contemporary society, they have also 'drawne', or contracted, the infection they meant only to imitate in verse. Against his vision of the epidemic spread of destructive ambition Marvell sets the image of 'That candid Age', whose civic morality speaks for the cultural longevity of the Roman ideal in government and in epideictic poems. But

> These vertues now are banisht out of Towne,
> Our Civill Wars have lost the Civicke crowne.

> (ll. 11–12)

Although the initial idea of this couplet may seem to flow naturally from the part of literary pastoral tradition that codifies anti-city feeling, it is probably a graceful reference to the court of Charles I and its exile from London. To say that the antique virtues have been banished with the king is appropriate in a poem to Lovelace; and it also serves as a contemporary instance of the values of the 'candid Age'. But, typically, Marvell is not so uncritical as this. To point out that the nation has 'lost the Civicke crowne' is not to indict the Parliamentary side alone. Marvell must have been aware of the irony implicit in the very phrase, 'Civill Wars'; throughout his career as poet and prose pamphleteer he shows a constant awareness of how much of value must be sacrificed when values themselves are fought over. No strife can be less civil than that which tears the fabric of society. The civic crown is not simply the oak-wreath traditionally awarded to the martial hero; it is the crown of civility which is the fruit of a healthy and mature culture.

The Caroline love lyric may also be seen as a fruit of that culture; its decorous manner, its witty, conceited dialectic, its polished elegance, all purported to express that 'civility' which supposedly

39

underlay its courtly code. As an apprentice Marvell was conspicuously self-conscious about his use of genre, perhaps even ironic in his approach to the poetic forms he was training himself to imitate and master.[2] Most often when Marvell is following a familiar convention, we can observe that he adapts it to his special interests and needs. For example, in 'The Gallery',[3] a conventional trope—the loved one's face 'graven in the heart'—has been converted into a governing conceit by Marvell's tactic of interpreting it literally and then extending its logical implications to the edge of absurdity. But we see that the series of portraits, each one a variation on Clora's destructive beauty, is completed and explained by a vision of virginal loveliness that takes the poem out of the realm of the amatory exercise and raises it to the level of a statement about nostalgia and innocence.

When the poet asks Clora to view the gallery of his heart and to tell, 'Whether I have contriv'd it well', he points to one of the central problems of the poem, the dedication of art to unsuitable ends, and the larger problem of the nature of artifice. This gallery is meant to show Clora the roles and disguises she has adopted; and the poet enjoys his ironic assurance that she will be pleased with the display, unaware that true praise is reserved for the last portrait, whose simplicity and innocence overshadow her worldly success as 'Murtheress' and 'Venus'. Clora will indeed think he has 'contriv'd it well', since she will see herself in her most seductive guises. The lover's unspoken question, however, is 'Is this well?' What he has spent most art in painting is precisely what he rejects most passionately. In working out the conceit of the Soul as a gallery Marvell wants to enforce the notion that the Soul, which has normally 'several lodgings', many passions that divert it, has, by its consuming passion for Clora, been swept clear of everything but her image. The 'Arras hangings' of other interests and other loves have made way for Clora alone. The tacitly ironic point is that the single-minded lover must still view a variety of portraits, since Clora is as mutable as he is constant.

In portraying Clora against the background of Petrarchan disdain, the luminous fertility of classical mythology, the darkling, fitful passions of Latin elegy, even biblical metaphors of eroticism, Marvell makes a dialectical point of the lack of relation amongst the various roles Clora chooses to play. In consequence, the final portrait must make clear its implicit rejection of the preceding ones.

But, of these Pictures and the rest,
That at the Entrance likes me best:
Where the same Posture, and the Look
Remains, with which I first was took.
A tender Shepherdess, whose Hair
Hangs loosely playing in the Air,
Transplanting Flow'rs from the green Hill,
To crown her Head, and Bosome fill.

(ll. 49–56)

Unlike the 'curled Hair' of the 'Murtheress' of stanza II, the shepherdess's hair 'Hangs loosely playing in the Air'; unlike Aurora or Venus, she is neither supine nor passively 'a float'. Rather, she is intimately connected with her setting; she uses the flowers to adorn herself, and the implication of 'To crown her Head, and Bosome fill' is that these flowers alone are fit to crown *her* beauty. The adjectives and adverbs that describe her insist on her gentleness and lack of artifice. Nevertheless, there is nothing explicit in the stanza that can explain the categorical rejection of Clora's previous transformations. The pastoral vision is set against the guises of the court and the world, and judgment is given. Miss Bradbrook remarks that 'at that point where the satiric intention reveals itself, there is a clear direct metaphor of natural beauty, which recalls to the mind something more satisfying and more lovely than is known in this world of polite society'.[4] But it is precisely this 'something' that is altogether elusive in 'The Gallery'; as a consequence the poem seems wrenched to make a point. The last stanza does not so much answer the earlier ones as simply turn from them. The attitudes that determine the movement are not yet articulated.

In roughly similar ways, 'The unfortunate Lover'[5] seems to accumulate fantastic conceits only to build up to its exquisitely precise and poignant final line. In this poem the *first* stanza illustrates qualities of diction and theme that associate it with Marvell's major poetry; and yet it is related to the body of the poem in only an indistinct manner. Marvell has seized on the oft-portrayed 'bleeding lover' of the chivalric and Petrarchan traditions and written an imaginary biography, couched in the visual images of an allegory and fashioned around a series of emblematic illustrations of the lover's 'progress'.[6] But the poem begins with a scene radically unrelated to the biography that follows.

Alas, how pleasant are their dayes
With whom the Infant Love yet playes!
Sorted by pairs, they still are seen
By Fountains cool, and Shadows green.
But soon these Flames do lose their light,
Like Meteors of a Summers night:
Nor can they to that Region climb,
To make impression upon Time.

(ll. 1–8)

The 'Tyrant Love', whom we meet again in lines 45–46, shooting arrow after arrow into the lover's breast, is a familiar figure; but this 'Infant Love' is a comparative stranger, especially when he is met out of the company of his mother, Venus. This is not the childish Cupid, but a particular infant god who rules over the dim retreat where these 'pairs' walk. The calm and distant natural scene forms a contrast with the highly coloured agonies of the unfortunate lover; and the young lovers themselves, 'Sorted' as they are, presumably, by the playful infant god of love, are presented as essentially passive. Like the shepherdess's 'green Hill', the setting hints at a paradisiacal innocence; the 'Fountains cool, and Shadows green' suggest both the Edenic garden and the garden of the mind Marvell will sketch in 'The Garden'; it is a place where figures move obscurely, out of the light of the sun. But it is of the essence of this visionary state that it be transient; not even the purest of sublunary lovers can avert the effects of time. The mixed awareness of spiritual values and the natural forces that threaten their extinction is rendered in the thought, 'But soon these Flames do lose their light'. Here, 'flame' stands for both passion and the imaginative power of the mind;[7] thus love is equated with intellectual purity and inspiration, and the inevitable demise of infant passion is made to coincide with the death of the spirit and the clouding of the mind. So, at least, we must interpret the metaphor implicit in 'light'; as a universally potent symbol it speaks of any illumination of the human spirit. And if Marvell seems to be saying, somewhat cryptically, that the quenching of this light is a concomitant of growing into adulthood, he is also trying, through the identification of the lovers with 'Meteors of a Summers night', to suggest the special quality of their hopelessness. The summer meteors are in themselves phenomena familiar enough, although they have emerged in a comparison to a metaphor of flames-and-lovers. But, as the verse pivots on 'Summers night' as if it were the middle term in a syllogism, the 'Region' of the meteors, the night sky, is named the realm of Time. It is clear that what separates the meteors from the background against which we see them is the same distance that separates eternity from the phenomena of the world of becoming.

The introduction of Platonic concepts is an implicit comment on the rest of the poem; for if the plotless fable of the first stanza does not 'frame' the story of the unfortunate lover, at least it states the fixed moral point from which he will diverge. The entire poem is an extended footnote on the necessity of that divergence, as it traces the unintelligible agonies suffered by the spirit caught in the undertow of sensuality. The wit of the emblematic stanzas represents an attempt to salvage some meaning from the chaos of adult emotion. The lover in Marvell's poem earns his bloody wounds by fighting at the command of 'angry Heaven', and Love awards his title; thus ennobled by his losing combat the unfortunate lover triumphs, if at all, in his distinguished position in the static realm of the heraldic device. The consistency with which he has followed the pattern decreed by the hostile gods of erotic love has its own kind of ordered beauty. Thus he can be granted the hypostatized existence of 'In a Field *Sable* a Lover *Gules*'. The figure painted in his own blood stands out clearly against the unrelieved blackness of his fantastic history.

Marvell shows the same skill at extracting the logical and expressive essence of literary convention in other, slighter, poems. 'The Match'[8] is clearly an exercise in the urbane and hyperbolical compliment. The conduct of its argument depends on the simple logic of commonly available terms from physical science and what passed for natural philosophy among laymen; but these neutral terms, or words which have unmistakable concrete significance, are made to carry very broad symbolic connotations. Thus when Marvell mentions the 'Treasure' of Nature's 'choisest store' he is relying on the wealth of suggestion implicit in the idea of Nature's 'Treasure'. By contrast, in the fourth stanza the elements of the basic conceit have been chosen so precisely that merely by naming them in order Marvell completes his argument.

> But likeness soon together drew
> What she did separate lay;

43

Of which one perfect Beauty grew,
And that was *Celia.*

(ll. 13–16)

The pellucid simplicity of the lines hides the skill and audacity with which Marvell has merged the philosophic notions of innate correspondence between entities and the transcendant nature of perfection.[9] Once he has defined perfect beauty by naming it Celia, Marvell shifts immediately to the second part of the poem's structure, the chemical fable of Love's magazine. The only integral connection between the two parts is the implied comparison between Nature's fear of decay and Love's fear of growing chilled and aged. Using the techniques not of allegory but of the symbolic sketch, Marvell develops a metaphor of diversity melting into unity, which, in the last two stanzas, touches on the concept of the loved one's including all the substances and values of earth and heaven.

The same impulse to enlarge the compass of conventional diction can be traced in other early poems, in which Marvell is beginning to work at his emerging themes of innocence, youth, and symbolic pastoral. 'The Fair Singer'[10] proposes that visual beauty and music are comparable in their effects upon the lover.

To make a final conquest of all me,
Love did compose so sweet an Enemy,
In whom both Beauties to my death agree,
Joyning themselves in fatal Harmony.

(ll. 1–4)

The major terms, and all the verbs, are drawn from musical terminology; but the point is that all the activities traditionally associated with reconciling differences, with connecting dissimilarities, with bringing order to chaos—and these are all understood within the love convention as acts of creativity and generation—are here shown in the service of cruelty and destruction. The last couplet of the stanza, 'That while she with her Eyes my Heart does bind,/ She with her Voice might captivate my Mind' (ll. 5–6), alludes to a division of the human faculties which was a commonplace. The heart is traditionally vulnerable to the impressions of the eye; Marvell's significant variation is to make the mind the peculiar object of the assaults of musical harmony, an idiosyncratic notion that will reappear at a crucial point in a great poem, 'A Dialogue Between The Resolved Soul, and Created Pleasure'.[11]

The mind, in Marvell, is threatened always by the allure of external beauty and by the tides of mutability; and while the mature poems meet these threats with a witty ingenuity of argument that can grow only out of unillusioned clarity, sometimes Marvell's early *essais* fall into the grotesque or the obscure in their attempt to dispel the paradoxes of experience. 'Young Love' has seemed to some not only a strange but also a perverse poem.[12] But the strange pastoral vision through which we move into the melodramatic world of 'The unfortunate Lover' helps to explain some of the assumptions which underlie this invitation to love, addressed ostensibly to a child. 'Young Love' lauds the joys of love while rejecting the satisfaction of the senses. It proposes that man can evade the ravages of time by loving before he is able to consummate his love. Despite the overingenious bravura of these formulae, it is not difficult to perceive, in the light of those 'Meteors of a Summers night', that Marvell is again considering the ways in which age and decay reflect the decline from primal innocence into the gules and sable universe of passionate, erotic love. As in 'The Picture of little T.C. in a Prospect of Flowers', Marvell has extended the central figure of a beautiful child toward an image of perfection seen against a menacing background of mutability.

We have seen that in poems concerned with civil or institutional values Marvell will often draw his figure from the analogical world of pastoral; within the conventions of the courtly lyric of love or compliment he must also supply figures for perfection, and he quickly moves beyond the familiar congeries of spheres, circles, Orient pearls, fountains of light, tears, and the other outpourings of nature's 'choisest store'. He devises a method of defining beauty or supreme excellence which seems to rely on basic perceptions that are metaphysical or strictly epistemological in nature, touching on the identification of an example with its abstract type, or a phenomenon with its setting. As might be expected, these occur most frequently in those poems which seem most clearly to have been written under the influence of Donne—although Crashaw, and most probably Cleveland, are as likely to have suggested such techniques to Marvell—poems which depend heavily on the conceit for their argumentative structure. Another resemblance to Donne is to be found in the pose assumed by the poet—one of cynical, yet painstakingly polite disbelief in the constancy of woman. 'Mourning',[13] for example, is based on the pretence of trying to determine the genuineness of Chlora's grief by examining the implications of her tears. One criterion by which they are to be judged is the relation among eyes, tears, and the crystalline spheres of the cosmos, a formula to be found in Sidney, Shakespeare, Donne and others. In the poem's second stanza

> Her Eyes confus'd, and doubled ore,
> With Tears suspended ere they flow;
> Seem bending upwards, to restore
> To Heaven, whence it came, their Woe.

(ll. 5–8)

Here Marvell forces the correspondence one step further, until it becomes a mirror image. By playing on 'confus'd'[14] he wills us to see both eyes and tears as a linked figure composed of liquid, repeated, spheres. Thus he can suggest that the tears will appear *above* the eyes, and justify the notion that they are tending again toward the sky from which they came.[15] The same technical device, that of turning concrete physical details into evaluative symbols through the powers of abstraction and analogy inherent in the conceit, can be seen at work a few stanzas later, where Marvell attempts to mythologize his description of Chlora's weeping: 'She courts her self in am'rous Rain; / Her self both *Danae* and the Show'r' (ll. 19–20). On the surface the lines follow the familiar device of identifying *persona* and natural phenomena; but here the pervasive tone of qualified politesse is deepened. 'Am'rous Rain' suggests that Chlora's self-love is as warm as Jove's for Danae, and the myth enhances the value of 'those precious Tears' by comparing them to gold.

Many of these techniques are highlighted in 'Eyes and Tears',[16] a poem which owes as much to Marino, Gongora, and Cleveland as it does to Donne. Its conceits are grounded in the premises that the faculty of sight can procure only grief and that, therefore, eyes and tears are so closely allied in their purposes that they may be identified. The poem attempts to derive from this playful reworking of the *contemptus mundi* theme a proof of the theory that if the world is inevitably a panorama of sorrow then only sorrow can be a good, because it elicits tears and thereby makes possible true sight and insight. Part of the strategy must then be to attack the

credibility of the sense of sight, usually considered the noblest of
the senses. Marvell begins the attack by noticing that:

> . . . since the Self-deluding Sight,
> In a false Angle takes each hight;
> These Tears which better measure all,
> Like wat'ry Lines and Plummets fall.

(ll. 5–8)

In alluding to the notorious fallibility of the senses—the point here
is that sight deludes the 'self', or Soul—Marvell turns for his criteria
of judgment to the celestial sciences, intending to exploit the
ambivalence of their terminologies in his attempt to design a
geometry of emotion. 'Angle' can be simply a line of observation—
as in the use of a sextant or astrolabe—or it can refer to the astrological 'house' from which the elevation of a heavenly body, or
'hight', is measured. In any case it is clear that the explicit metaphor
of astronomical judgment is linked to the suggestion that 'hight' can
represent other kinds of elevation—moral, social, intellectual.
These, too, are rendered deceptive by the treachery of 'Sight'. The
last couplet, however, resolves these metaphors into the single one
of surveying, by comparing the falling tears to plumb-lines. In
their directness and simplicity, the poem declares, tears are not
subject to the divagations of the eye as instrument. Throughout the
poem 'the good' is being redefined as that which is seen by an eye
not deceived by the apparent beauties and joys of the world. And
although the work of redefinition is often hampered or obscured
by spasms of overingenuity, the idea of a 'Sight more true', an
inward illumination fired by the realization of the world's inadequacy, emerges slowly. The paradoxical assertion that this clearer
vision is enhanced by a film of tears is commented on by an allusion
to the Magdalene; and then a set of negative comparisons turns the
theme to the praise of the *beauty* of tears.

> Not full sailes hasting loaden home,
> Nor the chast Ladies pregnant Womb,
> Nor *Cynthia* Teeming show's so fair,
> As two Eyes swoln with weeping are.

(ll. 33–36)

But this beauty is found in images of plenitude, pregnancy, promise
of grief. Indeed, the next stanza reminds us that tears bring the

47

inevitable extinction of fleshly passion, yet another statement of the purity and unworldliness that characterize the 'Sight more true'. And as the poem moves toward its concluding imperatives Marvell draws another set of comparisons.

> The Incense was to Heaven dear,
> Not as a Perfume, but a Tear.
> And Stars shew lovely in the Night,
> But as they seem the Tears of Light.
>
> (ll. 41–44)

The first couplet follows one recurring technical device of the poem by altering a traditional attribute to one that fits the poem's scheme; it was not the odour but the upward motion of incense which was grateful to the gods. The sense of the line demands that it be seen from the standpoint of the heavens; but the stars can appear as tears of light only when seen from below. The reader's 'sight' is manipulated, but in such a way that he is made aware of the analogies that hold the realm of event and the realm of value together, the analogies that make possible this discourse on tears which becomes a sermon on the excellence of sorrow.

Marvell never abandoned completely these uses of the conceit; but in his later work he turned the essentially logical and superficial qualities of the conceit into a mode more heavily symbolic, one in which word-play was focused on a central, dominating concern in each poem. In the early poems we have been glancing at, his sense of genre is matched always by an ability to charge a familiar trope with a new and intense meaning. This may be observed in clearest relief in those parts of 'Young Love', 'The unfortunate Lover' and 'The Gallery', where the epithets that characterize youth and pastoral simplicity combine to portray a world of values opposed to the urbanity of the poems' subjects. The opposition is essentially a stylistic one, but it generates the dialectic of a theme which is now to absorb Marvell—the consequences of man's dual nature.

The convention of a dialogue or debate within a pastoral poem was well established, even as early as Theocritus. It had some basis, obviously, in the actual custom of shepherds competing for a prize by the exercise of their special skills. This was transferred easily to the figure of the shepherd-poet, the contest becoming a singing competition, and the prize most often an elaborate cup with symbolic details. Furthermore the dialogue form offers a convenient and expressive way to present the arguments of flesh and spirit dramatically, as we shall see in 'Clorinda and Damon'* and 'A Dialogue between Thyrsis and Dorinda'. In these early poems an attempt is made to maintain the fiction of pastoral *personae*, and the philosophy is often dilute. Later, in 'A Dialogue Between The Resolved Soul, and Created Pleasure' and 'A Dialogue between the Soul and Body', Marvell concentrated on the central issue of the dialectical struggle, and on creating speaking abstractions that yet manage to display more idiosyncratically impressive 'characters' than the pastoral figures of the more jejeune dialogues. But even in 'Clorinda and Damon' he makes rich use of the other advantages of the pastoral, which are those of conventional symbols and epithets, mythological allusions, and the implicit connotation of the innocent purity of the natural life. But where the Elizabethans had seen the Muses' Elysium as a version of the earthly paradise, where uncorrupted desire was sanctioned by the gods, Marvell is suggesting that even unsophisticated indulgence of 'natural' impulses is not the perfect 'state of man'. Earlier phrasings of this idea, as in Ralegh's reply to Marlowe's 'Passionate Shepherd', had stemmed from the realization that transiency is the inevitable limit to even the most innocent pursuit of worldly goods. The bitterness of the anti-naturalistic reply had the savour of many medieval treatises on morality; and it was, after all, only the other aspect of the *carpe diem* theme in love poetry. The contemplation of death's unavoidable approach leads with equally compelling force to the exhortation to enjoyment and to the embracing theme of *contemptus mundi*.

In 'Clorinda and Damon', however, Marvell barely touches on the theme of the decay of earthly beauty. The force behind Damon's argument against indulgence is the force of a religious conversion, and we must understand the tone of his lines as that of a recent convert. The tone is a vital part of the argument itself, since it conveys the moral stance and attitude of one who feels himself to be of the elect, or of a soul who feels without question its intimate connection with the divine. It is instructive to recall the speech of Nature in the 'Cantos of Mutabilitie'.[17] After the lengthy and powerfully convincing argument of Mutabilitie, Nature's answer is framed in eighteen lines; and the authority of her reply is strengthened by the simple device of vanquishing so many words with so few. Each word is thus invested with a power and a sanction for which Mutabilitie's volubility disqualifies her. It is the old theatrical technique of 'protesting too much' that convicts her almost as successfully as Nature's monolithic, commanding power. We shall observe that there is in Damon's replies the same elliptical note of utter conviction.

The poem begins on the mildly disconcerting note of a shepherdess's invitation to love. It is not a major innovation, but it is unusual enough to make us aware at the outset that this will not be the expected poem of coyness and persuasion, ending in dalliance. Marvell announces the dialectical issue by having Damon answer, 'No: 'tis too late they went astray' (l. 2), pointing at the similarity between the responsibility of the shepherd for his flock and that of the individual for the state of his soul. Clorinda is then given two couplets in which to describe the attractions of the life of natural innocence—the longest speech in the poem, with the exception of the four-line choral epode that closes it.

> I have a grassy Scutcheon spy'd,
> Where *Flora* blazons all her pride.
> The Grass I aim to feast thy Sheep:
> The Flow'rs I for thy Temples keep. (ll. 3–6)

Marvell has used heraldic reference and terminology before, especially in 'The unfortunate Lover', but there is no obvious reason for the heraldic escutcheon to appear here. Nevertheless, Clorinda uses her terms accurately; the colours and emblems of Flora's shield are, properly, flowers and grass. Meadows and flowery hillsides were often called Flora's blazons in Elizabethan pastoral poetry; and the deliberate mixture of military terms and descriptions of flora was a convention which held place with the more frequent Petrarchan description of love as an armed combat. Many instances of the use of 'blaze', 'blazon', and the various forms of 'scutcheon' occur, of course, in Spenser's work; but the most obvious example is in the song in praise of Eliza in the April Eclogue of *The Shepheardes Calender*. Not only does Hobbinol implore the muse to help him 'blaze' the excellence of the 'Queene of shepheardes', but the third stanza of the ode might be a formula for the painting of an actual escutcheon.[18]

This grass and these flowers, however, are not to remain static symbols of beauty or pastoral divinity; they will be utilized for nourishment and a kind of secular worship. Yet it is inevitable that 'grass' call up the biblical dictum that makes of green, growing things an earthly symbol of mortality. Indeed, Damon himself reminds Clorinda of this by saying, shortly, 'Grass withers; and the Flow'rs too fade'. But because 'Clorinda and Damon' is meant to be an inversion of the 'persuasion to love' Marvell must allow the erotic elements of the genre to establish themselves convincingly. Thus, Clorinda's next assault on Damon's new-found sacred devotion is: 'Seize the short Joyes then, ere they vade./Seest thou that unfrequented Cave?' (ll. 8–9). The grotto is as venerable a place of assignation as the grove, but we may note that it presents an appearance equally attractive and menacing.[19] That Clorinda tries to lead her idol to a cave informs us immediately that the love she speaks of is categorically profane; it shuns the light which is both the common symbol of goodness and the proper illumination of the innocent loves of the pastoral world. She can mean only wanton carnality, the 'Cave' tells us, and the point is driven home by the abrupt, clipped exchange of line 10.

> D. That den? C. Loves Shrine. D. But Virtue's Grave.

The monosyllabic line furthers our sense of the hopeless division between the two speakers, a division made all the more radical by the fact that Clorinda, clearly, does not yet understand what it is she is arguing against. Damon's replies are meant to reveal what separates their views by redefining the objects that surround the antagonists. There is even a degree of development in their disagreement, as Clorinda's 'Cave' becomes, in Damon's word, a 'den'. She insists that it is 'Loves Shrine'. If this is the shrine of earthly love then we may wonder how it is that Flora's flowers can be offered to the temples of the shepherd-lover.

The mixed form of allegorical pastoral relied heavily on personification for many of its metaphorical effects, and it is noteworthy that 'Clorinda and Damon' makes constant use of this figure. Perhaps the instance that shows the greatest compression of figurative force and meaning is 'Virtue's Grave'. In quite another connection the thought will recur in 'To his Coy Mistress', and it is a conceit that can be traced with ease to the preoccupations of certain of Donne's love poems. But its interest for us in 'Clorinda and Damon' is in its use as a moral perception directly opposed to the way in which it would appear normally in an example of the *carpe diem*. There the image of beauty lying unenjoyed in a grave would be the most compelling exhortation to indulgence. Here the death of virtue is imagined as the active enjoyment of physical lust and beauty. In the same way, when Clorinda mentions the attractions of the cave, 'In whose cool bosome we may lye/Safe from the Sun' (ll. 11–12), our knowledge of the convention warns us instantly that a pure love does not hide from openness and light. Moreover, the coolness of a cave is desirable only when day's heat becomes uncomfortable—and it is Clorinda who sees and feels the sun as intruder and oppressor.

There is a further comment on the conventions of naturalistic love poetry in Damon's next rejoinder, 'not Heaven's Eye'. This is not precisely a pun, but a deliberately pointed choice of one of the several epithets for a familiar symbol; in the act of choice his moral position is illuminated. Damon, in effect, reminds Clorinda that she cannot limit the sun arbitrarily to its astronomical existence; it is not simply that heavenly body which gives light and reveals sin. For light is also of the spirit, and so there is point in calling the sun 'Heaven's Eye'—it can see and reveal even where there is physical darkness. This dialectical probing of the proper uses of religious symbols continues in the four lines that follow, probably the best known in the poem:

> C. Near this, a Fountaines liquid Bell
>   Tinkles within the concave Shell.
> D. Might a Soul bath there and be clean,
>   Or slake its Drought?
>
> (ll. 13–16)

This ultimate defeat in the frustrating game of enticement-and-rejection provokes Clorinda to the exasperated 'What is't you mean?'; and we can sympathize with her to the extent that we hear in Damon's tone the patronizing expertise of the newly initiate. As we soon discover, 'great *Pan*' has just 'The other day' revealed to him pleasures of the soul that are greater than the delights of the cave.

Christian commentators on the Old Testament found the Song of Solomon particularly rich in antitypes and symbols which prefigured the Christian dispensation. One such is the fountain mentioned in 4:12; the 'spouse' is first referred to as 'a spring shut up, a fountain sealed', where the adjectives convey the same meaning as in *hortus conclusus*, an enclosed garden, kept pure from contamination by the world. Later she is called 'a fountain of gardens, a well of living waters, and streams from Lebanon'. The images translated themselves quite easily into the iconography of Christian grace and redemption. The nineteenth symbol in Henry Hawkins' *Partheneia Sacra* (1633) is the fountain and, as we might expect in a Jesuit emblem book, the elucidations of the symbol include the portrait of the Virgin as a fountain of grace. Crashaw, among the myriad terms of comparison he finds for Mary Magdalen in 'The Weeper' (1646), does not refrain from calling her an unceasing fountain of tears of grief for sinful man. But these are both Roman Catholic readings of the symbol, and are too closely tied to specific dogmas to explain the wider significations of the fountain. George Herbert uses the metaphor of washing in a flowing stream which both refers particularly to the sacrament of baptism and generally to the spiritual cleansing which comes with the influence of grace.

> Sometimes, when as I wash, I say,
> And shrodely, as I think, Lord, wash my soule,
> More spotted then my Flesh can bee.
> But then there comes into my way
> Thy ancient baptism, which when I was foule
> And knew it not, yet cleansed mee.   (ll. 7–12)†

The same group of symbols, including one of the many Christian connotations of 'shell',[20] appears in 'The Pilgrimage', attributed to Sir Walter Ralegh. The poem opens with the request 'Give me my scallop-shell of quiet', the shell carried as a commonly-understood symbol of the pilgrim. A few lines later, describing the pilgrimage of the soul toward heaven, Ralegh says:

> Over the silver mountains,
> Where spring the nectar fountains:
>   There will I kiss
>   The bowl of bliss;
> And drink mine everlasting fill
> On every milken hill.
> My soul will be a-dry before;
> But, after, it will thirst no more.[21]

These are examples of the tradition of religious reference which lies behind Damon's pointed answer to Clorinda's praise of the fountain.

But it must be remembered that the cool and mellifluous spring has an important place in the genres of love poetry and descriptions of place. Most often the fountain is taken as an analogue of the weeping, grief-stricken lover, as in Donne's 'Twicknam Garden'. But in 'Clorinda and Damon' it is clearly one of the expected accoutrements of the natural setting which conduces to erotic love. Damon makes the point unmistakably by dismissing 'Pastures, Caves, and Springs' in one gesture as 'enticing things' that have no power over him any longer. The phrase is a brief catalogue, almost a vignette, of the typical pastoral settings to be encountered in the idylls of Suckling, Cartwright, Randolph, and other naturalists. Marvell's argument is that these sensuous refreshments no longer answer the demands of the soul; in short, Damon's thirst, a thirst for sanctity, cannot be slaked by the fountain that 'Tinkles within the concave Shell' of a pagan landscape. However, it is typical of Marvell, Spenser, and Milton, that the antagonist be allowed to present a genuinely forceful and appealing case, lest the victory of the righteous seem too facile, and consequently worthless. Clorinda's couplet on the fountain is melodious; the soft 'l' sounds and the easy flow of the line-and-a-half following the first caesura ensure that Damon is not rejecting an existence without strong intrinsic beauty and attraction for him. The active faith advocated by Puritanism demanded that the struggle against evil and temptation be a worthy and unending one.[22]

The final illustration of Marvell's adherence to the characteristics of the genre in which he is writing is the role of Pan in 'Clorinda and Damon'. The closing lines of the dialogue give an explanation of the shepherd's conversion.

> C. And what late change? D. The other day
>   Pan met me.   C. What did great Pan say?
> D. Words that transcend poor Shepherds skill,
>   But He ere since my Songs does fill:
>   And his Name swells my slender Oate.
> C. Sweet must Pan sound in Damons Note.
> D. Clorinda's voice might make it sweet.
> C. Who would not in Pan's Praises meet?

(ll. 19–26)

One could multiply examples of Pan's appearing in Christian pastoral poetry as a type of Christ; the locus classicus is the May

Eclogue of *The Shepheardes Calender* and its gloss, in which E. K. explains:

> Great pan) is Christ, the very God of all shepheards, which calleth himselfe the greate and good shepherd. The name is most rightly (me thinkes) applyed to him, for Pan signifieth all or omnipotent, which is onely the Lord Iesus.[23]

The 'Words' Pan spoke to Damon are, apparently, mysterious and not to be told carelessly to the uninitiate. Marvell again keeps scrupulously within the diction of the pastoral dialogue by reminding Clorinda and the reader that the pastoral was by common critical consent a genre committed to the 'low' style and therefore unfit for expressing spiritual revelation.[24] The 'poor Shepherds skill' cannot reach the exalted phrases of Pan's message and so Marvell claims that Damon's pastoral ditties will henceforth be *inspired* by Pan, that he will 'fill' the songs and 'swell' the oat with spiritual insights that Damon can only reverence, not analyse. Marvell has modulated the poem into the vocabulary of Christian liturgy, while sustaining the fiction of Pan and Damon. 'Words', 'Songs', 'Name', and 'Praises' are not only the everyday elements of Christian worship but also part of its special terminology.

The resolution of the debate is achieved in a pithy, almost offhand way, as Clorinda accedes to Damon's new-found faith. Even so, Marvell cannot resist the final pun on 'meet'; it refers to the musical term for a concord of voices, but also to the new basis for the meeting of Damon and Clorinda, the worship of Pan. Thus economically the idea of 'meeting' in the cave, and all that it implied, is ultimately cast aside. The final Chorus contains a further allusion to the Spenserian technique and ethos which to some extent have governed 'Clorinda and Damon'.

> Of Pan the flowry Pastures sing,
> Caves eccho, and the Fountains ring.
> Sing then while he doth us inspire;
> For all the World is our Pan's Quire.[25]
>
> (ll. 27–30)

Line 28 can only have been intended as a tribute to the beautiful refrain of *Epithalamion*, one of whose variants is 'That all the woods shal answer and theyr eccho ring'. But Marvell is not simply constructing an emulative compliment to Spenser; the same line that records his debt to his master in the genre also makes a point for 'Clorinda and Damon' itself. The caves and fountains whose significance had divided the antagonists earlier now join the chorus in praise of Pan; the natural scene has been converted to divine worship, as have its denizens. The metaphorical 'all the World is our Pan's Quire' is a version of the pastoral convention which required, usually, that the landscape reflect the mourning posture of the love-stricken shepherd. Not infrequently nature mirrored human joy, but the concept of a choir of praise made up of the elements of created nature is closely related to the conventions of nature as the 'Book of God' and to other analogical tenets of natural theology.[26]

Finally, the exhortation 'Sing then while he doth us inspire' is a precise interpretation of what Damon has said above about Pan's influence on his songs. 'Inspire' means, literally, to fill with breath or spirit; and just as Pan's inspiration has made Damon capable of singing his praises with nothing but the oaten flute and slender skill of pastoral poetry, so the natural world can chant its worship only so long as the god's spirit is immanent in it.

'A Dialogue between Thyrsis and Dorinda'[27] is firmly embedded in the pastoral genre; and its main point is the description of a celestial world which is to be desired above the beauties of nature. Throughout the poem, Dorinda's speeches are compounded of ignorant simplicity and a surprisingly intellectual cleverness in the use of words. Thyrsis, in contrast, speaks in a manner which reveals a full acquaintance with the mythological and symbolic conventions of the pastoral; but he is not given to word-play. To his answer that he and the shepherdess will go to 'the Elizium', Dorinda rejoins, in a line that echoes Clorinda but adds a note of ingenuous curiosity, 'oh where i'st?' Thyrsis' reply recalls the grudging instruction of Damon: 'A Chast Soul, can never mis't'. A good deal could be made of the assumption in this line that purity of spirit is the equivalent in the moral sphere of pure knowledge in the intellectual sphere.

Dorinda misses the subtle point, however, and can only exclaim with a naïveté carefully contrived by Marvell, 'I know no way, but one, our home;/Is our cell Elizium?' (ll. 7–8). In Dorinda's question there is the pathos of one who is disabused of an illusion long and fondly held. It has been an important habit of the pastoral poets to speak of the natural countryside as Elysium; comparisons to the earthly paradise were commonplace, and to the various symbols of sublunary perfection, such as the Isles of the Hesperides. But these are being swept aside by Thyrsis with one gesture, as he turns Dorinda's eyes to heaven.

> Turn thine Eye to yonder Skie,
> There the milky way doth lye;
> 'Tis a sure but rugged way,
> That leads to Everlasting day.

(ll. 9–12)

'The milky way' alludes both to our galaxy and to the Promised Land of milk and honey.[28] The adjectives collect around 'way' in "Tis a sure but rugged way' as if Marvell were reluctant to leave a word which can speak in so many guises of the journey of the soul toward God. The 'milky way' leads to 'Everlasting day', a phrase that will occur in a more impressive context in 'On a Drop of Dew'; it is a symbol that has been illuminated for us by the exchange between Clorinda and Damon concerning the sun as the eye of heaven. Here endless daylight is seen as the very image of heaven, not as oppressive heat or as an obstacle to the fulfilment of love.

Dorinda, quite sensibly, asks how they are to reach the sky without wings; obviously, she is unacquainted with the symbolic tradition that pictures the soul as a winged being, in recognition of its original birth in heaven and its constant longing to return.[29] Thyrsis does not even pause to enlighten her, but resorts to an analogy with fire, and a pun on 'aspire' which combines both the usual sense of 'hope for' and one of its Latin meanings, 'climb up to'. His point is that the natural motion of the soul is upward, so that the mention of fire is not an idle one. But Dorinda insists on translating Thyrsis' noble metaphors into a language she can grasp; she wants to know 'how do they/Pass Eternity away?' In its utter simplicity it is a question that dramatizes the gap between an existence bound by time and one where permanence and perfection rule. And for once Thyrsis is gracious enough to speak in a way she can understand; his description of eternity might be taken from any pastoral paean to the Golden Age. It is a place where fear is absent and, Thyrsis remarks pointedly, hope as well. This is natural enough, since the spirit's goal has been reached and it can want nothing more. Even the shepherd's pipe is replaced by the music of the spheres; the pastoral life has no justification here, or at least that part of it which is concerned with actual labour, privation, and apprehension. Thyrsis goes on to paint the pastoral of eternity in lines 31–38, and we may notice that it, too, is made up of the standard items of the Elysian catalogue.

It is this highly conventional passage that immediately precedes Dorinda's invitation to Thyrsis to join her in a drugged passage to the other world. She is 'sick' with longing for the delights he has described, and wants only to hasten her arrival in 'Elizium'. It is doubtful that Marvell was being so subtle, but it can be noted that after Thyrsis' first description of a heavenly place where there is no fear, Dorinda merely wishes to 'Antidate' her 'future state' by thinking quietly about it and by talking about 'Elizium'. But once she has heard of its soft and musical beauty, and of the promise that she will be a pastoral queen, she rushes to embrace death. I can only suggest that the final lines of 'Thyrsis and Dorinda' parallel Spenser's interest in the problem of the soul's weariness of the burdensome tasks put upon it by belief in the supernatural and by the exigencies of the natural world.

Marvell does not always cast his religious dialectic in the dialogue form; 'On a Drop of Dew'[30] is simply an extended conceit. Its structure is bare to the point of being skeletal; the picture of the dew-drop is painted in eighteen lines, followed by eighteen lines on the soul. The last four lines seal the correspondences that have been drawn in the body of the poem, in a tone very much like the statement that concludes a successful geometric proof. But the proposition 'a equals b' is only the frame of 'On a Drop of Dew'; the accumulation of similarities to illuminate the first premise is the mark of Marvell's virtuosity. In this poem he varies his verse forms widely to suit an involved argument, and creates a rhyme scheme far more subtle and flexible than anything he has yet attempted—both innovations suggest the influences of Donne and Herbert, especially since 'On a Drop of Dew' exhibits something like a stanzaic organization.

The first eight lines of the poem will demonstrate all these characteristics, but they will also reveal the very difficult syntax that makes the interpretation of several lines problematical.[31]

> See how the Orient Dew,
> Shed from the Bosom of the Morn
>   Into the blowing Roses,
>   Yet careless of its Mansion new;

For the clear Region where 'twas born
Round in its self incloses:
And in its little Globes Extent,
Frames as it can its native Element.

(ll. 1–8)

It is not usual for Marvell to begin a meditative or descriptive poem with an imperative, so we must assume that 'On a Drop of Dew' is meant to be a hortatory exemplum. The same tone appears in the demonstrative 'Such' in line 37. What we are invited to examine is the 'Orient Dew' in its pristine beauty, dropping into the earthly beauty of the rose. Empson's difficulty about the tense of 'Shed' can hardly be a real one; if, as he says, 'Frames' is the first verb in the sentence that can be clearly associated with the dewdrop, then there can be no justification for assuming that 'Shed' is in the perfect tense. It must be a past participle, referring to the fall from 'the Bosom of the Morn'.[32] 'Orient', although it is a conventional hyperbolical adjective, is particularly fitting in this verse, because it describes the dewdrop as lustrous and at the same time reminds us of the comparison to a pearl, and deepens our sense of a shining sphere. Further, it calls into play the other associations of the word with the East, always the poetic source of jewels; and this establishes a link with 'the Morn' which is both eastern and shining. From the second line the roseate colour of the dawn is carried into the image of the 'blowing Roses'. The Latin is even more intricately interwoven; in the lines *Cernis ut Eoi descendat Gemmula Roris,/Inque Rosas roseo transfluat orta sinu* (ll. 1–2), the epithet *roseo* is transferred to *sinu* (the bosom of the dawn), where it can mean either 'full of roses' or 'blooming'. Since *roseo* is juxtaposed immediately to *Rosas* the comparison between the present and previous homes of the dewdrop is driven home with epigrammatic conciseness, and *transfluat* provides the exact verb to convey both motion and interpenetration.[33]

From the beginning of the poem it is evident that Marvell is conscious of the seemingly paradoxical attitude of both the dewdrop and the soul, in that they reject categorically a world whose physical beauty is never minimized by the poet. Permanence is chosen above transience, perfection above imperfection which is yet lovely; the distinctions are clear, but not crude. In specifying the rose as the receptacle of the dewdrop Marvell has chosen deliberately the universal symbol for the most perfect state of earthly beauty. He is speaking only of created beauty, not the rose's significance as a symbol of divine love; and the force of 'blowing' reminds us that the moment of its perfection is also the moment before the onset of decay. It is important that we feel the perfection of the rose's beauty because the fact that the dewdrop is 'careless' of it then becomes more impressive. The reason for this superb indifference is given in the lines, 'For the clear Region where 'twas born/Round in its self incloses' (ll. 5–6); but the syntax here is at its most ambiguous. As Grierson points out,[34] the Latin says, quite clearly, 'incloses itself in its own orb'. But Margoliouth's opinion that 'Line 5 gives the reason for l. 6'[65] supports what seems to be the main direction of the conceit. In brief, with an ellipsis typical of the poem, Marvell omits a pronoun. If we supply the omission the lines yield the meaning: 'the dewdrop is not affected by the beauty of the rose because, by reflecting the heavens from its own shining, spherical surface, it "incloses" the "clear Region" where "'twas born", and thus is provided with the sustenance that it disdains to draw from the earth'. As if to insist on this reading, Marvell rephrases and repeats the idea in: 'And in its little Globes Extent,/Frames as it can its native Element' (ll. 7–8). To be sure, Marvell is aware of the practical absurdity of 'framing' heaven in a dewdrop; but such an objection is averted by the concessive 'as it can'. Marvell deflates the hyperbole consciously, while retaining the communicable truth of the original conceit. It is eminently worth observing how he converts the poise and shimmering motion of the dewdrop into psychological states in the following passage.

> How it the purple flow'r does slight,
> Scarce touching where it lyes,
> But gazing back upon the Skies,
> Shines with a mournful Light;
> Like its own Tear,
> Because so long divided from the Sphear.
> Restless it roules and unsecure,
> Trembling lest it grow impure:
> Till the warm Sun pitty it's Pain,
> And to the Skies exhale it back again.

(ll. 9–18)

Notice that in almost every case the imputation of human feelings to the dewdrop is rationalized in the next line by a reference to its physical state. Thus, if we find that the notion of a drop of dew slighting the flower it rests upon is too fanciful for belief, our objection is met by the descriptive 'Scarce touching where it lyes'. The line is justified by its precise observation of the way a dewdrop retains its spherical shape while resting on a flat surface—and by the perception that this paradoxical physical behaviour can indeed represent the reluctance of purity to endure contact with something less pure than itself.[36]

In lines 11–13 the reflection of heaven shines in a way that suggests another sphere, thus making the dewdrop resemble 'its own Tear'. The image is not unusual in itself, but it does reinforce the cardinal metaphor of the entire poem—that of lesser entities that identify themselves with greater ones by containing the larger bodies within themselves, if only by reflection or analogy. As if to remind us that the poem is concerned, too, with the origin of both the dewdrop and the soul, line 14 explains that the 'mournful Light' with which the drop shines is elicited 'Because so long divided from the Sphear'.[37] We need pause over 'Sphear' only long enough to point out that, aside from the reference to heaven in general and to the spheres of influence of the Renaissance cosmologists, the word carries with it the connotation of perfection, since the sphere in both Platonic and Aristotelian philosophy was the very image of the perfect. Naturally enough, Marvell is at pains to continue the variations on this figure in the latter half of the poem, since the soul cannot be said to have the obvious physical qualities of the spherical dewdrop. But he manages, with the use of 'circling', 'wound', and 'round', to establish a degree of continuity in the poem's diction.

The dewdrop's grief at being separated from its proper sphere leads to an instability which is both physical and psychological.

> Restless it roules and unsecure,
>   Trembling lest it grow impure:
>   Till the warm Sun pitty it's Pain,
> And to the Skies exhale it back again.

(ll. 15–18)

It is possible that Marvell intended 'unsecure' to refer not only to the precarious position of the drop on the petal, but also back to

the 'careless' of line 4; he would have known that one of the
meanings of *securus* was 'carefree', and the drop at this point is
very evidently in danger of becoming uncarefree.[38] But the sun
which reigns over it has something of the character of the sun
in 'Eyes and Tears' (ll. 21–24), in so far as it (or He) feels pity for
the world's lot. In offering a conceited explanation for the process
of evaporation and, indeed, for the entire cycle of precipitation,
Marvell recalls Crashaw's lines from 'In memory of the Vertuous
and Learned Lady Madre de Teresa that sought an early Martyrdome':

> Like a soft lumpe of Incense, hasted
> By too hot a fire, and wasted,
> Into perfuming cloudes. So fast
> Shalt thou exhale to heaven at last,
> In a disolving sigh. . . .

> (ll. 114–118)

Marvell makes no attempt to disguise the joints of the poem; the
strict comparison between the dewdrop and the soul is begun with
a direct 'So', as if we were to enter into an epic simile.

> So the Soul, that Drop, that Ray
> Of the clear Fountain of Eternal Day,
> Could it within the humane flow'r be seen,
> Remembring still its former height,
> Shuns the sweat leaves and blossoms green.

> (ll. 19–23)

The lines on the soul, like those on the dewdrop, make pointed use
of the figures of personification and identification. 'That Drop, that
Ray/Of the clear Fountain of Eternal Day'—by calling the soul
two different names Marvell stresses the double significance of the
symbolic fountain. It is not only the sun that is being glanced at
here, although the implicit reference would seem to be to line 17.
It is also the source of the soul's being, something for which 'sun'
is only one among many possible names. But if Marvell is going to
cast the second eighteen-line strophe in terms predominantly of
light, he must maintain the fabric of his analogy by stressing,
initially, some metaphors that relate the soul closely to the dewdrop.
Thus the epithet 'Drop' and the naming of the sun, or Son, 'the
clear Fountain'. The qualities of water and light are deliberately

intermingled in the figurative strategy that has characterized the poem thus far. One more detail is added to the analogy in a line which should really be parenthetical, 'Could it within the humane flow'r be seen'. If the soul can be compared to a drop of dew, then the body that contains the soul, and from which the soul yearns to flee to its home in heaven, can be compared to the flower that contains the uncontaminated dewdrop.

And just as the drop is said to gaze mournfully back at its heavenly home, so the soul,

> Remembring still its former height,
> Shuns the sweat leaves and blossoms green;
> And, recollecting its own Light,
> Does, in its pure and circling thoughts, express
> The greater Heaven in an Heaven less.

(ll. 22–26)

The 'height', of course, is that of both heaven and the exalted soul itself before its descent into an earthly body. But by the time the soul has turned away from the 'sweat leaves and blossoms green' it is apparent that no cause is assigned *within the poem* to the act of renunciation. Or, more accurately, the emphasis is always put heavily upon the attractions of divine beauty, and never at the expense of earthly beauty. This presents Marvell with a taxing technical problem—how to support the positive epithets attached to heaven without attributing sensuous qualities to it? The solution is found in resorting to a very simple diction that is yet charged with religious connotation. Thus line 24, while it is the parallel in its metaphoric structure to 'Frames as it can its native Element', makes a more profound point, since 'its own Light' creates a conscious ambiguity between the meanings, 'its proper, generic light' and 'the light the soul creates itself'. There is no doubt that the former is the dominant meaning; but there is just enough suspense between the two possible interpretations, and the image of 'collecting again' that the verb introduces, to intensify the relation between the soul and the source of its light.

By the same token, 'pure and circling thoughts' in this context, is almost redundant; the circle stands universally for purity and perfection. In so far as the soul possesses these qualities it can 'express/The greater Heaven in an Heaven less'.[39] And it is important if we are to understand Marvell's dialectic here to see that the emphasis is equally divided in 'an Heaven less'. Perhaps the distinction would be clearer if the lines that follow were better; but the last part of the discourse on the soul adds little meaning to those already established. It does give Marvell an opportunity to extend the catalogue of analogies which thus far has been the spine of the poem. But what is missing from the final passage is precisely that delicacy of selection that assured the doubling of each effect in the first twenty-odd lines by a metaphor or an epithet mirrored or reinterpreted within those same lines. Instead we have:

> In how coy a Figure wound,
> Every way it turns away:
> So the World excluding round,
> Yet receiving in the Day.
> Dark beneath, but bright above:
> Here disdaining, there in Love.
> How loose and easie hence to go:
> How girt and ready to ascend.
> Moving but on a point below,
> It all about does upwards bend.   (ll. 27–36)

We know nothing of Marvell's part in collecting or editing the *Miscellaneous Poems*; the strong probability is that he had no hand in it at all. We cannot, therefore, charge him with the capricious punctuation of this passage; rather, we must simply deplore the casual attitude of most seventeenth-century printers and compositors toward the niceties of 'pointing'. Here, at least, the sense is not obscured. Whether the 'Figure' is physical or rhetorical is not clear, and 'Every way it turns away' is the clumsiest sort of verbal gymnastics. But the disputed 'So the World excluding round' is easy enough to decipher, even without the help of the Latin.[40] However difficult the line might be at first it would yield its not very heavily veiled meaning as the contrast emerges in 'Yet receiving in the Day'. As if the categorical distinction between 'the World' and 'the Day' had not been established firmly enough, Marvell adds the qualifying: 'Dark beneath, but bright above:/Here disdaining, there in Love' (ll. 31–32). 'Excluding round' refers only to the plane which surrounds the soul and to the one below it; the soul is still open to influence from above. 'Dark beneath, but bright above' is the baldest possible employment of the figurative language of Christianity and Platonism; coming after the subtleties of the first twenty lines it begins to justify the charge of 'appauvrisse-ment' that Legouis lays against the poem.[41] It is possible, however, that Marvell intends a secondary reference to the moon, which indeed could be described thus, and which might have been recog-nized as a Plotinian analogue of the soul.[42] Marvell introduces his astronomical reference as casually as he alludes to his observations of the surface tensions of liquids. Science and pseudo-science leave their traces frequently in Marvell's poetry, but rarely does he allow their significance to become organically important in a poem; a reading of Donne, Chapman, Lord Herbert, or Fulke Greville will show that other 'metaphysicals' made more integral use of con-temporary theories and experiments than Marvell ever did.

But the lines on the dark-light, moon-sun contrasts resolve themselves into line 32, 'Here disdaining, there in Love', which displays some measure of the verbal wit encountered at the beginning of the poem. 'Here' alludes obviously to the world, 'there' to the sun, or 'Day'; but at the same time the words point to the imagined parts of the soul itself that are alternately darkened and illuminated. By making the directive words refer both to the soul and to the universe around it Marvell adds one more kind of identification to the many which fill the poem; he also looks ahead to the physical metaphor of lines 35–36: 'Moving but on a point below,/It all about does upwards bend'. Thus an abstract entity is made to seem an object precariously balanced, as was the dewdrop in lines 10 and 15–16. Both the balance and the precariousness are important, because the first dramatizes the position of the human psyche, caught between heaven and earth; and the second empha-sizes the longing of the soul to return to heaven, a figure that repeats and varies the simile of the dewdrop's gazing up 'Like its own Tear'.

To conclude the poem Marvell must find a symbol which will combine physical and religious reality with economy and expressive power. Thus the last two couplets turn, with a scant appearance of consistency, to a familiar image of divine intervention in the affairs of the world.

> Such did the Manna's sacred Dew destil;
> White, and intire, though congeal'd and chill.
> Congeal'd on Earth: but does, dissolving, run
> Into the Glories of th' Almighty Sun.   (ll. 37–40)

The lines glance at the recurrent theme of distillation, and the adjectives 'White' and 'intire' reiterate in different symbolic terms the values of perfection, sphericalness, and purity that have governed the entire poem.[43] Now congealing cold is added to the opposed values of darkness and impurity; and the opposition is given added force by the dominating 'Glories' of heat and light in the final line. 'Dissolving' is a precise metaphor for melting and for the untying of the bonds between the heavenly and the earthly. And, although 'run' is primarily an image for the precipitate flight of the soul to Christ (the Son), it also carries on the idea of melting. Although Marvell does not paint the world as a place of unmitigated evil, there can be no doubt that in 'On a Drop of Dew' the soul is seen only as the most unwilling prisoner in its cage of flesh.

This emblematic concept[44] is examined most fully in 'A Dialogue between the Soul and Body',[45] which presents the claims of the flesh and the spirit not so much to resolve and choose between them, as to dramatize each in a way that will not allow of an obvious or arbitrary resolution. The initial image is ubiquitous in Christian poetry of the era; a reading of Donne's 'Second Anniversary' will turn up any number of lines such as:

> Thinke that no stubborne sullen Anchorit,
> Which fixt to a pillar, or a grave, doth sit
> Bedded, and bath'd in all his ordures, dwels
> So fowly as our Soules in their first-built Cels;
>
> (ll. 169–172)

or this, from the verse letter 'To The Countesse of Bedford' that begins 'T'have written then . . .'

> Let the minds thoughts be but transplanted so,
> Into the body, and bastardly they grow.
> What hate could hurt our bodies like our love?
> Wee (but no forraine tyrants could) remove
> These not ingrav'd, but inborne dignities,
> Caskets of soules; Temples, and Palaces:
> For, bodies shall from death redeemed bee,
> Soules but preserv'd, not naturally free.

As men to'our prisons, new soules to us are sent,
Which learne vice there, and come in innocent.

(ll. 51–60)

It will be seen immediately that the tenor of Donne's treatment is
different from Marvell's poem; there is no true debate there since
the questions of relative value have long since been decided.
Furthermore, Donne's lines are more closely imitative of a treatise
or sermon in that they seem to teach and exhort, where Marvell's
verse attempts to give voice to the many parts of the paradoxical
experience at the heart of much Christian thought. A similar
approach to the theme can be found in William Hammond's 'A
Dialogue upon Death', between Phillis and Damon.[46] Hammond is
no less certain of the eventual answer to the problem posed, but
there is in his poem at least a semblance of the cogency which
Marvell gives to the arguments of his 'Soul'.

> *Phil.* How can that be, when sense doth keep
> The door of pleasure? That destroy'd,
> The soul, if it survive, must sleep,
> Senseless, of delectation void.
> *Dam.* Sense is the door of such delight
> As beasts receive; through which, alas,
> Since Nature's nothing but a sight,
> More enemies than friends do pass:
> Nor is the soul less capable,
> But naked doth her object prove
> More truly; as more sensible
> Is this fair hand stript of its glove.

(ll. 25–36)

Even before Damon has crushed debate with the sanctioned reply,
Phillis has begged the true question by permitting sense to be the
door only of pleasure. The colouration of this description had been
sufficient for many ages of faith, since the agony of questioning
the nature of knowledge did not touch the conviction that God
maintained the intelligible fabric of the world. The great revolution
in this respect occurred in Marvell's own century; and even so
conventional an exercise as 'A Dialogue between the Soul and
Body' shows signs of the awareness that the senses are the gates
not only of sinful pleasure but also of knowledge and perception
essential to the continuing vision of the soul and the mind.

The sermon literature of the century is filled with exemplary discourses on the theme of the caged soul; one can hardly read three consecutive pages in Donne, Andrewes, or Jeremy Taylor without coming upon a sentiment of the same character as Joseph Hall's 'I account this body nothing, but a close prison to my soul; and the earth a large prison to my body',[47] which in itself is reminiscent of Donne's 'Our prisons prison, earth'.[48] Marvell's poem is distinguished from both the meditation and the strict debate by the device of having its antagonists address themselves to an imagined judge or listener.[49] The poem is primarily a study of the interdependent effects wrought upon the soul and the body in the fated union of irreconcilable faculties; Marvell devotes as much intellectual energy to the body's painful awakening to consciousness through the agency of the soul as he does to the more conventional picture of the torments of the soul enshrouded in the clay of the flesh. In fact, the very disposition of the poem's four stanzas creates one of the important ambiguities in its meaning; the Soul, naturally enough, speaks first—but this permits the Body to have the last word, and thus to make the poem's final impression. Rather than take this as evidence of faulty structure, we should see it as a strong indication that Marvell, as always, was more interested in the true content of a paradox than in resolving it through logic or lyric. The Body in its final stanza is even given two extra couplets in which to drive home its arguments, and there is nothing in this poem to compare to the final, triumphant chorus of 'A Dialogue Between The Resolved Soul, and Created Pleasure'.

The portrayal of paradox, indeed, dominates the Soul's opening speech; and much of what it says could be exemplified easily from the works of Crashaw, Herbert, Donne, or the sermon-writers.

> O who shall, from this Dungeon, raise
> A Soul inslav'd so many wayes?
> With bolts of Bones, that fetter'd stands
> In Feet; and manacled in Hands.
> Here blinded with an Eye; and there
> Deaf with the drumming of an Ear.
> A Soul hung up, as 'twere, in Chains
> Of Nerves, and Arteries, and Veins.
> Tortur'd, besides each other part,
> In a vain Head, and double Heart.   (ll. 1–10)

68

The initial question is in some respects rhetorical, since every believing Christian knew that salvation through the grace of God would free the spirit eventually from the bonds of the flesh. But the dramatic effect is dependent upon the soul's situation *during* its imprisonment, when it may be assumed that the body clouds its perception of the truth. The correlating conceit—the body as prison—is posited in the mention of 'Dungeon', and the stanza then goes on to revivify, by reinterpreting, the very phrase we have just used, 'the bonds of the flesh'. 'Bolts' is a synonym for fetters, and thus stands in apposition to the fetters and manacles of lines 3 and 4. The paradox of the embodied soul is implicit in the word 'in', which is an ellipsis for 'in having'. Thus, from the soul's viewpoint, hands themselves are manacles.

This trope, redefining the avenues of perception and motion as perfect bars to vision and growth, continues through the lines on 'blind eyes' and 'deaf ears', biblical phrases that reverberate through much seventeenth-century religious prose and poetry.[50] Marvell introduces a slight innovation in the next lines, where the visual image alludes to anatomical science and to a body hanging from a gibbet.

The metaphor shifts from conventional paradox to graphic comparison, since the muscular and circulatory networks of the body may indeed be seen as an enchaining web. But in the final couplet he reverts to the first mode of the poem and adds its first note of deliberate punning. 'Vain' carries equally the meanings of 'empty' and 'foolish', as well as the modern connotation of 'self-regarding'; and the 'double Heart' is both a precise description of the ventricles and auricles and a reference to the duplicity and deceptiveness of passion. The first ten lines, then, constitute an agile restatement of the received doctrines on the relation of soul to body.

However, the poem's originality begins to reveal itself in the parallel appeal of the Body against its tormentor. And this time the opening question (although it, too, is answered by the doctrine of bodily redemption) poses a greater challenge.

> O who shall me deliver whole,
> From bonds of this Tyrannic Soul?
> Which, stretcht upright, impales me so,
> That mine own Precipice I go;

And warms and moves this needless Frame:
(A Fever could but do the same.)
And, wanting where its spight to try,
Has made me live to let me dye.
A Body that could never rest,
Since this ill Spirit it possest.

(ll. 11–20)

This is the voice of Matter, protesting against being stirred out of the inert mindlessness to which it had been consigned by Plotinus and his followers. It speaks with unknowing irony when it refers to its 'needless Frame', since only the soul can inform the body of its true needs.[51] And in its 'stretcht upright' can be heard the tone of the worldling objecting to the moral rectitude of the devout, which seems only self-righteousness to the eye blinded by unbelief.[52] While the Soul regards the Body only as a lumpish, unpurposeful burden, the Body is articulate in ascribing actively hostile motives to the Soul. Marvell adheres scrupulously to decorum in differentiating between the passive materialism of the flesh and the active spirituality of the soul, even in the smallest detail.

In lines 18–20 Marvell might almost have been paraphrasing Plotinus or John Smith[53] in describing the soul breathing the life of the spirit into the inert flesh. The Body complains that it has been forced into life only to be let die, an argument that evades the Puritan sentiment that the life of vigorous moral conflict was the only way to earn the rewards of virtue and holy living. So sure is this Body that it has been unfairly imposed upon that it compares its invasion by the Soul to the state of possession by a demon. In both cases, peace would follow exorcism of the 'ill Spirit', but peace for the body is a return to the motionless unconsciousness of pure matter.

Marvell carries the allusion to black magic into the next stanza, where the Soul shows signs of having learned from the Body's habits of verbal irony. It does not yet pun; perhaps the corruption has not spread so far. But it does indulge in a kind of freedom of paradoxical statement that is more clearly humorous than its first speech.

What Magick could me thus confine
Within anothers Grief to pine?
Where whatsoever it complain,

I feel, that cannot feel, the pain.
And all my Care its self employes,
That to preserve, which me destroys:
Constrain'd not only to indure
Diseases, but, whats worse, the Cure:
And ready oft the Port to gain,
Am Shipwrackt into Health again.

The humour is in the Soul's awareness that the Body has induced in it sensations that, according to all theologians, necromancers, and natural philosophers, the soul is unable to feel. Thus, though it 'pines' for another's grief, that grief has been made peculiarly the Soul's own by what is seen in this stanza as a supremely wry joke. That the Soul shares at least some of the aspects of the joke is indicated by the play on 'Care', where the double meaning of 'interest' and 'trouble' is extremely apposite. The Soul's ironic insight is developed sufficiently to see that its very task is the necessary cause of its greatest suffering, for in informing the body with the life and meaning of the spirit, it also keeps alive its loathed fleshly prison.

The last two couplets turn back upon the Body's previous speech and adopt the metaphors of ill health, but with a difference. Here the life of the flesh is seen as indeed 'this long Disease'; but the Soul converts the bitterness to acid wit by reminding us that the soul's curative efforts not only cure the flesh of its innate evils, but prolong it in its life of repeated falls from perfection. Beneath these lines is a subdued but continued reference to death as the desired end of the soul. Thus, the cure of bodily disease is a sharper disappointment to the Soul than the illness itself; and the 'Port' which one meets in so many devotional poems, that port which is to be the harbour of the storm-tossed spirit after its earthly journey,[54] is seen here as frustratingly unattainable. Instead we have the humorous conversion of 'Health' into a calamity for the Soul—its 'Shipwrack' is the recovery of the body, another failure to reach the haven of souls in death.

The Body's final rebuttal is phrased so that it includes the terms of magic, physical science, and medicine that have already been established in the poem. But where the Soul has interpreted the body's welfare as its own illness, here the Body characterizes as diseases, first, the emotions to which the soul is subject, and then,

71

the mental faculties that are its distinctive features. Thus hope is a
'Cramp' and love a 'Pestilence'; and part of the amusement inherent in the Body's expression of outrage is in our sense that in
another poetic genre—the contemporary love lyric—the epithets
would be perfectly in place. But this is not the despairing lover
deploring his enslavement to a cruel mistress, it is the very essence
of the flesh crying out against the feelings that the world believes
to be, above all, fleshly. The distinction Marvell draws in

> Joy's chearful Madness does perplex:
> Or Sorrow's other Madness vex,
>
> (ll. 37–38)

may owe something to *The Anatomy of Melancholy*[55] but the concepts of memory and knowledge in

> Which Knowledge forces me to know;
> And Memory will not foregoe,
>
> (ll. 39–40)

are his own. That which must be known and not forgotten in the
couplet is the sum of emotional experience just described. The mental functions are seen here as personified forces which impose their
special activities upon the body; the point, I take it, of the personifications is that the soul contains the forms of all mental faculties,
and that its perfect apprehension of Knowledge creates the possibility
of 'knowing' within the body. But this 'Body' is not to be imposed
upon so easily; taking its cue from the Soul's characterization of
bodily health as spiritual disease, it converts the Soul's faculties
not only into torturing 'ulcers' and 'palsies' but directly into 'Sin'.

> What but a Soul could have the wit
> To build me up for Sin so fit?
> So Architects do square and hew,
> Green Trees that in the Forest grew.
>
> (ll. 41–44)

In these concluding lines the poem achieves two climaxes: first, the
bitter irony of the Body reaches its height in the word-play of the
first couplet; and, secondly, the final couplet introduces a judgment
which appeals to a world of activities and values that hitherto has
been only implied. The multifold meanings of 'wit' in the
Renaissance are not at issue here; all that is intended is to convey

the scorn of the body for the skill of the soul in rendering it subject
to pain and damnation. In a different way, 'for' implies both 'suited
to' and 'equipped to commit sin'. In either case, the Body's ironic
comment is revealed, ironically, as its own prejudiced mis-
understanding of the purpose of the devoted labours of the soul.
Thus, the mention of the professional skill of the architect in the
last couplet leads to an evaluation of similar complexity. The Body
sees the Soul as comparable to the architect who reshapes matter
to suit a pre-existent, abstract idea of form. It has often been thought
that the architect is being criticized for treating nature brutally
and mechanically, 'hewing' it to shapes it would never assume
without the harsh touch of thought and design. But we must
remember that it is the Body speaking here; and the Body has
been throughout the poem the irreconcilable enemy of all sensation,
intellection, art, and aspiration. In 'A Dialogue between the Soul
and Body' the major concern is not with the relation between
nature and artifice, but with the recalcitrance of both elements
in the human compound; and the Body, as it has pictured itself
in the poem, is not entitled to compare itself to the forest trees.
It has not been an unconscious but growing thing; rather, it has
been the essence of fruitless inertia. One sign of the extravagance
of its complaint is that there is nothing in the architectural comparison that can justify a reference to sin. All that relates the building
made from trees and the Body who speaks these lines is the form
that both have been given by an intellect that interferes with their
natural inclinations. Only the Body can interpret this as an invitation to sinfulness.

This critical indecision may be caused by the lack of direct
dialectical conflict in the parallel complaints of Soul and Body,
but no such disability results from the arguments presented in 'A
Dialogue Between The Resolved Soul, and Created Pleasure'.[56]
Not only is the debate acted out in its most stringent form, but
Marvell attempts to give each contestant a characteristic tone,
vocabulary, and verse metre. The poem is not so much a debate as
the dramatization of a temptation and its failure. It reveals a
distinct dramatic structure, and one which is closely tied to certain
conventional ethical and theological doctrines. The contest opens
with a hortatory chorus addressed to the soul; the action begins as
Pleasure attacks each of the five senses in order, and after the
successive attacks have failed, the chorus once again encourages

73

the Soul. The next series of assaults by Pleasure follows the pattern of temptations set originally by Satan's temptation of Christ in the Synoptic Gospels and rehearsed by Spenser in Book II of *The Faerie Queene*, Milton in *Paradise Regained*, and Giles Fletcher in *Christ's Victory and Triumph*. The vices aimed at are lust, avarice, the hunger for worldly power, and the 'hydroptique' thirst for knowledge. Marvell is thoroughly conventional in his choice of temptations and in their order of presentation, except that in the first part of the poem the sense of hearing usurps the place of the usually pre-eminent sense of sight. This results in a slight disalignment of the poem's structure; if the topmost points of each scale are to match, sight, on the scale of the senses, should be equated with knowledge on the scale of desired goods. But Marvell resorts to music as the figure for universal harmony; and in this poem it will once again stand for the most beautiful part of creation and the most powerful temptation of the mind.

The exhortation to the soul that opens the poem is weighted with the terminology of the armourer. This conforms to the conception of the 'Dialogue' as a mortal combat and extends the sources of the poem's references to that part of Christian symbolism which is predominantly military. One can find iconographical explanations for the shield, the helmet, and the sword,[57] but it is more important to recognize that, thus clothed, the Soul would appear in the *persona* of the archangel Michael. And it is Michael who, in Revelation 12: 7–9, fights and kills the dragon that is also 'that old serpent, called the Devil, and Satan', and who is as well the guardian of the Church Militant against the Devil. The armed warrior would recall to Marvell's readers St George too, as well as Redcrosse as he is shown in the engraving that precedes Book II of *The Faerie Queene*. Above all, the poem's first four lines echo the words of St Paul in Ephesians 6, where the saints of Ephesus are commanded to 'Put on the whole armour of God', which includes 'the shield of faith', 'the helmet of salvation', and 'the sword of the Spirit, which is the word of God'. However, it is not the biblical allusion alone which gives Marvell's lines meaning; it provides a background against which his verbs acquire secondary meanings. Thus: 'Courage my Soul, now learn to wield/The weight of thine immortal Shield' (ll. 1–2), suggests not only that this soul is inexperienced in moral conflict, but that the shield of faith, although impenetrable, is not grasped and employed

74

without effort and study. The same sense of difficulty to be overcome is implicit in 'Ballance thy Sword against the Fight' (l. 4),
where to balance means to hold erect.[58] One consequence of
Marvell's choice of imagery is the immediate realization that this
soul will not triumph simply by soaring back to its original home,
that this debate will not be settled by disdain or by mutual re-
crimination; rather, we are to witness the trial by combat of the
spirit of the 'true warfaring Christian', and from the tone and the
content of the Soul's speeches will emerge Marvell's most fully
conceived portrait of one particular kind of Puritan ethical attitude.

This attitude assumes that it is essential that the enemies of
virtue be perceived and understood in the full strength of their
attraction and menace. Moreover, the Christian spirit is not allowed
to rest in the assurance of faith; while faith may be unquestionable,
it must also defend itself unsleepingly against a foe who is both
subtle and overwhelming. We shall see in Marvell's poem that
Pleasure's case is not a mere gesture to feign genuine temptation; it
has, indeed, all the power the world possesses to distract the spirit
from its ordained path. To support this sense, the beginning of the
poem is truly an exhortation to battle and not a complacent
announcement of the Soul's inevitable victory. That the outcome
is meant to be seriously in doubt is shown in,

> Now, if thou bee'st that thing Divine,
> In this day's Combat let it shine:
> And shew that Nature wants an Art
> To conquer one resolved Heart.

> (ll. 7–10)

The 'if' is not gratuitous; the enemy has been described already as
'strong as fair', and now we are informed that the army in the
field against the Soul is Nature itself, whose 'silken Banners' stand
for the myriad regiments of earthly beauty.[59] And it is at this point
that the pun is added to the technical resources of the dialogue. The
'Art' that Nature lacks alludes to the skill required to defeat the
armed Soul, but refers also to the artifice with which Nature
enables men to adorn 'natural' beauty and to create images of beauty
of their own. Similarly, 'resolved' can mean either 'determined',
'stripped of doubts'—or it may be a fleeting reference to the musical
process that brings concord out of dissonance. If we recall the

'double Heart' of 'A Dialogue between the Soul and Body', the importance of resolution in the Soul will be understood.

The trochaic tetrameters of Pleasure's initial address give it, and all its speeches, a jaunty, reckless, yet forceful air, which is clearly contrasted to the subdued, assured iambics in which the Soul replies. Yet there is intelligence and cunning behind Pleasure's exuberant invitation.

> Welcome the Creations Guest,
> Lord of Earth, and Heavens Heir.
> Lay aside that Warlike Crest,
> And of Nature's banquet share.

(ll. 11–14)

The epithets in line 12 are true to the received concept of man's position on earth; what is strange is that 'Creations Guest' is also a precise term, but one that undercuts Pleasure's argument. Exactly because Christian doctrine regarded man as only a sojourner in the world, 'Guest' describes him accurately and explains why he is at last eager to leave his temporary home. There is a deeper irony in Pleasure's dislike of the 'Warlike Crest'; it sees the helmet only as a martial threat, while the Soul knows it to be the helmet of salvation. But Pleasure speaks more wisely than it knows, since the helmet is part of the Christian armour that represents the concrete aspect of Christ's promise to bring 'not peace, but a sword'. Whatever tension we may feel about the outcome of the temptation is intensified by Pleasure's apparent confidence in the inability of the Soul to resist the snares of the world. It is essential to the poem's drama that Pleasure's enticements appear reasonable, and part of that reasonable tone is based on the possibility that the Soul may succumb.

Thus, the first temptation stems from the conventional 'argument from abundance', which we may meet in the Bower of Bliss, in Comus' enchanted wood, or in any number of persuasion-to-love poems. The logic is cogent—if the world was created for man's delight and government, then the proper worship of the Creator is to make use of his gifts. The unspoken reply, however, is equally cogent—man *per se* is not the antagonist here, but the resolved soul, that recognizes only heaven as its provenance and the source of its true nourishment. Marvell seems almost to acknowledge this, and perhaps to allude briefly to the contemporary debates on the corporeality of spirits,[60] when Pleasure offers not material dainties, but a banquet 'Where the Souls of fruits and flow'rs/Stand prepar'd to heighten yours' (ll. 15–16). The subtlety in these lines lies in the suggestion that the 'souls' of vegetables stand in the same relation to the Resolved Soul as the vegetative soul does to the rational soul. Much depends on the intended meaning of 'heighten'; for the subordinate parts of the soul indeed enable the rational soul to survive by maintaining the life and sensitivity of the body, but they can do nothing to affect its inherent superiority. But Pleasure goes further into error, and in a way that reminds us very powerfully of the complaint of the Body in the previous dialogue; here again created nature sees the soul as something with extension, something that measures its spiritual exaltation by physical height. The Soul, indeed, tries to correct this misinterpretation in its typically clipped rejoinder, but the effort goes into stating the case correctly, not into clarifying Pleasure's view: 'I sup above, and cannot stay/ To bait so long upon the way' (ll. 17–18). This at least makes clear that the proper food of the soul is not earthly abundance, and it makes the point by adopting the metaphor of Pleasure's banquet and then revising it.

The appeal to the sense of touch, which follows, is marked by numerous soft 'l' sounds, and by its reference to the epitome of sybaritic luxury in the tale of the prince so sensitive that he could feel, with pain, the disarrangement of a single rose-petal in the flowery bed beneath him. The Soul's reply takes up the tacit image of the bed and converts it into a play on the religious concept of reward and spiritual sustenance: 'My gentler Rest is on a Thought,/ Conscious of doing what I ought' (ll. 23–24). It seems strange that the Soul resorts here to hyperbole; but the point is made that an abstraction can be 'softer' and more tranquil than the finest plumes and roses of the sublunary world.[61]

The rejection of the 'Perfumes' that Pleasure offers next introduces another aspect of virtuous knowledge and submission. To 'show/Like another God below', enveloped in fragrances the gods themselves admire, is not only to fail to be a god but also to step beyond the limits of presumption, as the Soul points out. Its answer includes as well the dictum that due humility is pleasing to God in itself and also fulfils the duties of the soul as an entity: 'A Soul that knowes not to presume/Is Heaven's and its own perfume' (ll. 29–30). It is precisely this conviction that is challenged in the temptation of the sense of sight. Not the beauties of the earth are summoned to distract the Soul, but its own image, in a mirror that can stand for the physical universe, or for the Soul's own consciousness. The trap is in the doctrine that the soul is a reflection of the beauty and perfection of its Creator; it can hardly fail to agree that it is the most beautiful denizen of earth, without slighting its maker. Marvell may touch here on the problem of the identity between the knowing mind and the thing known, but he is also characterizing, with some wit, Pleasure's conviction that the Soul is a passionate solipsist and can be seduced into the rapt contemplation of its own beauty. The Soul escapes by an argument that displays more inventiveness than logical power: 'When the Creator's skill is priz'd,/The rest is all but Earth disguis'd' (ll. 35–36). Here again is the appeal to an abstract form, this time the supreme artifice of God's shaping powers; compared to the art itself, says the Soul, the products of that art are only bits of matter glorified by the touch of the artist, but possessing no intrinsic beauty.

The first episode of the poem ends with the assault on hearing and the temptation through music. Pleasure, thoroughly pagan, naturally alludes to the Orpheus myth in speaking of the power of music to control nature. The mistake lies in assuming that a resolved soul is as subject to music's charm as are the elements. But Pleasure is not naïve; this speech contains one of the most audacious and sinister puns in the entire poem: 'Heark how Musick then prepares/For thy Stay these charming Aires' (ll. 37–38). 'Stay' represents the invitation to 'stop' on earth; but at the same time it is a synonym for 'bond', an image that will be the centre of the Soul's reply. And it is also a reference to the 'gentler Rest' the Soul has spoken of, since Pleasure now proposes that music can serve as the prop and spiritual support of the Soul. The pun is sinister because this stay is made of 'Aires'; the musical term is imposed upon its homonym to enforce the impression that this most beautiful of all earthly delights is yet as insubstantial and deceptive as the others.

The meaning of the Soul's singling out of music as the one creation that might tempt it to 'lose time' may be related simply to questions of Marvell's personality and preferences. But at least his choice is justified by any number of theological and poetic texts that characterize music as the very symbol of universal harmony and thus as a worthy figure for the highest degree of perfection attained in the world. Certainly the Soul's turning from music is accomplished with a convincing reluctance that rings through the punning lines, 'None can chain a mind/Whom this sweet Chordage cannot bind' (ll. 43–44).[62] The intervening chorus departs from the couplet in a stanza rhymed *abbacc*, and we shall notice that in the second half of the poem the speeches of Pleasure, too, will change from the couplet to quatrains rhyming *abab*. Thus Marvell marks the shift from the temptations of the senses—which may legitimately be thought of as related more closely to the soul as embedded in the body—to the temptations of the mind, which parallel the episode of Christ and Satan in the desert. The middle chorus tunes itself to the proper degree of exultation at the victory the Soul has won thus far, but recalls the Soul to the coming combat and promises it a 'crown' if it triumphs in the next siege, that same crown that appears in innumerable Puritan (and Anglican) sermons as the sign of the soul's reward for devotion to 'holy living'.

The first of the series of mental temptations is addressed apparently to the vice called 'lust of the eye', but actually to the intellectual lust for the beauty of perfection and harmony. Pleasure's promise is that

> All this fair, and soft, and sweet,
> > Which scatteringly doth shine,
> Shall within one Beauty meet.
>
> (ll. 51–53)[63]

The adjectives of line 51 suggest that this temptation is not aimed solely at sight, but at the Soul's sense of earthly beauty that is compacted of all possible material good. Despite the Soul's reply, 'If things of Sight such Heavens be,/What Heavens are those we cannot see?' (ll. 55–56), what is being proffered is that ideal beauty which transcends its effects on any one sense. And the Soul, in rejecting even this, vitiates the concept by finding it illusory beside the invisible (insensible) beauties of the divine. The premise of the Soul's argument, like that of the Soul in 'A Dialogue between the Soul and Body', is that the purest perception of a bodily sense is truly blind when compared to the perception of the spirit. Once again, the logic of the Soul's case is effective only if its premises are granted outright, for it is not logic that will win out over the powers of Created Pleasure, but the certainties of faith.

There is a note of perfunctoriness in the next two temptations, which attack the vices of avarice and the hunger for wordly dominion; and it may arise from Pleasure's growing realization that a soul that will not be diverted by beauty or the passions of the senses is not likely to swerve because of the drive for power or possessions. The exchange is lightened only by the Soul's insistent use of paradox and its habit of turning the words of Pleasure back upon their author by the by-now familiar process of inverting their initial meanings. Thus, in answer to the offer of unlimited gold the Soul counters 'that's worth nought that can be sold' (l. 62). The play on price and worth has, again, a biblical reference, and it does its work by denying the very terms and values in which the challenge has been posed.[64] Similarly, to Pleasure's offer of a world made up equally of slaves and friends, the Soul rejoins: 'What Slaves, unless I captive you?' (l. 68), implying that the idea of slavery itself has no meaning unless the Soul can enforce the only true and necessary slavery—that of the world to the spirit. Something of the revolutionary fervour of the Gospels in converting old rituals and values into radically new ones makes itself felt in the two middle temptations, but it cannot keep the verse from growing less interesting as the feigned tension of the combat becomes less credible. Even the final temptation, although it touches on ideas and on human faculties of the utmost importance, seems more than anything else a last gesture demanded by the established pattern of the poem.

> Thou shalt know each hidden Cause;
> And see the future Time:
> Try what depth the Centre draws;
> And then to Heaven climb.

> (ll. 69–72)

The quatrain ranges from Aristotelian metaphysics to contemporary physics, from clairvoyance to universal knowledge; but we must not disregard its clustering reminiscences of Christ, Aeneas, Odysseus, and all the heroes of pagan and Christian epic who were allowed to see the future or made the perilous descent into hell in the quest of some form of knowledge. The temptation to see into the 'hidden Cause', to know the secrets of earth and heaven, to attain to the knowledge of the gods, Pleasure knows full well, is the critical one for a man of the seventeenth century. The sin of pride is being gradually replaced by the ubiquitous *libido sciendi* as the epidemic vice of the late English Renaissance, and Marvell is as intimately aware of it as Milton will show himself to be in

Books VIII and IX of *Paradise Lost*. The Faust legend has come down to us in such undiluted strength that the Soul's climactic rejection of this most dangerous of temptations may seem to lack the power of phrasing to match the power of its moral perfection: 'None thither mounts by the degree/Of Knowledge, but Humility' (ll. 73–74). The couplet could be attacked on the same grounds that provide a basis for charging Milton with anti-intellectualism in Book IV of *Paradise Regained*. But there is no gainsaying the Soul. Here is the extreme development away from the Thomistic faith in the power of human rationality and in the essential correspondence between human reason and the intelligible plan of God for the universe. The Soul is in all respects doctrinally correct in stating that knowledge of whatever profundity cannot achieve either salvation or divine illumination of the intellect. Only humility can guarantee that, and in these lines humility stands for the just apprehension of man's position in the hierarchy of values and essences. Thus the Soul ends its battle on another paradox—that the understanding of the soul's inferiority to the divine is the only way to achieve union (or reunion) with God.

Paradox, as we have seen, is limited to the speeches of the antagonists in the poem; and the final chorus is explicit both in its paean to victory and in its promise of the reward prefigured in the crown in line 50. The final quatrain is marked by the juxtaposition of lines composed primarily of monosyllables and lines composed of words of two to four syllables, and by the mixture of iambic and trochaic metres, as if to suggest that the distinctions maintained during the progress of the dialogue have broken down now as the tension is released in an access of joy.

> *Triumph, triumph, victorious Soul;*
> *The World has not one Pleasure more:*
> *The rest does lie beyond the Pole,*
> *And is thine everlasting Store.*

(ll. 75–78)

Nevertheless, Marvell is not so firmly seized by the ecstatic moment that he neglects the opportunity to complicate his poem with veiled internal references. Line 76 reports not only the exhaustion of Pleasure's arsenal but the banishment of Pleasure itself from the World. 'The rest', those pleasures of the invisible heavens that were invoked in lines 55–56, refers to the support and surcease mentioned in line 23. Finally, the use of 'Store' in line 78 recalls Nature's store in 'The Match', with the qualification that *this* store is everlasting; it is, therefore, a fitting reward for the spirit that has eschewed earthly temptations, and can indeed be identified with the soul's 'rest', because it is a treasure house not of mortal beauty but of the imperishable excellences the Soul has clung to throughout its trial.

'The Coronet',[65] in its passionate and uncompromising disavowal of secular verse, marks Marvell's closest approach to pure devotional poetry. Perhaps a discussion of 'The Coronet' is out of place before a consideration of the pastoral poems and the 'Mower' series that it criticizes so explicitly; but it represents the climactic stage of the development of certain religious and ethical themes in Marvell's poetry. When we turn to Marvell's pastorals we shall examine the attitudes and poetic interests that 'The Coronet' is concerned to discredit; but for the moment we shall have to assume that opposed to this poem stands a body of secular poetry that includes both poems of courtly compliment and the pastoral discourses on the debate between art and nature.

'The Coronet' finds its place in the tradition of the palinode. Within Marvell's own century and during the previous one many poems were written attacking the prevalence of secular poetry and calling for a return to the role of the poet as a guide to the proper worship of God. In 'Jordan I' Herbert puts forward the proposition that poetry need not be limited to 'fictions' about 'enchanted groves' and 'purling streams', or to allegorical obscurities or finely worked lines whose only excellence is in the wit of their construction. He proposes, a neglected subject for poetry, simply 'truth.' In the second 'Jordan' poem Herbert deplores his own pride in the skill with which he has wrought his poems in the past. At many points his lines reveal obvious parallelisms to the thought of 'The Coronet'.

> That I sought out quaint words, and trim invention;
> My thoughts began to burnish, sprout, and swell,
> Curling with metaphors a plain intention.

(ll. 3–5)

Later he speaks of weaving his own desires and vanities into the 'sense' of the poem, a figure which is suggestive of Marvell's serpent, inevitably interwoven with the flowers. Although the first sonnet of the *Corona* series describes Donne's poems as an offering to God rather than as something of which he is ashamed, Donne nevertheless implores: 'But doe not, with a vile crowne of fraile bayes,/Reward my muses white sincerity' (ll. 5–6). Again, when we think of Spenser's October Eclogue or of one of the possible interpretations of the last line of 'Lycidas', the farewell to secular (or, more particularly, pastoral) poetry emerges as nearly a genre in itself. Another reason for believing that 'The Coronet' is best understood within this genre is the fact that the poem is constructed almost entirely of symbols and allusions drawn from conventional religious and pastoral poetry.

We do not expect to encounter in 'The Coronet' the verse patterns that were pertinent to the structure and subjects of the dialogues, since it is clearly a meditative poem. Marvell invents a rhyme scheme that begins with *abba* quatrains, goes on to an unmarked stanza rhymed *ababcc*, and concludes with eight verses rhymed *abcabcdd* (the sets of rhymes in each case are different). Although word-plays, puns, and double allusions are present in the usual degree, 'The Coronet' depends strongly for its verbal intricacy on complex syntax, as befits the twists and turns of its argument. The best example in the poem is its first clause, which resembles the opening of 'On a Drop of Dew' in its suspense.

> When for the Thorns with which I long, too long,
>> With many a piercing wound,
>> My Saviours head have crown'd,
> I seek with Garlands to redress that Wrong.

(ll. 1–4)

The delay in revealing the object until the third line makes it possible to misunderstand the first two lines so that 'long' can seem to mean 'yearn' and the wounds to be the speaker's. The point of the diction is to underscore the grief of the 'I' of the poem before we are permitted to know its real cause. The repetition in 'long, too long' is unusual in Marvell and suggests the affinities we have already noticed with the devotional poems of Donne and Herbert. The irony in the 'crown'd' of line 3 is thoroughly conventional, as indeed is the very phrase 'crown of thorns'. But Marvell's characteristic note appears in the fourth line, where the pun on 'redress' is not only patent, but reinforces the meaning of the 'Garlands'. It is still not clear that the flowers are to be identified with secular poems, even though this is not an infrequent comparison in the seventeenth century. But our uncertainty allows Marvell to write several lines whose surface meaning is replaced by the desired symbolic meaning only after we have reached the end of the first 'stanza' at line 12. Consider how the knowledge that the poet has been referring to his own verse affects a reading of:

> Through every Garden, every Mead,
> I gather flow'rs (my fruits are only flow'rs)
> Dismantling all the fragrant Towers
> That once adorn'd my Shepherdesses head.
>
> (ll. 5–8)

We shall explore those meads and gardens when we examine the pastoral poems; but what is conveyed immediately is that for all their undoubted beauty they have provided only ephemeral, decorative emblems, and not the nourishing creations of true fertility. We learn, too, that some of these flowers have been gathered at the sacrifice of the love poems already written.[66] The painfully culled garland, the poet's 'store' (l. 9), is to be devoted to weaving a rich 'Chaplet', and the implication is that somehow the substance and art that created the poems which have now been cast aside will be able to join in the new form of worshipful praise. But:

> Alas I find the Serpent old
> That, twining in his speckled breast,
> About the flow'rs disguis'd does fold,
> With wreaths of Fame and Interest.
>
> (ll. 13–16)

The 'Serpent old' should need no gloss, except to point out that the glinting of the snake's burnished back through the leaves and flowers and grass of the Garden of Eden was a favourite subject for tapestries, allegorical paintings, and other iconographic works.[67] And the significance of the serpent is heightened by the adjective 'speckled', for in the analogical world of seventeenth-century poetry any example of variety was equally an example of discord and potential evil.[68] More important, however, are the 'wreaths of Fame and Interest', since we need no instruction in the utter moral contradiction between true devotion and pride of artifice in writing a devotional poem. The same struggle exists in Herbert's two poems,

and a different light is shed on the conflict by Milton's lines on
fame in 'Lycidas'. In so far as the desire for fame represents an
involvement with the dictates of the world it must be suppressed
by the religious poet. But the appearance of the ineluctable serpent
amongst Marvell's choicest flowers is a sign that he is tormented
by the question of how to write without skill, or without being
conscious of his skill. It is a Christian dilemma *par excellence*, since man
is commanded to devote his best energies to God, and yet forbidden
to be aware of the quality of his own devotional exercises.

The resolution in 'The Coronet', as in 'Lycidas', comes through
an appeal to the God to whom the poem is written as an act of
worship. (We cannot ignore the paradox of this poem's being
about the moral struggle of a poet trying to purify his verse of the
slightest taint of worldly ambition, while the poem is constructed
with obvious skill and conscious art.)

> But thou who only could'st the Serpent tame,
> Either his slipp'ry knots at once untie,
> And disintangle all his winding Snare:
> Or shatter too with him my curious frame:
> And let these wither, so that he may die,
> Though set with Skill and chosen out with Care.
>
> (ll. 19–24)

Christ is asked either to repeat his famous victory and thus crush
the evil within the poet, or, if the serpent's wreaths are indeed part
of the fabric the poet has woven, then to destroy the flowers with
their corrupter. The accumulation, in three lines, of 'curious',
'Skill', and 'Care' makes it possible to feel, as many have done,
that the exhortation is mingled with sadness and great reluctance
(even though 'Care' may as well refer to painful concern as to pains-
taking). But I think it would be more faithful to the obvious intent
of the poem to understand these phrases as Marvell's way of
impressing upon us the gravity of the sacrifice—which nevertheless
is seen as necessary and worthwhile. The closing couplet, 'That they,
while Thou on both their Spoils dost tread,/May crown thy Feet,
that could not crown thy Head' (ll. 25–26), dwells on the paradox
of sacrifice while it exhibits the cross-patterning so evident throughout the poem, the external sign of the intertangled predicaments it
dramatizes. Lines 19–26 offer several examples of qualification,
alternation, and reversal in the argument of the poem; and each of

these syntactical movements contributes to the sense of complication and difficulty resolved that prevails. If the last line reminds us
of Crashaw, the ones that preceded it show the impress of Herbert;
the modesty and self-awareness of the one temper the excessive
wit of the other, and the major invention remains Marvell's own.

If the mood of acceptance of the final lines seems unable to match
in intensity the self-scrutiny of the earlier parts of the poem—or if
the climax has none of the exultant certainty of 'A Dialogue Between
The Resolved Soul, and Created Pleasure'—we must remember that
'The Coronet' is written in the meditative mode, wherein triumphs
are won over oneself and are therefore not celebrated without a
sense of loss. Furthermore, in order to create a language that will
enact inner spiritual struggle, Marvell has had to compress, into a
very restricted set of expressive symbols, themes and images of
experiences which are the major subjects of other poems. Until we
have discovered what kinds of beauty and richness mark the
'Towers' made for Marvell's shepherdesses we cannot appreciate
the gesture that regretfully casts them aside. The controlled, modest
agony of 'The Coronet' tells us much about the poet's reaction to
the desire to transcend his own art; but the control exerted everywhere in the poem over structure and tones allows only highly
distilled and emblematic uses of pastoral motifs. To understand
the ground of the struggle 'The Coronet' depicts we must survey
the landscape that Marvell drew in this most unambiguous in-
vestigations of pastoral concepts.

Notes

1 M. C. Bradbrook, *Andrew Marvell*, pp. 28–29.

2 Bradbrook, loc. cit.

3 Margoliouth, *Poems and Letters of Andrew Marvell*, I, pp. 29–30.

4 Bradbrook, op. cit., p. 30.

5 Margoliouth, I, op. cit., pp. 27–29.

6 Joseph Summers, in his Introduction to *Marvell*, in the Laurel Poetry
   Series (New York, 1961) is only the most recent of Marvell's editors to
   feel impelled to say: 'I have no idea what "The unfortunate Lover"
   means'. More recently still Mrs Ann Berthoff, in 'The Voice of Allegory:
   Marvell's "The unfortunate Lover" ', *MLQ*, XXVII, 1 (1966), pp. 41–50,
   has offered an interpretation of the lover's story as an allegory of the
   history of the soul's conflict with the world.

7 See *Oxford English Dictionary*, under 'Flame', s.v. 6: a, b, c. Examples

are given from Cowley's *The Mistress* (1647) and Denham's *Cooper's Hill* (1642).

8 Margoliouth, op. cit., I, pp. 39–40.

9 Margoliouth, op. cit., I, p. 218, suggests a similarity to Cowley, 'The Soul', ll. 17–19; *Poems*, ed. A. R. Waller (Cambridge University Press, 1905), pp. 82–84. Similar figures may be found in Donne's 'An Anatomy of the World', ll. 175–182; *Poems*, I, pp. 231–245,and in Lord Herbert's 'Madrigal', ll. 8–14; *The Poems English and Latin of Edward Lord Herbert of Cherbury*, ed. G. C. Moore Smith (Oxford University Press, 1923), p. 18.

10 Margoliouth, op. cit., I, p. 31.

11 See ll. 37–44.

12 Margoliouth, op. cit., I, pp. 25–26. See Legouis, *Andrew Marvell*, p. 91.

13 Margoliouth, op. cit., I, pp. 31–32. Miss Wallerstein, in *Studies in Seventeenth-Century Poetic*, p. 155, refers to Marino: '*Eyes and Tears* and *Mourning* are Marinistic not merely in their subjects and in their imagery at once witty and sensational, but in the handling of their tetrameters also'.

14 It means both 'intermingled' and 'flowing together'.

15 For a more beautiful version of a similar image, cf. Lord Herbert's 'An Ode upon a Question moved, Whether Love should continue forever?', ll. 133–136; *Poems*, pp. 61–66. Cf. also Crashaw's 'The Weeper', l. 19; *The Poems English Latin and Greek of Richard Crashaw*, 2nd ed., ed. L. C. Martin (Oxford University Press, 1957), pp. 308–314.

16 Margoliouth, op. cit., I, pp. 15–17.

17 *The Faerie Queene*, VII, vii, st. 58, 59.

18   See, where she sits upon the grassie greene,
         (O seemely sight)
        Yclad in Scarlot like a mayden Queene,
         And Ermines white.
        Upon her head a Cremosin coronet,
        With Damaske roses and Daffadillies set:
         Bayleaves betweene,
         And Primroses greene
        Embellish the sweete Violet.

The Shepheardes Calender, 'April', ll. 55–63.

19 Cf. Spenser's descriptions of the caves of Mammon and of Morpheus in *FQ*, II, vii, and I, i.

20 In Christian iconography the shell appears both as the standard symbol of pilgrimage and as the usual setting for a fountain in the enclosed garden. See George Ferguson, *Signs & Symbols in Christian Art* (Oxford University Press, 1954), pp. 25, 220, 254, 323. D. W. Robertson, Jr., in 'The Doctrine of Charity in Mediaeval Literary Gardens: a Topical Approach through Symbolism and Allegory', *Speculum* XXVI, 1

(January 1951), pp. 24–49, points out that a well or fountain 'appears often beneath the Tree of Life'.

21 Ralegh, 'The Pilgrimage', ll. 11–18. There are many printed and manuscript versions of the poem. See *The Poems of Sir Walter Ralegh* ed. A. M. C. Latham (Routledge and Kegan Paul, 1951), pp. 49–51 & 140–143.

22 Cf. Cassirer, *Platonic Renaissance in England*, p. 45: 'Just as puritanism sets up the ideal of an active faith, so empiricism sets up the ideal of an active philosophy. They both reject mere contemplation and speculation'; and William Haller, *The Rise of Puritanism* (New York, 1938), pp. 153–154: 'If he [man[suffered no sorrow for the unrighteousness which he partook with the old Adam, he should partake none of the joy that ensues upon the righteousness of the new; he was not of the elect. The ordeal of the flesh was the victory of the spirit. So long as sin vexed him, he might know that God was with him. All he had to do was to continue to be vexed, and he was sure to triumph, because all existence is the conflict of Christ against Satan, the fore-ordained outcome of which is the triumph of the elect'.

23 *The Poetical Works of Edmund Spenser*, I, p. 56.

24 See Wallerstein, *Studies in Seventeenth-Century Poetic*, p. 156; '*Clorinda and Damon* . . . reflects the older tradition of the pastoral elegy no less in its motifs and in its epithets than in its dialogue, its allegory, and its mythology'. Cf. Sir Philip Sidney, *An Apologie for Poetrie*, in *Elizabethan Critical Essays*, I, pp. 175–176; William Webbe, *A Discourse of English Poetrie*, in Smith, I, pp. 262–265; George Puttenham, *The Arte of English Poesie*, in Smith, II, pp. 39–40.

25 In the original the text of this passage is entirely in italic type, with the exception of Pan's name.

26 The finest example of this figure is the morning prayer of Adam and Eve in *Paradise Lost*, V, ll. 153–208.

27 Margoliouth, op. cit., I, pp. 19–20. Margoliouth gives variant readings from the 1681 Folio and from the Additional MSS in the British Museum. See Margoliouth, I, p. 221, for his remarks on the collation. Hugh Macdonald in *The Poems of Andrew Marvell* (Routledge & Kegan Paul, 1952), p. 186, has an excellent note on versions of the poem that appeared in pre- and post-Restoration collections, especially in books of 'ayres', which would suggest that it was a popular song. Macdonald also emends 'Cold' in line 34 to 'cool' on the authority of the version printed in John Gamble's *Ayres and Dialogues* (1659). Given the paradisiacal picture Thyrsis is painting, 'cool' is obviously preferable to the Folio's 'Cold'.

28 Cf. Ralegh's poem quoted above. See also, in *The Works of George Herbert*, ed. F. E. Hutchinson (Oxford University Press, 1941), 'Affliction

(I)', ll. 19–20 (pp. 46–48), and 'Prayer (I)', ll. 9–12 (p. 51), where a similar pun is made on this phrase; and Crashaw, 'The Weeper', (1646), ll. 20–21; *Poems*, p. 79.

29 The most famous instance of this symbol in Marvell is of course in stanza VII of 'The Garden'. So many examples could be adduced from the poetry of the seventeenth century that it would be pointless to begin listing them. To give one of the most popular—of the fifteen emblems in Book I of Francis Quarles' *Hieroglyphikes of the Life of Man* (1638) seven include the figure of a winged soul.

30 Margoliouth, op. cit., I, pp. 12–13.

31 In *Seven Types of Ambiguity*, 3rd ed., rev. (Chatto and Windus, 1953), p.80, William Empson has protested against the ambiguity of these lines and offers the disgruntled suggestion that the syntax 'conveys the delicacy of the dewdrop, and how sickeningly likely it was to roll off the petal'. He also points out that the first line of *Ros* is grammatically clear and complete. For Margoliouth's note on the interpretation of lines 4–6, see I, p. 219.

32 The first line of *Ros* simply describes the dewdrop as falling—*descendat Gemmula Roris*. Although the English is not so direct it seems clear that 'falling' or 'having fallen' is posited of the dewdrop as it first appears, and that it is meant to be inactive until line 6.

33 *Ros* is no more a Latin version of 'On a Drop of Dew' than the latter is a translation of *Ros*. H. J. C. Grierson, in *Metaphysical Lyrics and Poems of the Seventeenth-Century* (Milford, 1921), pp. 239–240, has a note on the relations between the poems. We will notice *Ros* only in so far as it sheds light on 'On a Drop of Dew'. But it must be said that the Latin poem, although close in many respects to the English one, is more expansive and elaborate and contains many classical names and allusions, as befits its genre.

34 Grierson, *Metaphysical Lyrics*, p. 240.

35 Margoliouth, op. cit., I, p. 219.

36 The relation between 'touching' and 'lyes' is another means of demonstrating how Marvell achieves his effect. The syntax decrees that the dewdrop is performing the action of both verbs simultaneously. The difference between the two verbs defines the 'attitude' of the dewdrop.

37 'Mournful' is the only adjective in the poem that is not validated by physical realities. The only attempt to justify it is the description of the reflected light as a tear. The logic is circular but the defect most probably goes unnoticed because the conceit is so easily grasped.

38 It is less probable, but still possible, that Marvell was thinking of the adverbial use of *impurus* in line 16.

39 Marvell must have had in mind several meanings of 'express' derived from *exprimo:* to articulate, to imitate, to force out, to represent. All

these emphasize the discrepancy between the agent and the model.

40 *Ros* has *oppositum Mundo claudit ubique latus*; Margoliouth (I, p. 219) paraphrases: 'thus shutting out the world on every side'.

41 Pierre Legouis, *André Marvell: poète, puritain, patriote 1621–1678* (Paris, 1928), p. 81.

42 The comparison is ubiquitous in Plotinus, since the moon, as a lesser heavenly body that shines only with the Sun's reflected light, has obvious relation to the philosopher's theory of the soul. See *The Enneads*, trans. S. MacKenna, 2nd ed., rev. (Faber & Faber, 1956): I, ii, pp. 33–36; II, iii, pp. 269–270; IV, iv, pp. 290–315; V, vi, pp. 419–423.

43 J. E. Saveson, 'Marvell's "On a Drop of Dew"', *NQ*, N.S. V, 7 (1958), pp. 289–290, interprets the lines on manna as a reference to the Eucharist and a conceit referring to man's salvation through Christ. I cannot see that such a specific allusion is intended, especially since nothing in the poem thus far has relied on particularized Christian doctrines or usages. Furthermore, the comparison between manna and a dewdrop was fairly common. Cf. Hawkins, *Partheneia Sacra*, pp. 65–66.

44 Cf. Quarles, *Emblems* (1634), Book V, Emblem X, where the engraving is of the soul (not winged this time) in a huge birdcage. The verse begins: 'My Soule is like a Bird, my Flesh the Cage'.

45 Margoliouth, op. cit., I, pp. 20–21.

46 In *Minor Poets of the Caroline Period*, ed. G. Saintsbury. 3 vols (Milford, 1905–1921), II, p. 509.

47 *Meditations and Vows* (London, 1851), p. 61.

48 'The Second Anniversary', l. 249; *Poems*, I, pp. 251–266.

49 It is true that in line 32 the Body speaks to the Soul as 'Thou', but this is the only deviation from third-person address.

50 Cf. Matthew 13: 13–15

51 'Frame' recalls the anatomical description of ll. 3–8 and emphasizes the belief that the soul 'informs' a body that is essentially a carnal receptacle for it.

52 To clarify 'Precipice' Margoliouth (I, p. 221) cites *The Rehearsal Transpros'd*: 'After he was stretch'd to such an height in his own fancy, that he could not look down from top to toe but his Eyes dazled at the Precipice of his Stature'. Rosemond Tuve, *Elizabethan and Metaphysical Imagery*, p. 163, says of 1.13 the 'relation between concretion and abstraction is shown in this "impaling" which allows the Body to blame the Soul for its own self-caused "falls".' I am not sure that the abstract meaning here is as important as Miss Tuve would suggest. Although life on earth was often characterized as a series of moral falls repeating the pattern and significance of Adam's fall, Marvell's point is that the Soul'r spiritual stature has forced the Body to live precariously, has made is vulnerable to all ills—indeed, has made it mortal. Therefore, the sheet

physical sensation of the danger of moral consciousness is what is being dramatized here, whatever the underlying allusion to 'a fall' may be. If one can add a footnote to a footnote, it is barely possible that Marvell was also playing on another meaning of 'impales'—as it appears, for example, in Herbert's 'The Church-Porch': 'God hath impal'd us'— that of enclosing or limiting. Just as the Soul has roused the Body to awareness, it has closed it off from utter passivity—an action that is equally responsible for its becoming its 'own Precipice'.

53 See Plotinus, *Enneads*, IV, viii, pp. 358–363; John Smith, *Select Discourses*, Discourse IV, 'On the Immortality of the Soul', Chapter VII.

54 The figure is, of course, a commonplace in Renaissance love poetry as well. See 'The unfortunate Lover' for Marvell's parodic version of this form.

55 See Robert Burton, *The Anatomy of Melancholy*, Part I, Section 2, Member 3, Subsections iv and xiv.

56 Margoliouth, op. cit., I, pp. 9–12.

57 Cf. Ferguson, *Signs & Symbols in Christian Art*, p. 303; R. Gilles, *Le Symbolisme dans l'Art religieux* (Paris, 1943), p. 136.

58 Cf. 'An Horatian Ode', l. 116. 'Against' means both 'in opposition to' and 'in preparation for'.

59 Cf. Song of Solomon 6:4.

60 See, for only one study of the question, Marjorie Nicolson, 'The Spirit World of Milton and More', *SP*, XXII,4 (1925), pp. 433–452. Milton's treatment is in *Paradise Lost*, V, l. 404 ff.

61 Henry Peacham's *Minerva Britanna* (1612) (Sig. C3ᵛ) contains an emblem depicting a woman leaning on a T-shaped cross, holding a book (the Bible) in her right hand. The verse is: 'My hope is heaven, the crosse on earth my rest'.

62 Empson, *Seven Types of Ambiguity*, pp. 105–106, gives a full exposition of the wordplay in these lines. Cf. Lovelace, 'A forsaken Lady to her false servant that is disdained by his new Mistris', l. 26; *The Poems of Richard Lovelace*, ed. C. H. Wilkinson (Oxford University Press, 1953), pp. 35–36.

63 Margoliouth (I, p. 11) points out that many editors prefer Cooke's text, which reads 'All that's costly, fair and sweet'.

64 It may be observed that Pleasure's lines, 'Till thou purchase all below,/ And want new Worlds to buy' (ll. 59–60), have a possible double significance. Pleasure refers to the pagan legends of Pluto, Plutus, Mammon, and other possessors of the earth and the underworld. But the Soul, and we, can perceive an allusion to Christ's sacrifice (which 'purchased' all below), to His harrowing of Hell, and to His establishment of a new kingdom.

65 Margoliouth, op. cit., I, pp. 14–15.

66 To 'dismantle' means both 'to take apart' and 'to strip of its covering', and we can follow Marvell's metaphor by seeing an allusion to the structure and the conceited 'adornments' of his secular poems.

67 Cf. *The Faerie Queene*, III, xi, 28.

68 Cf. the Pict's 'party-colour'd Mind' in 'An Horatian Ode', l. 106, and the 'double' Pink in 'The Mower against Gardens', l. 9.

*Margoliouth, I, p. 18.

†"Love, a poem in the Williams MS. not included in *The Temple*; *Works*, pp. 201–202.

3

Shepherds and Mowers

I

Prominent among 'the goodly exil'd train/Of gods and goddesses' whom Donne had banished from English poetry[1] were many of the mythological figures we have already encountered in Marvell's work. Carew felt that 'the Muses garden' was 'O' rspred'with these 'pedantique weedes', that Flora, Pan, Apollo, and Daphne no longer represented the vital centre of the poet's concerns; and Donne's innovations in language had been matched by his creation of new *dramatis personae*. Pagan gods were replaced by types of the *bourgeois* world, emblems were discarded in favour of the jargons of contemporary enterprises; and the terminologies of the sciences and theology became the instruments to perform anatomies upon the thinking mind and the passionate heart. And we can feel some sympathy for Carew's enthusiasm in the light of a dedicated reading of *England's Helicon*, Davison's *A Poetical Rhapsody*, or even of the more arid stretches of William Browne's *Britannia's Pastorals* or Drayton's *Muses Elizium*. It is hard to account for the indefatigable Elizabethan taste for pastoral verse, but there is no obstacle to feeling that much of the poetry it elicited is worth little except as documentary evidence of a passing, but powerfully gripping, fancy. As we read one of the pastoral anthologies the mythological names soon lose their precise meaning, as does a word repeated too often in one's mind; the italics remind us only that these are gods and goddesses who would look very ill at ease in Cumberland or the Wye Valley. One Coridon grows fairly like another, and the enticements or reproaches of a score of Phillises show few signs of individual distinction. And yet we cannot dismiss the entire phenomenon with quite the bravura of Carew. For one thing, we are hampered by the rigours of historical perspective; the knowledge we have accumulated forbids us some of the luxuries

93

of partisan prejudice. Scholarship can now trace the course of pastoral poetry, not only from its sources in Theocritus, but throughout its career in England; and we can demonstrate that it has had many recrudescences and has served many important purposes in its more than two thousand years of history. We cannot feel Carew's sense of urgent need for purgation of the style and subject matter of English poetry; Donne's own revolution has done its work, and much of it has been absorbed into the larger currents of our literature. We also know that on the other side of Donne's craggy fancy lay not only Marvell, but Milton—and that the pastoral mode would go on in its endless life of reinterpretation in Pope, Gray, Thomson, Blake, Wordsworth, Arnold, and Robert Frost. The catalogue of names proves only that there seem to be as many 'versions of pastoral', almost, as there are poets to perceive its relevance to their condition and their artistic needs.

For other reasons, too, Carew's formula is inadequate for the modern point of view. The uses of the pastoral in the English Renaissance ranged from Sidney's epic and romantic setting in the *Arcadia* to Shakespeare's songs, and the portrait of Eden in *Paradise Lost*. Apparently the poets of the time saw much more in the antiquated furniture of shepherds, shepherdesses, and empathetic landscapes than Carew allowed. An artistic or a specifically literary convention is comparatively easy to observe and even to describe, if one limits observation to echoes and more obvious imitations of one author by another. The more generalized the imitation, the more difficult it is to single out its conventional aspect. What we rarely can know without immense labour and thinking that is both trenchant and synthetic, is how a particular convention seized the mind of a particular writer, how, in short, it presented itself to him as a way to say something he could not express otherwise. Ultimately, of course, we can never truly know such a thing; but we can, sometimes, see that literary conventions satisfied large and important demands, and were not always limited to problems of particularized expression. The costuming of Malvolio or Zeal-of-the-Land-Busy was 'conventional' in that the audience would know their political and moral positions by the cross-garters or the steeple-hat; but the appearance and placing of such conventional figures were related to the entire critical strategies of *Twelfth Night* and *Bartholomew Fair*. There was nothing about the dress or diction of a stylized Puritan that would tell the audience what the playwright's purpose was in introducing him; that task remained to the play, and it would figure as only one of the play's many interrelated meanings. The appearance of Colin Clout in Book VI of *The Faerie Queene*, for another example, would have been understood with ease as a thoroughly venerable convention. To portray the poet in the guise of a shepherd was a comfortably familiar procedure; its use in *Colin Clouts Come Home Againe*, too, would justify even the conclusion that Colin, in some undefined sense, was meant to stand for Spenser himself. But the convention *per se* takes us no further than this; it will not explain what Spenser means by having Colin pipe *to* the Graces, nor who Rosalind is nor what she represents—and it is frustratingly helpless to explain the meaning of the incident of Calidore's intrusion into the pastoral-poetic scene. These are questions we attempt to answer only in the context of Spenser's work as an artistic whole.

Pastoral as a literary convention has been discussed often enough;[2] we noticed some of its aspects in the previous chapter. It is important to recognize that many Renaissance poets, faithful to the doctrine of 'kinds', believed that pastoral verse was the proper apprentice work for an ambitious writer. With a nice sense of decorum that embraced all the ways of looking at poetry, Renaissance rhetorical theory decreed that, as pastoral represented the youth of a poet's career, so it represented the youth of poetry itself; they even adduced what passed for historical documentation to substantiate this view. It followed, therefore, that the least of 'kinds' should be written in the lowest kind of diction. What Puttenham or Webbe thought of as 'low' is a difficult question in itself, but we know that they thought archaisms suitable for pastoral poetry, and also a carefully contrived 'roughness' that would simulate the actual speech of rustics, in the manner of Theocritus himself. We can see these theories operating in *The Shepheardes Calender*; but we can also see there the theories of Clément Marot and the poets of the Pléiade, who were far more interested in purifying and revivifying vernacular French than they were in recreating the rural diction of some fabulously distant Arcadian world. The very fact that these men could write treatises and learned glosses on the precise way to introduce rustic talk into a poem is a sign of one of the many anomalies in the theory and practice of the pastoral.

There have always been at least two major strains in pastoral poetry. At its very beginning, Theocritus wrote both realistic and allegorical eclogues about the rural Sicilian scene. The realistic pastoral poem made some attempt to recreate the language, the manners, the very atmosphere of the life of shepherds and farmers. To speak of the allegorical pastoral in Greek times is simply to point out that very quickly the eclogue form revealed its usefulness as a means to discuss public affairs and the nature and problems of poetry itself, and to form a critique of urban and sophisticated cultures. Once the criticism of society became a major intent of the pastoral poet and not just a tacit implication of his natural description, it was essential that allegory enter the poem. In no other way could Bion, Moschus, or their followers justify the shepherd who sang in perfectly-modelled metres or, indeed, the lavish eloquence of all the inhabitants of their rural paradise. It should be clear that 'allegory' in early pastoral poetry has nothing to do with the complex system of symbolic expression developed in the middle ages and throughout the European Renaissance. There are no 'levels' in Bion's lament, no 'mystical' or 'anagogical' interpretations to be sought. Pastoral allegory limits itself rather rigorously to the device of personification and to the representation of typical figures within a given culture. These types are constructed from a collection of gestures, qualities, and material objects that are not so much symbolic as referential; they rely on accepted beliefs and tacitly assumed values. Thus, the reed pipe of the shepherd, although it has its actual counterpart among working keepers of sheep,[3] is more important to pastoral in that it refers to the legend of Pan and Syrinx, and because it bears obvious relationships to music and, therefore, poetry. The fact that the Pan-Syrinx story probably arose as a literary transmutation of the experience of real shepherds is less germane to the purposes of pastoral art than the equal probability that the fable was intended to give literary form to the experience of creating verse or song. What does matter is that the legend serves as a repository for commonly understood elements of all pastoral verse, so that Pan becomes the tutelary deity of all pastoral landscapes, and the reed pipe the characteristic instrument of the poet-shepherd.

But to say that literary tradition has sanctified the identification of the poet and the shepherd is not to explain why the shepherd was chosen as a representative figure originally. Within historical knowledge there is as much reason to connect the origins of poetry with religion, or agriculture, or warfare. And even Western literary history alone, in the Hesiodic and Homeric canon, has shown that poetry grows naturally in other settings than the pastoral. Attempts have been made to analyse the 'psychology' of the pastoral impulse,[4] however, and many of them suggest that the creation of a pastoral 'world' as an exercise of literary art is a recurrent and persistent habit of the Western imagination. Beyond that the accounts tend to disagree. For example, Renato Poggioli finds that 'the psychological root of the pastoral is a double longing after innocence and happiness, to be recovered not through conversion or regeneration, but merely through a retreat'.[5] There is no doubt that pastoral poetry in general opposes the values of rustic simplicity to the ambitious and sophisticated worldliness of the city and the court. But to say that the pastoral excludes the necessity of spiritual regeneration is to limit its meanings too arbitrarily. Recognition of this need is implicit in the pastoral's traditional interdependence on the ubiquitous myth of the Golden Age. From Hesiod and Ovid through Spenser and Sylvester's Du Bartas the myth has demonstrated its powerful imaginative grip.[6] It can be seen as a pre-Christian explanation of the loss of innocence in a world grown complicated and shabby; or it can express in a naturalistic manner the universal applications of the biblical story of Eden. In either case it serves two immensely important functions in literature; as evidence for the argument that the growth of civilizations is an unending process of decay from a state of primal perfection, and as a continuing image of that perfection.

We have noticed that Marvell's interpretations of the Golden Age select innocence and youth as its most salient characteristics. Only in 'A Dialogue between Thyrsis and Dorinda' does he make use of other, more commonplace, traits, such as the gentleness and beauty of the natural world in the imagined paradise. But even this sort of description is not the most usual version of the Golden Age landscape, the version we meet in Spenser, Drayton, Sidney, Browne, Jonson—even in Suckling, Randolph, or Cartwright. In these poets the metaphoric emphasis is on *otium*, the classical concept refined by Horace and rehearsed by nearly all of the seventeenth-century poets of 'retirement'. The Golden Age was innocent not so much because of its natural beauty as because the earth gave of its bounty so generously that man was not driven by any desire for achievement or acquisition. And ambition is uniquely charged with bringing men into conflict with each other, so that from the primal sin, greed, arise all the others with which the world is burdened and corrupted. The myth, to be found in the *Metamorphoses* and elsewhere, translates the moral judgment into the story of the first invasion of earth's sanctity by a man digging for gold, thus wounding the creature that had nurtured him, for the sake of a treacherous, glittering lure. And from the pursuit of gold (and all that it represents) follows the development of industry, competition, urban society—every institution that contradicts and invalidates the pastoral vision.

It is easy to understand how this peculiarly pointed mythology can be viewed as an elaborate apology for the non-competitive spirit. But this is to retreat to the method of 'explaining away' rather than explaining. If we think of the pastoral only as a venerable form of wish-fulfilment we shall miss the aspect of its meaning that can help to explain its perennial power over the imagination. For the classical world, after all, the contemplative life was something more than a defeated withdrawal from a world grown too brutal and demanding to be coped with. On the contrary, contemplation was held to be the highest goal, and certainly the most perfect achievement, of a being whose pride and distinction was the faculty of reason. Under the Christian dispensation, contemplation continued to be the most virtuous activity, although its object changed from metaphysical perfection to God. And the rejection of worldliness was converted with no difficulty into the rejection of the world *per se*. Many elements of the pastoral proved to have easily identifiable Christian counterparts. We have noticed already in Marvell that the fountain and the cave had perfectly clear connotations within the secular and religious traditions. But it might be useful to mention once again the importance of Pan as an antitype of Christ, a conventional formula that is repeated widely in Renaissance pastoral poetry and prose. It is a case of concentrating one's emphasis on only one segment of a wide range of symbolic reference. Pan as satyr, Pan as wood-god, Pan as rural deity of fertility and god of misrule—all these *personae* are sheared away and forgotten, leaving only Pan as protector of shepherds, Pan as the archetypal shepherd. And from that figure to the figure of Christ as the great shepherd tending his flock of faithful sheep is not an enormous leap of the imagination. The very diction of the Gospels forms the foundation for the metaphor, and the developing structure of the Church follows the lines laid out by the metaphor. The vision of a flock of innocents guarded by their pastor against the menacing evils, and temptations, of the world that surrounds their idyllic countryside remains strangely constant when it occurs in Longus' *Daphnis and Chloe* or in *Paradise Lost*. Renaissance Christianity imposed its doctrinal values on classical pastoral in a way that paralleled the Renaissance penchant for confusing, deliberately, the boundaries of erotic and devotional poetry. The Christian pastoral, like the plea to the 'divine' mistress, widens its scope by fusing the resources of two major kinds of literary and moral expression. In doing so it also enriches its potential for irony and allegorical complexity since it not only maintains but depends on an underlying ambiguity of reference. The Christian values implicit in the poem comment tacitly on the purely naturalistic meaning, and the natural scene offers a means of comparison and evaluation for the spiritual meaning.[7]

However, as is usual in any true ambiguity the double nature of the Christian pastoral encumbers it with what appears to be an inherent, irreconcilable contradiction. The pastoral, however it may be understood to exalt the virtues of contemplation and retirement, is quite unambiguous in its praise of earthly beauty. The delights of the typical 'pleasance' are not merely ornamental to the pastoral tale; they are integral parts of the way of life that pastoral poetry recommends by implication and by assertion. The truth of this is attested by the prevalence of the notorious 'pathetic fallacy' in pastoral poetry. By Ruskin's time it may have been true that references to grieving trees and laughing brooks were simply outworn bits of anthropomorphism; but in Renaissance poetry the literary habit of speaking of nature as if it shared human moods and emotions was neither so trivial nor so self-conscious. It represented, rather, one aspect of the mental habit of perceiving analogous truths in the worlds of material creation and of thought. Part of the point of the Golden Age myth was truly to identify the young and innocent world with the youth and purity of essential man. Christian doctrine has it that Adam's sin cut him off from God's grace; pastoral poetry shows us man wrenched from his original sympathy with created nature by the corruption of greed and self-seeking. This arouses a momentary temptation to equate nature with God, but it is obvious that the pastoral is pulled in two directions by its own governing myth. A possibility of reconciliation is present in the image of Eden, since it can represent both man's primal innocence and the uncorrupted, nourishing world from which his sin thrust him.

The deeper contradiction lies in the fact that for the traditional pastoral the image of the Golden Age includes perforce a consistent view of man as 'natural' and his appetites as untainted. Lust, gluttony, and greed enter the pastoral world only as incursions from without, or as the direct result of succumbing to sinful temptation. Sexual feelings are usually regarded as innocent, court-ship as an instinctive miming of the activities of fertile and joyous nature. It is noteworthy that in the classical pastoral the narrative rarely goes beyond the announcement of the wedding of shepherd and shepherdess. Rapes and seductions are threatened or attempted by evil shepherds, by pirates, by passing courtiers out hunting; but the solicitations of Daphnis or Coridon are pictured always as passionately naïve. The pastoral world has no place for children, no acknowledgment of the relation of cause to effect, no recog-nition of the rigour of events in actual life. The act of imagination that first sketched the pastoral knew that it could not accommodate the dimensions of the real world. To do so would be to jeopardize its task of presenting a coherent alternative to the acceptance of 'reality' in the world's own terms. Plato would say that the world of the pastoral is a 'remembered' reality; a Christian would describe it as a recognition of the potential reality within each man. Modern criticism rejects both views and sees, as the only reality in pastoral literature, the projection of feelings of guilt and the desire to simplify and purify man's tormenting consciousness.

But the Renaissance was not so subtle, or at least not subtle in this way. Naturalist, or *libertin*, poets took the pastoral vision at face value, and glorified the flesh and its impulses with the same energy and assurance that went to paint the beauties of nature. Their argument goes something like this: if nature is God's creation, then whatever is natural is good and to be enjoyed; and if pastoral love affairs are innocent and natural, then they may be described and praised and imitated in terms that know nothing of the Christian vocabulary of sin and depravity. Variations on these themes are as frequent in the sixteenth and seventeenth centuries in England as are the many versions of explicitly Christian pastoral ideas. If the work of Spenser and Sidney has come down to us as examples of the latter, poems such as Carew's 'A Rapture', Herrick's 'Corinna's going a Maying', Randolph's 'A Pastorall Courtship', and Lovelace's 'Love made in the first Age', epitomize the naturalistic pastoral in a way that makes the distinction sufficiently clear. Sin and alienation from God are not the threatening forms of retribution that hover over this world of indulgence; death alone is the event against which the joys and fruits of life are measured. The moral world of the naturalists, in short, is the one we find in every poem that celebrates the theme of *carpe diem*, a theme that maintains its tenacity during the long transition from the classical world to the modern.

Marvell's poetry distinguishes itself repeatedly by appearing to accept common assumptions and literary conventions, and then by proceeding to reinterpret them by revealing, with scrupulous precision and objectivity, their latent contradictions or hidden inconsistencies. I do not mean to suggest that his only purpose in writing verse was to anatomize the literary materials he inherited from the classical and English traditions and that he learned from his contemporaries. But the bent of his mind was to examine the myriad ways in which words and symbols represent or fail to represent the ideas they were meant to express. We have already seen how, in his poems most obviously sprung from the traditions of courtly compliment and of religious paradox, part of his intent is revealed in an implicit, and sometimes ironical commentary on the very type of poem he pretends to be writing. We shall find that the same intellectual habit is no less common in his pastoral poems. The 'Mower' poems in particular are immensely complicated examples of his incessant modifying and re-examination of literary forms. But before discussing them it might be advisable to glance at the few other poems he wrote explicitly in the pastoral genre. And in doing so we shall notice that the members of this small group are very different from each other. The minor poems, 'Daphnis and Chloe' and 'Ametas and Thestylis making Hay-Ropes', are unmistakably related to *libertin* pastoral poetry; indeed the latter is so perfect an example that despite its wit it bears few marks that we can identify with assurance as Marvell's. But as a representative of the other strain within the pastoral, the absorption of classical conventions into the Christian moral framework, we shall turn to 'The Nymph complaining for the death of her Faun',[8] a poem that has caused a good deal of controversy in recent years, and most of it generated by critical uncertainty as to what the poem is really intended to do.

The difficulty, one is led to believe, arises from the fact that Marvell has recreated the lineaments of at least two poetic genres so perfectly that it is almost impossible to decide which one he intended to be dominant. Miss Bradbrook feels that although 'the poem opens with straightforward and charming naturalism' in the end 'the love of the girl for her fawn is taken to be a reflection of the love of the Church for Christ'.[9] In a more carefully qualified account, Professor Bush once suggested that 'if this [the poem] have any ulterior meaning, it may be an Anglican's grief for the stricken Church'.[10] Now these opinions are responding to the presence in the poem of images and ideas drawn quite obviously from the Song of Songs and the extensive literary tradition founded on it. Perhaps St Jerome's commentary on the biblical text was the original sanction for the interpretation of the Song that viewed it as a metaphorical paraphrase of the relationship between Christ and the Church, but medieval and Renaissance writers both expanded the embryonic notion and took immense liberties with it. It became, indeed, part of the strategy of the *libertin* poets to base their intermingling of erotic and religious imagery on the example of the Song of Songs. Marvell's poem, it is true, is 'about' love in several ways, but it becomes progressively more clear that his use of the biblical imagery is heavily dependent on its spiritual connotations.

The other side of the debate is best represented by a study by Professor D. C. Allen which ventures to identify 'The Nymph' with the traditional pastoral *epicedium*, a lament for the death of a beloved person, but occasionally, as in Catullus III, for the death of a cherished animal.[11] Professor Le Comte[12] recalls the episode in *Aeneid* VII where Ascanius kills the pet stag of Sylvia, and thereby precipitates the battle between the Trojans and the Latins. The purport of both articles is that these classical and secular references are predominantly important in 'The Nymph', and that the poem's relation to the tradition of religious allegory in the line of Solomon's Song is at best peripheral. Even so, Professor Allen goes on to adduce many examples from medieval literature of the commonly understood allusion to Christ in the mention of a sacred deer or a white hart. But he offers as explanation of these apparently contradictory themes only the statement that 'through the skill of allusive annotation, Marvell is able to follow a simple course and at the same time complicate our intellectual pursuit by covering his trace with intimations drawn from the rich literary assembly of his mind'.[13] This sounds very much as if Professor Allen believes that Marvell thought of himself as a sacred deer pursued by sharp-eyed, wanton troopers of literary criticism. But I find it difficult to feel that Marvell is at pains to conceal any 'trace' whatsoever; on the contrary, the poem is full of all sorts of literary and religious traces, all of which invite us to track them as far as we can. However, the trail marked 'Virgil' does not promise to lead very far, since a stag is very different from a fawn, whose symbolic value is clearly in the line of pure sacrificial victims reminiscent of Christ, as Professor Allen himself recognizes. And if the analogy is based on the similarity between Sylvia and Sylvio, the Nymph's false lover, one might suggest with equal cogency that Marvell came upon the name in Robert Heath's *Clarastella* (1650), where Sylvio is the name of a pre-eminently inconstant lover engaged in a dialogue with the lady Mirtillo.[14] This 'source' has at least the advantage of a similarity in sex as well as in name.

Nevertheless, Professor Allen's argument has the virtue of adhering to the poem itself, and does not carry us off into a discourse on Marvell's projected sympathy with dumb animals that suffer at the hands of cruel men. Legouis chooses to comment on this rather baseless idea, extending his discussion to the role of tenderness for animals in the literature of England.[15] True, he is a bit puzzled by other remarks of Marvell, in both the poems and the prose works, that indicate he had an interest in field sports (especially falconry) quite usual in an Englishman of his time; but Professor Legouis is not the first to have been bemused by the juxtaposition in the English national character of a love for fox-hunting and a strong instinct for 'fair play' with regard to brute nature. However, the solution of that anomaly is hardly relevant to Marvell, and certainly not to a poem whose tone is that of 'The Nymph complaining for the death of her Faun'.[16]

Of course, there is good reason for this confusion of opinion. The poem's naturalism is shattered early, when in the ninth line the Nymph first refers to the hoped-for efficacy of her 'simple Pray'rs'. Still earlier, the scene of the poem itself, which we would expect to be a fairly conventional pastoral landscape, was altered by the presence of 'The wanton Troopers'. Sacred deer and milk-white harts were more often killed by the arrows of greedy hunters or evil shepherds;[17] the troopers do not quite fit the world of the Nymph, and they give some reason to believe that a reference is intended to the armies that were still at large in England whenever the poem was written. In fact, 'Troopers' suggests the Parliamentary army more nearly than the regiments of Royalist cavalry, but there is no overwhelming reason to believe that the phrase is aimed at Cromwell's (once Fairfax's) troops. The possibility of such an allusion gives support to the idea that the fawn, in some sense, stands for the Anglican church, although it would be unlike Marvell to characterize the Presbyterian attack upon Episcopacy as wanton and gratuitous. His famous statement that 'the cause was too good to have been fought for' is the remark of a man who can understand the power of an abstract issue to create opposed passions, and a man who is always hesitant to see in certain kinds of partisan-ship only unrelieved villainy.

But the reading that leaps to the conclusion that Marvell is writing political allegory proves to be a false start. Whatever the poem may say about the state of organized religion in mid-seventeenth-century England, it is not an unqualified attack upon Roundheads. It is more important to notice that, in whatever sense the fawn is intended to represent Christ, the Nymph's early lines specifically cut the troopers off from all hope of redemption by its death. There is a measure of audacity in thus limiting the essential omnipotence of Christ as redeemer, and yet the point is made very clearly.

> nor cou'd
> Thy death yet do them any good.   (ll. 5–6)

> Though they should wash their guilty hands
> In this warm life-blood, which doth part
> From thine, and wound me to the Heart,
> Yet could they not be clean: their Stain
> Is dy'd in such a Purple Grain.
> There is not such another in
> The World, to offer for their Sin.   (ll. 18–24)

Line 24 has been cited as evidence for the allusion to Christ in the fawn, yet I do not recall that anyone has mentioned that the line says, if the allusion is truly there, that *this* sin is irredeemable by the blood of its sacrifice. One could go far afield in search of references to the ritual of blood-sacrifice in other religious traditions, and it might be possible to compare the washing of guilty hands to the meaning of the Eucharist; but I am not sure that such a hunt, or its trophies, would illuminate the poem any more distinctly than does its own clear statement. It might be more profitable to notice that in the use of 'Purple' Marvell combines the traditional symbolic colour for Christ as martyr and the equally traditional colour of royal sovereignty; thus, if the subject of the poem is in fact the perilous position of the Anglican Church, there may be an allusion here to the threatened (or accomplished—we do not know the date of 'The Nymph') execution of Charles I.

But there is also the possibility that lines 23–24 are an instance of the hyperbolic style that often accompanies the physical description and abstract praise of the beloved in a pastoral poem. That Marvell is dealing constantly in the poem in pastoral as well as religious conventions is apparent in the all-too-familiar pun on 'Heart' in line 20. This particular pun is of course a major item in the stock-in-trade of the naturalist poets of both the sixteenth and seventeenth centuries, since the comparison between the shy woodland creature and the emotions of the beloved woman is an inviting one. But Marvell, while bringing this standard piece of word-play into his poem, is also preparing the poem's diction for the further comparison between the fawn and Christ, a comparison with equal authority. One of the puzzling qualities of 'The Nymph' is precisely this high incidence of word-play, since we can never be quite sure whether the Nymph herself is conscious of the puns she voices. There can be little doubt that she is meant to appear as not only innocent but naïve, although we must always be careful in speaking of figures in Marvell's poetry as if they were endowed with the consistency of a dramatic character.

The transition between the opening passage on the sinful troopers and the unique sacrificial fawn, and the beginning of the Nymph-Sylvio narrative is awkward. Speaking of the fawn (indeed, speaking most likely over his bleeding body) the Nymph, with some psychological realism, goes back in thought to the time when Sylvio presented it as a gift. But the realism does not accommodate the abrupt modulation in the symbolic mode; from clustered allusions to Christian dogma and ritual we subside to the diction of erotic pastoral verse with its puns and stock emotional attitudes. Although

Sylvio is characterized for us with great economy, his 'counterfeit' qualities function more particularly as a dramatic foil to the developing relationship between the fawn and the Nymph.

> Said He, look how your Huntsman here
> Hath taught a Faun to hunt his *Dear*.
> But *Sylvio* soon had me beguil'd.
> This waxed tame, while he grew wild,
> And quite regardless of my Smart,
> Left me his Faun, but took his Heart.
>
> (ll. 31–36)

This is as meaningful as good repartee, but it is remarkable in its power to render the Nymph's personality for us, that curious melange of obtuseness, melancholy wit, and childlike generosity. Marvell catches the very accent of Sylvio's clever worldliness, but the point is in the Nymph's parallel pun, on 'Heart', which reveals not only her awareness of the painful irony in Sylvio's joke, but also her blindness to the irony of the substitution of the fawn for her lover's heart.

The simply-stated contrast between 'tame' and 'wild' does more than underscore the reversal of civilized and barbaric qualities in the animal and the lover. It also poses for us the question whether Marvell is emphasizing the meaning of 'wild' or of 'grew'. We can understand 'wild' in a very simple sense, and regard Sylvio's disaffection as an incident not unfamiliar in the pastoral world of evanescent passions and cruel, inconstant lovers. Whether Marvell thought 'wildness' the inevitable concomitant of maturity we cannot say; if he did, he nevertheless made it clear that the Nymph sees nothing necessary in her betrayal. She does, however, generalize about the faithlessness of man and about the uncertainty of human love when compared to the innocent and unspeaking affection of an animal. But even this opinion is qualified.

> Had it liv'd long, I do not know
> Whether it too might have done so
> As *Sylvio* did: his Gifts might be
> Perhaps as false or more than he.
> But I am sure, for ought that I
> Could in so short a time espie,

Thy Love was far more better then
The love of false and cruel men.

(ll. 47–54)

The passage immediately preceding these lines is a description of
the idyllic life the fawn had introduced to the Nymph, wherein
she was content to spend her 'solitary time'. The transition, then,
seems motivated only by the dramatized recollection of Sylvio.
Marvell's procedure here suggests that the poem may be related to
the tradition of the epistolary monologue exemplified in Ovid's
Heroides and Daniel's *Complaint of Rosamund*. 'The Nymph' of
course is not framed as a letter, but it does share with the genre
the careful attention to the characteristics of individual speech
style, the intermingling of narrative and commentary, and the
deliberate introduction of dramatic event and tone into a monologue.

The forty-odd lines that follow the Nymph's musings on the
careless depravity of Sylvio are devoted to a portrait of the fawn
that is marked both for its insistently hyperbolic style and for the
consciously biblical tone of its imagery. The physical characteristic
singled out for exaggeration is the whiteness of the fawn, as if to
prepare the way for the religious symbol that is to develop out of
this strange figure in a pastoral tale.

And oft
I blusht to see its foot more soft,
And white, (shall I say then my hand?)
NAY any Ladies of the Land.

(ll. 59–62)

The only reason to pause over so conventional a comparison is to
note that the fawn is said to possess feminine qualities more perfect
than those of women themselves. We should remember that Sylvio
left the fawn in place of his heart; the point is that 'hart' is one
technical name for the adult male deer, and that 'fawn' is usually
applied to a yearling deer of either sex. The fawn of the poem, then,
has been exchanged by Sylvio for the freedom of his own adult
maleness; and the fawn remains by definition of indeterminate sex,
so that the comparisons to women that the Nymph makes are
consciously ambiguous, and dramatically poignant. A similar point
is made a few lines later when she says of the fawn: 'For it was

nimbler much than Hindes;/And trod, as on the four Winds'
(ll. 69–70). Again, we cannot be sure whether the Nymph is
sensitive to her own pun, but 'Hindes' can equally well refer to
adult female deer (which would stand for the Ladies and the Nymph
herself) and to men in general, 'hind' being an archaism with about
the same breadth of reference as 'wight' (a pun that Marvell here
denies himself).

The full symbolic tide of the poem sets in at line 71 and does not
abate until line 92; the dominant metaphor in this central passage is
that of a creature absorbing the attributes of its surroundings so
completely that it becomes indistinguishable from the attributes, not
only indistinguishable from the surroundings. This is an extremely
roundabout way to speak of metonymy—but what Marvell is
writing is not precisely metonymy. First we are given the Nymph's
description of her garden, in terms that suggest, and are meant to
suggest, the imagery of the Song of Songs.

> I have a Garden of my own,
> But so with Roses over grown,
> And Lillies, that you would it guess
> To be a little Wilderness.
>
> (ll. 71–74)

Interpretation is complicated by the ever-present question of how
much the Nymph understands of what she is saying. It is quite
imaginable that she is meant to appear unconscious of the unavoidable echoes of the garden of Canticles or Eden; and we may
be willing to grant that she is not aware of the force of her comparison of the garden to a wilderness, a comparison that relies on
the Renaissance taste for 'natural' settings. It is even possible that
she is meant to understand the sweeping reference implicit in 'Roses'
and 'Lillies' to secular and spiritual beauty. But it seems unlikely that
she is supposed to recognize the ironic note in 'over grown'—the
garden has produced a super-abundance of the roses of earthly
beauty, and 'grown' carries us back to Sylvio's growth into wildness, perhaps even to the idea that growth is tantamount to evil.[18]

The flowers in the Nymph's garden are in themselves a complex
symbol. Their colours, white and red, are the commonplace visual
signs of carnal beauty in the female; the rose, separately, stands
for natural beauty, and the lily for purity and innocence of spirit.
Taken together the flowers can only be reminiscent of liturgical

imagery of Christ and, most particularly of the 'beloved' in the Song of Songs.[19] Up to this point Marvell's technique of manipulating conventional references bears some resemblance to Spenser's syncretistic way with the symbolism of colours and natural objects. But as the Nymph's speech goes on the lilies and roses take on significances that are not circumscribed altogether by either the sacred or the profane tradition.

> For, in the flaxen Lillies shade,
> It like a bank of Lillies laid.
> Upon the Roses it would feed,
> Until its Lips ev'n seem'd to bleed:
> And then to me 'twould boldly trip,
> And print those Roses on my Lip.
> But all its chief delight was still
> On Roses thus its self to fill:
> And its pure virgin Limbs to fold
> In whitest sheets of Lillies cold.
> Had it liv'd long, it would have been
> Lillies without, Roses within.

(ll. 81–92)

The simile in lines 81–82 is enforced by the repetition of 'Lillies' so that the prevailing sense of whiteness is created not by saying that the fawn was as white as the lilies, but by saying that among lilies the fawn looked like lilies—we are left to understand 'white', even though this is the sole point of the simile. This same effect is the climax of the passage, in the famous 'Lillies without, Roses within', but it is approached by essays in less radical kinds of hyperbole. Whatever the meaning of the fawn's eating the roses, the comparison of the stains of colour to blood is meant to detain us, if not to make us think that the fawn's martyrdom is being foreshadowed. But the next image is that of 'printing' the roses on the Nymph's lip, where the visual focus has changed from blood back to the petals' colour—except that the idea of blood cannot be forgotten or forced out of the poem now. The Nymph and the fawn are connected by a serious metaphor, and their innocent games assume some of the graver colouration that the metaphor demands. That part of the growing seriousness comes from religious, or Christian, undertones in the imagery is made perfectly clear in the lines that identify the fawn's 'virgin Limbs' with the 'Lillies cold'. And the last couplet of the passage completes and justifies the various rhetorical gestures that have preceded it by driving the visual imagery to logically extreme statement: 'Lillies without, Roses within'. It is comparatively easy to see how this radical vision stems naturally from the preceding ten lines; it is less easy to phrase its relation to the biblical tradition it recalls. I do not think that the line is intended to say anything about the relative value or position of body and spirit. Rather, the conceit is a triumphant final touch to cap a succession of witty variations on themes that are kept throughout the poem suspended between serious and mocking treatments. What it does say is that certain natures will, through the power of analogy in the intelligible universe, become the very things for which they have the strongest affinities. If the fawn could have enjoyed immortality and purity simultaneously, its own essence would have dissolved into the qualities of 'rose-ness' and 'lily-ness', and it would have fused their various meanings within its own body.

It must be recognized, however, that Marvell is really not concentrating on subtleties such as these, although his diction may be meant to excite precisely this kind of speculation. Having reached the climactic point of his metaphorical exercise, he turns abruptly once again to the narrative—and this time we are brought back to the present, the actual moment of the fawn's death. And here the religious undertones become quite frankly overtones, although the analogy between the fawn and Christ becomes superficial in the process. The simplicity of 'dye as calmely as a Saint' is abandoned immediately for the typically metaphysical expatiation on tears and trees that exude sap. The technique has developed since 'Eyes and Tears', where the tears themselves were forced to suggest progressively more elaborate intellectual comparisons. Here the initial conceit leads us through a series of similes in which each step is a more widely meaningful analogy, as if Marvell were writing a paradigm of the word 'tear'. It begins with the generic comparison to the gum tree, which suggests the behaviour of the balsam in particular. Not only was the product of the balsam considered a sovereign specific, but its healing powers were regarded with something like religious awe. Further, the mind habituated to allegorical perception was not slow to perceive a correspondence between the tree that gave off healing balm when 'wounded' and the martyred beneficence of Christ.[20] The balsam gives way to a mention of frankincense, which can be an exudate from any one of a number of trees, but which is distinguished by its use as incense in religious ceremonies. The final comparison in the series retreats from the specifically Christian to a classical allusion, but one, nevertheless, that can sustain the underlying metaphor on Christ's sacrifice: 'The brotherless *Heliades*/Melt in such Amber Tears as these' (ll. 99–100). The couplet is effective because the emphasis is on 'Amber'; the word carries a complex allusion to the *value* of all the kinds of tears that have been mentioned previously, since it was a standard way to indicate the fixing, the congealing, of attributes of great beauty or worth. Of course knowledge of the myth only deepens the pertinence of the lines; the Heliades were turned into willows, and their 'tears' to amber, when they grieved for the death of their brother Phaeton, the sun. The Christ-sun analogy need not be insisted on, but we may observe that in describing the fawn's tears the Nymph has come upon a comparison which better fits her situation than the fawn's. Nor could Marvell have been unaware of this; it is only a small detail within the large device he is constructing through the poem, that of the identification of the Nymph with the fawn.

Another detail is added in the lines that follow, lines that depend also on the wide range of imaginative correspondences elicited in metaphysical poetry by the idea of tears.

> I in a golden Vial will
> Keep these two crystal Teares; and fill
> It till it do o'reflow with mine;
> Then place it in *Diana's* Shrine.

> (ll. 101–104)

There is no inconsistency in calling the tears amber at one moment and crystal at the next; both adjectives convey the expected sense of perfect, unchanging beauty. The Nymph's tears are to be mingled with these unique jewels, as she promised in lines 11–12, and the mixture dedicated to Diana. No goddess could more properly receive the offerings of a Nymph and a virginal fawn, and the name itself continues the metaphor of whiteness that has throughout the poem stood for innocence and pastoral purity. Perhaps the Nymph does not think of Diana's connection with the hunt; if she does, the irony is almost too strong.

The last lines of the poem are reminiscent of the puzzling conclusion of 'Thyrsis and Dorinda', not alone in the picture of
'Elizium'[21] but also in the perfectly straightforward assumption
that death is desirable. Of course in 'The Nymph' suicide is seen
as the result of a metamorphosis very much like the ones already
described in the myth of the Heliades. But there is no question of
her clearly dramatized wish to follow the fawn to the realm of
'milk-white Lambs, and Ermins pure'. And surely her apparent
afterthought, the statement that she need not 'bespeak' the grave
monument, is meant to be a touch of psychological verisimilitude.

> For I so truly thee bemoane,
> That I shall weep though I be Stone:
> Until my Tears, still dropping, wear
> My breast, themselves engraving there.
> There at my feet shalt thou be laid,
> Of purest Alabaster made:
> For I would have thine Image be
> White as I can, though not as Thee.

> (ll. 115–122)

The legend of Niobe is behind the visual image, but the passage
must also be studied for its climactic word-play. There is a minor
conceit in the idea of tears engraving the stone of her unnaturally
weeping statue, for 'engrave' meant both to etch and to reproduce
visually. But more important, the final four lines toy wilfully
with this notion of reality and its representation. The 'thou' of
line 119 is the sculptured image of the fawn, as we learn in the next
line; and the next couplet makes a clear distinction between the
statue and the animal. But the 'I' that is the standard of whiteness
for the alabaster is not the Nymph, but the monument into which
she has been transmuted by her grief. The implication is that just
as the fawn was more perfect than she in life, so its image in death
cannot approach the purity of its spiritual perfection. And the
measure of comparison is that the Nymph, or the statue, can be
white as the fawn's image, as if death could bring her closer to a
community of innocence and virgin beauty with the fawn. Just
as the tears of pure grief become immortal amber, so the Nymph
in her mourning will be converted into the immutable earthly
perfection of alabaster, a stone traditionally symbolic of heavenly
purity.

The contrast between the playful gravity of 'The Nymph complaining for the death of her Faun' and the grave insouciance of the two pastoral dialogues is instructive. For one thing, it illuminates the materials from which Marvell constructed the attitudes that will govern the 'Mower' poems. Both the secular, erotic style and the allegorical pastoral have their place in the 'Mower' series, but those poems represent, essentially, a departure from the norms that Marvell had already explored and exploited. 'Ametas and Thestylis making Hay-Ropes',[22] for example, is a thoroughly trivial exercise in the love-banter that passed for seductive wit in so many poems of the period. If it were more ambitious it might be laid under Dryden's charge along with Donne's poems, since Ametas 'perplexes the minds of the fair sex with nice speculations of philosophy, when he should engage their hearts, and entertain them with the softnesses of love'.[26] Not that Thestylis languishes for lack of 'entertainment'; she is, as Legouis says, 'not too coy',[24] and the ease of Ametas' conquest prevents the development of any dramatic tension and throws our interest back upon verbal by-play.

Although 'Ametas and Thestylis' seems to begin with a smutty joke, it quickly moves on to the single conceit on which its frail structure depends, the intertwined hay-rope that stands for the reciprocity of physical love. As line 4 states so bluntly, 'Love binds Love as Hay binds Hay'. We can assume throughout the poem that 'Love' with its capital L refers both to the personification and to the individual lovers, since the constant allusions to binding and twisting are not simply images of abstract passion. Thestylis' reply is even a greater piece of casuistry than Ametas is yet guilty of, but it contains some double meanings that are meant obviously to contribute to the poem's dialectic rather than to characterize the mind of Thestylis. She says:

> Think'st Thou that this Rope would twine
> If we both should turn one way?
> Where both parties so combine,
> Neither Love will twist nor Hay.

(ll. 5–8)

The logic is specious, relying as it does on the device of taking Ametas' figurative argument literally and then exposing its untruthfulness to literal fact. But we have seen Marvell practising before now on the various meanings of 'way', and there is in 'turn' the latent notion of conversion or even physical metamorphosis. In line 8 the word 'twist' is rich with connotations that range far beyond the simple one of twining, although Marvell uses only the specific sense of the verb. 'Twist' could also, at this time, be applied to a weak support upon which important matters depended; it was a cant term for an intimate sexual union, and its use in slang referred to any voracious appetite. But these are mere conjectures, and we can find a more certain pun in 'Hay'. Editors and critics have been quick to point out that the mention of 'Hay' in 'Upon Appleton House' (l. 426) refers to a country dance; but none has mentioned that the Hay was performed by two lines of dancers constantly weaving in and out, so that the dance became a contemporary synonym for anything sinuous and interwoven. Every mention of hay in 'Ametas and Thestylis', therefore, has behind it not only the image of the hay-rope itself, but also the common memory of the dance, whose movement the poem imitates.

Ametas' answer is impatient and scornful, but not so hasty that it cannot indulge in a typical metaphysical play on the comparison between physical and mental phenomena: 'And Love tyes a Womans Mind/Looser then with Ropes of Hay' (ll. 11–12). Superficially this is the same genre as the 'Fetters of . . . Air' of 'The Fair Singer', but the point of the lines is precisely to deny the power of abstractions over the mind. And if there is any true humour in the poem it is in the very downright recognition of Ametas and Thestylis that metaphysical subtleties do not lead to consummation. As Thestylis says, 'What you cannot constant hope/ Must be taken as you may' (ll. 13–14), a gesture of discouragement that invites as it repels in a masterful example of ambiguity. But Ametas, at least, is not in doubt about her meaning: 'Then let's both lay by our Rope,/And go kiss within the Hay' (ll. 15–16).

The levity and swiftness of 'Ametas and Thestylis' provide a vantage for judgment of 'Daphnis and Chloe', since the latter poem appears to follow the same dialectical pattern until its surprising reversal in the last two stanzas.[25] It is based, as we learn from 'Lawes' in line 107, on the rules of amatory conduct set up in the French Courts of Love and maintained, with fluctuating seriousness and mockery, throughout the Renaissance in Europe. The rules decreed rigid poses for the beseeching lover and the disdainful beloved; but the decrees tacitly sanctioned a compassionate yielding when the drama had been played out. 'Daphnis and Chloe' is also true to its genre in relying primarily on personification for its figures, and on paradox for its means of progress. However, the ironic view of the two final quatrains is problematical. These last lines are spoken by the narrator, and we cannot credit the frustrated swain with the cynic viewpoint; but the actions described are those of Daphnis, as is the excuse offered.

The initial situation is Daphnis' imminent departure in despair over his unsuccessful suit. The mention of 'the dismal Hour' that must 'devour' all his hopes looks forward to the 'slow-chapt' Time of 'To his Coy Mistress', but only as a sign that Marvell is well aware of the traditional emblem of 'all-devouring Time'. However, the cannibalistic appetites of time and death are important concepts throughout the poem, and they are the basis of several extravagant and almost repellent images later on. The explanation of Daphnis' gloom is left to the paradoxical statement, 'Nature her own Sexes foe' (l. 5), where 'her' is Chloe, and the enmity between Chloe and Nature is left unexplained, carrying the definite stigma of being 'unnatural'. That Nature should give lessons in coyness is Marvell's generalization about womankind, since the laws of courtly love were admittedly highly artificial. The next remark, 'But she neither knew t'enjoy,/Nor yet let her Lover go' (ll. 7–8), implies that whatever Nature teaches, she has not given Chloe the knowledge necessary to treat realities. (The sexual plays on 'knew' and 'go' are there but only as witty embellishment. They are the comments of the narrator, not the judgments of Daphnis.) Nature is as formidable an antagonist as Death in the poem, and her ambiguous benevolence is once again considered in:

> Nature so her self does use
> To lay by her wonted State,
> Lest the World should separate;
> Sudden Parting closer glews.
>
> (ll. 13–16)

Thus, beneath the glittering (and, by implication, hypocritical) appearance of alluring Nature lies the genuine animal appetite that struggles against discord and single sterility. The image of the 'World' summons up the Platonic myth of the universal significance of joined essences and bodies, but here it is meant to compress all lovers into the two who occupy us in this room. In the next line the psychological observation is turned into the kind of paradox of which the poem makes such constant use: 'Sudden Parting closer glews'.[26]

The following quatrain combines several of the themes we have just mentioned, and introduces the conventional military metaphor so frequently encountered in poems that either pursue or parody the Petrarchan style. Daphnis, although 'well read', does not yet know enough to understand the paradoxical ways of a woman who will yield the 'Fort' only when the 'Siege' has been raised. The incommensurability of what passes for knowledge in the world and true knowledge is but touched on in the quibble over 'Sence' in line 23, where the surface meaning seems to demand 'intelligence' but the deeper irony obviously suggests physical sensibility, particularly that of clear sight. This hint will now be developed into a full statement of the paradox of Daphnis' being both alive and dead— literally alive but dead in the entreaties of Chloe and the possibility of physical consummation. The ensuing humour arises from the poem's eagerness to exploit the notion that Daphnis is but a 'Lovers Ghost'—and to follow that with the narration of his supremely energetic dalliance after parting from Chloe.

Meanwhile he is described as 'undone' and 'rent', as if to present us with a concrete demonstration of that 'separation' Nature had feared in stanza IV. He is, indeed, separated from Chloe, and the metaphorical language of the poem equates this with being dead, and credits his death-stroke to Time.

> For, Alas, the time was spent,
> Now the latest minut's run
> When poor *Daphnis* is undone.
>
> (ll. 29–31)

Time itself declines along with Daphnis, as if time were in a very real sense the life's breath of the lover in this artificial world. By stanza XI Daphnis' death is taken as proved, and he is called 'this Lovers Ghost'; the fact that he takes his leave 'resolved' will permit an amused recollection of the Resolved Soul which, in its way, conducted the same defence of its purity against the temptations of the Created Pleasure represented by Chloe.

But Puritan, or simply Christian, allusions in this poem are gratuitous; for Daphnis to refer to Chloe as 'my Hell and Heaven Joyn'd' is merely to appeal to the force of a paradox as venerable as the myth of Genesis. Marvell expends a good deal of ingenuity in anatomizing the grisly idea of fattening the intended victim of an execution. He has time to blend personification and paradox in:

> Nor to my Departure owe
> What my Presence could not win;
>
> (ll. 59–60)

and in:

> Than my Losses to increase
> By a late Fruition,
>
> (ll. 63–64)

where the paradox is preserved only by our understanding that there is no possibility that Daphnis will have a change of heart. And this realization, at least, does suggest that his outpouring of illustrative analogies may be a warning of the promiscuity to come. For the tone is further from the tranquil confidence of the Resolved Soul than it is from Shakespeare's notorious Player Queen, who protested 'too much'. But there is also in Daphnis' speeches an echo of the obsession we have seen elsewhere in Marvell, the fascination with death as not only a threat but an enticing promise. It is but an echo, since his explicit rhetoric is directed at scorning the temptation to salvage some joys from the life he has abandoned. Death is called 'Fate' (l. 65), 'Executioner' (l. 67), and 'Canibal' (l. 72), and the delights proffered by Chloe are spoken of as 'Jewels' and food to 'fat' him up for the cannibal's dinner. In each case the device is to compare physical love to a profit that will be enjoyed only by the hungry maw of death; and in 'Daphnis and Chloe' this argument is the justification for the rejection of love rather than the most urgent persuasion to love, as it is most strongly in 'To his Coy Mistress'. There, and in most poems of *carpe diem*, the dominant idea is to snatch physical pleasure out of the jaws of death and time; here we are asked to dwell on the obscene appetites of these joint fates, and to reason about the propriety of denying them their feast.

And the question holds through necrophiliac visions, allusions to the wandering Hebrew tribes, and a reference to local English beliefs about the magical properties of ferns; it breaks down only before the justly famous quatrain,

> Gentler times for Love are ment
> Who for parting pleasure strain

> Gather Roses in the rain,
> Wet themselves and spoil their Sent,

> (ll. 85–88)

that reaches back openly to the world of pastoral symbols and
values that was the unspoken frame for the poem originally. Part
of the gentle shock this stanza administers derives from the abrupt-
ness with which the diction drops from radical simile to natural
description; another part is accounted for by the fact that while it
describes an absurd act, it is the kind of absurdity that men cannot
avoid because of the way their emotions lead them, not because of
vanity, superstition, or vicious appetite. Daphnis speaks here with
the voice of a kind of deified Prudence, but the accents of his image
betray a more compassionate viewpoint.

It must also be noticed that the phrase 'Gentler times', although
it is related to all the other references to time in the poem, introduces
an idea that is present nowhere else. It recalls 'Young Love', 'The
unfortunate Lover', and 'The Gallery'. While it undercuts the
sardonic tone of the final eight lines, it suggests at the same time
that the pastoral tradition is remembered here as the continuing
image of the proper setting for innocent love. The rain in 'Daphnis
and Chloe' is not the nourishing gift of heaven, nor is it lost in a
conceit about the Sun's tears over the spectacle of human folly.
Rather, it is equated with time, and darkness, and death—with all
the elemental forces that contrive to wither roses, drench the passions
of men and women, and spoil the 'Sent' of flowers, which is Nature's
form of incense, grateful to the senses of gods and men. Woven
into this delicate fabric is a repetition of the motif of the early
stanzas, the unnatural stress of separation against which Nature
struggles; this time it is equated with the attempt to 'strain' pleasure,
to devour too much pleasure just at the moment when pleasure
becomes irrelevant and unattainable.

The two stanzas that follow are more subdued in their imagery
than the earlier part of the poem, but they are fully charged with
paradox. The subject now is the intermingling of opposed qualities,
and the paradox is expressed through personification. But whereas
Daphnis says, 'Joy will not with Sorrow weave' (l. 91), he seems to
contradict himself immediately in saying:

> Fate I come, as dark, as sad,
> As thy Malice could desire;

> Yet bring with me all the Fire
> That Love in his Torches had. (ll. 93–96)

If joy will not 'weave' with sorrow, then at least the fires of passion (or remorse?) can lighten the darkness of sorrow. The flame has been stolen from Love's (Hymen's?) torches, but it is not at all clear what specific fuel it burns in Daphnis' hands. At any rate, his fire lights him no further than to the block, and the moment when he signals for the fall of the axe recalls the famous scene of Charles I's execution in 'An Horatian Ode'. For the prisoner to indicate the moment for the stroke was as customary as for the executioner to be granted the prisoner's effects,[27] and Marvell seems to have been well acquainted with the procedures of legal executions.

The transition to the closing comments is as abrupt as the axe's blow, and has as violent an effect on the movement of the poem. Daphnis, we are told, has rushed from his noble and philosophic rejection of Chloe's passionate overtures to the beds of Phlogis[28] and Dorinda; between these assignations he 'but rid to take the Air'. And the explanation the narrator gives is even more dismissive than the speed of Daphnis' hypocritical change of heart.

> Yet he does himself excuse;
> Nor indeed without a Cause.
> For, according to the Lawes,
> Why did *Chloe* once refuse? (ll. 105–108)

We noticed before that this appeal to the laws of love is both anachronistic and illogical. But it is difficult to read these lines unless we read them as a cold and mocking revelation of the unreality of Daphnis' warmly argued convictions. It is clear that the pastoral world of the dialogue is one from which innocence has been banished. In the 'Mower' poems we shall find it once again; but innocence is now an aspect of nature itself, no longer of man.

II

The 1681 Folio of Marvell's poems contains 'The Mower against Gardens', 'Damon the Mower', 'The Mower to the Glo-Worms', and 'The Mower's Song', in that order. The sequence has no discernible narrative structure, nor does it employ different verse forms in variations of pastoral conventions, as does *The Shepheardes*

Calender. But the poems are related to each other in so far as we are first acquainted with Damon the Mower in the full strength of his moral and philosophical attack on worldly excess ('The Mower against Gardens'), and then shown his progressive decline into despair because of his self-destructive passion for Juliana, the icy-bosomed goddess of death. Damon's precipitate fall is paralleled by the dissolution of his intimate ties to the natural scene in which the poems are set, ties that in one sense constitute the basic metaphor of the entire sequence. For the great subject of all the 'Mower' poems is the impossible reconciliation between man and the world of natural creation of which he is a part. The mind may mirror the order of the world, but it is the imagination that divides man ultimately from the field of that imagination. The problems at the heart of the apparently simple pastoral poetry of the 'Mower' sequence are, above all, paradoxical. And the flashing play of symbol and pun, the incalculable shifts of viewpoint and attitude, the ironies tacit and overt—all these are the instruments Marvell uses to probe the problems, as if poetry, itself the product of imagination, could in some fashion repair a schism slashed through Damon's world by his own imagination.

But before we are engaged by questions of this magnitude the poems present a more obvious but no less significant obstacle to interpretation—Marvell's choice of a mower rather than a shepherd for his pastoral *persona*. I think we can assume directly that the change was not made through caprice or because of a taste for arbitrary innovation. In every other respect the poems deal so thoroughly in recognizable versions of strict pastoral convention that we must account for the difference in the focal dramatic figure. It would seem obvious that the analogy at the heart of 'all flesh is grass' is sufficient as a clue to Marvell's meaning, since all the 'Mower' poems treat in one way or another the meaning and the experience of man's correspondence with the world he lives in. But a variety of other explanations has been offered in good faith by Marvell's critics. They range from Miss Sackville-West's simplistic remark that 'Marvell's Mower simply takes the place of the traditional shepherd. It was Marvell who discovered the scythesman as an ornament to poetry, and who for *bergerie* substituted *faucherie*',[29] to the rather baroque extravagance of Empson's 'I suppose he is not only the ruler but the executioner of the daffodils—the Clown as Death';[30] the supposition leaps a little too eagerly into the realm of personification, leaving the characters of the poems deflated and without the proper title to the roles Marvell gives them.

Miss Bradbrook believes that Damon carries some ethnocentric meaning, although why this should be more true of a mower than of, say, a Cumberland shepherd is hard to understand.[31] Such a theory encounters, too, the difficulty that 'The Mower against Gardens' at least directs its criticism against customs and fads that were European in scope; furthermore, the pastoral was a universal genre in the same sense that Latin had been the *lingua franca* of the European Middle Ages. True, one could find different local fairies, different dances, and even different proper names as the locale of the realistic pastoral varied—but shepherds *and* mowers passed current everywhere, none more English nor French than any other. M. Legouis, whom we might expect to be able to point out any traditional basis for Marvell's mower in French pastoral verse, says only that the change was sought for purposes of contrast,[32] supporting his view by reference to the passage in 'Damon the Mower' (stanza VII) that compares the mower to the shepherd, very much to the advantage of the former. But this seems to misplace effect for cause, and can hardly explain why Marvell should make a single alteration in a conventional scheme he adheres to so closely elsewhere. More important, Legouis' idea limits the possible significance of the mower figure to an extent that simply will not be reconciled with Marvell's obviously serious intentions in creating him. This is not to say that the 'Mower' poems are uniformly grave and philosophical; they are compounded of Marvell's usual proportions of humour, irony, absurdity, and pointed intelligence. But I hope to be able to demonstrate that the symbolic weight of Damon alone in his role of emperor of the meadows, with the dual powers of cultivation and destruction (Empson's point is valid to this extent), is of vital importance to the meaning of each of the four poems, and essential to an understanding of the series.

The burden of Damon's complaint against the formal and ornate gardens of the mid-seventeenth century is a familiar one, for it appears in one form or another in the many Renaissance debates over the proper relationship between nature and conscious art. The terms of the traditional opposition are epitomized in the Garden of Adonis and the Bower of Bliss in *The Faerie Queene*,[66] and again in the description of Nature's pavilion in the 'Cantos of Mutabilitie':

> Not such as Craftes-men by their idle skill
> Are wont for Princes states to fashion:
> But th'earth her self of her owne motion,
> Out of her fruitfull bosome made to growe
> Most dainty trees.
>
> (FQ, VII, vii, 8, ll. 3–7)

Professor Kermode cites as the *locus classicus* of the argument the exchange between Perdita and Polixenes in *The Winter's Tale* (IV, iv, 79–103) where Perdita scorns 'Nature's bastards', the 'streak'd gillyvors' because their colours have been artificially enhanced. Polixenes answers that 'Nature is made better by no mean/But Nature makes that mean. . . . This is an art/Which does mend nature, change it rather, but/The art itself is Nature'.[64] Perdita is more orthodox in her sense of the difference between the natural and the artificial. Or at least her orthodoxy is that of the conventional pastoral. Polixenes, however, has on his side the great majority of Renaissance theoreticians of rhetoric, since 'artifice' deserved no opprobrium in the mind of an Elizabethan author or critic. Rather, it was the sign of the controlled craft that was essential to the artist's task of giving shape to the chaos of created nature. But the critics were sufficiently in accord with Perdita to insist that the poet's art was not to be acquired solely by imitation and study, but must be founded in perceptions and imaginative insights that reflected the creative power of nature itself. To take only one example, Puttenham arrives at his distinctions by stating, first, that:

> though it be better to see with spectacles then not to see at all, yet is their praise not egall nor in any mans judgement comparable: no more is that which a Poet makes by arte and precepts rather then by naturall instinct, and that which he doth by long meditation rather then by a suddaine inspiration.[35]

But writing poetry is not quite the same thing as seeing, with or without spectacles, as Puttenham recognizes when he says that:

> Man also in all his actions that be not altogether naturall, but are gotten by study, discipline, or exercise, as to daunce by measures, to sing by note, to play on the lute . . . it is a praise to be said an artificiall dauncer . . . & player on instruments, because they be not exactly knowne or done, but by rules & precepts or teaching of schoolemasters.[36]

The decisive stage of the argument is reached when Puttenham points out that the arts of language share something of both the natural and the trained functions,

> so whatsoeuer a man speakes or perswades he doth it not by imitation artificially, but by obseruation naturally . . . because it is both the same and the like that nature doth suggest.[37]

This does not go far enough for Puttenham's satisfaction, however, since it skimps the importance of the artist's finely trained faculties in enabling him to 'speak or persuade' with a natural cogency that conceals the calculation beneath its power. His final qualification, therefore, is that:

> that in our maker or Poet which restes onely in deuise and issues from an excellent sharpe and quick inuention, holpen by a cleare and bright phantasie and imagination, he is not as the painter to counterfaite the naturall by the like effects . . . but even as nature her selfe working by her owne peculiar vertue and proper instinct and not by example . . . or exercise as all other artificers do, is then most admired when he is most naturall and least artificiall: and in the feates of his language . . . because they hold as well of nature to be suggested . . . as by arte to be polished. . . . Therefore shall our Poet . . . be more commended for his naturall eloquence then for his artificiall, and more for his artificiall well disembled then . . . ouermuch affected.[38]

The niceness of Puttenham's discriminations can be instructive for the reading of 'The Mower against Gardens' since Marvell is not dealing with the art-nature controversy in its crudest terms—that is, he is not saying simply that the natural is good and the artificial bad. As well as Puttenham and Polixenes he is aware that art can follow nature in its creativity; what Damon deplores is man's abuse of the fertile principles of art, and what the poem does is to give us an elaborately reasoned and figured account of the consequences of that abuse.

Nevertheless, Marvell's attitude is not that of sentimental primitivism. His penchant for describing natural scenes in terms derived from the formalistic arts of painting, landscape-gardening, and fortification has led some critics to declare that 'nature', to Marvell, is essentially a patterned and ordered reality rather than the picturesque wilderness extolled by later poets.[39] This is more faithful to Marvell's true preoccupations than the opinion of nineteenth-century critics who saw him as an unabashed pantheist, a worshipper of nature who had somehow hit upon the Wordsworthian mode of apprehension in the middle of the seventeenth century.[40] But while the former theory may receive some support from some parts of 'Upon Appleton House' it is not fully adequate to the ideas of nature that obtain in the 'Mower' poems.

The very opening lines of 'The Mower against Gardens', indeed, pose a problem that is only tangentially related to the controversy about the naturalness of art: 'Luxurious Man, to bring his Vice in use,/Did after him the World seduce (ll. 1–2).[41] The distinction is made almost in passing, but it is clear that 'Luxurious Man' is something apart from 'the World'; we must also remember that every word is spoken in the *persona* of Damon and that he, therefore, disassociates himself from the vicious betrayer of the natural world. The rich and open sounds of 'Luxurious' are better suited to the seventeenth-century meaning of the word; the texture of 'l', 'x', 'r', and 'u' gives a sense of languorous indulgence, a sense that will be reinforced in the following lines and that is not vitiated by the crisp play on 'seduce', which refers to its Latin connotation of 'lead apart, lead astray' as well as to its usual moral and sexual meanings. But the most important task of these two lines is to establish the relationship between man and the world; and we see it to be one of perverted and selfish exploitation.

The values opposed to those of 'Luxurious Man' are characterized succinctly in the next distich:[42] 'And from the fields the Flow'rs and Plants allure,/Where Nature was most plain and pure' (ll. 3–4). Thus we are informed that the garden is something less noble than the field, that the flowers are not only *dis*placed but *mis*placed. 'Plain' and 'pure' are self-defined values; their monosyllabic simplicity is the best assertion of what Nature stands for to Damon. In contrast to both the sound and sense of line 4, Marvell is lavish in his description of the archetype of the formal garden:

> He first enclos'd within the Gardens square
>   A dead and standing pool of Air:
> And a more luscious Earth for them did knead,
>   Which stupifi'd them while it fed.
>
> (ll. 5–8)

The diction of these four lines is almost an exercise in the expression of disgust. As if 'dead' and 'standing' were not enough to convey the sense of stifling decay, Marvell intensifies the underlying image of a stagnant pond by applying it to the air itself, making the garden enclosure even more unnatural and repellent. 'Luscious' repeats some of the sounds of 'Luxurious', and 'l', 'r', and 's' occur often enough to suggest a conscious pattern of softness and passivity. The measure of man's treachery is to be found in the idea of 'a more luscious Earth'; the process of nourishment is perverted, not by diverting or interrupting it, but by intensifying it to the point where fertility lapses into satiated, sterile stupefaction. The use of natural processes for purposes not their own is the theme and target of Damon's execrations for the next twenty lines. But the items of his indictment are not embedded in a random catalogue of unconnected conceits; they are arranged to have a cumulative effect in demonstrating man's taste for interfering with the inherent processes of nature: 'The Pink grew then as double as his Mind;/The nutriment did change the kind' (ll. 9-10). We have seen that doubleness of mind is a synonym for moral depravity; the further horror pictured here is that the flowers lured from Nature into the luxurious garden now mirror the moral evil of their seducer. The wit lies in thinking thus of the art of hybridization, which often depended for the creation of new colours and shapes in flowers upon artificially controlled mineral diets. It is only in Damon's outraged imagination that the nutriment can actually 'change the kind', or species of the plant. But it is precisely Damon's mind that limits and defines our view in this poem. The exaggeration of the statement is an index of the indignation he feels.

The same tone prevails in lines 11-15, where the imagery is drawn from flowers but refers, obviously, to the use of cosmetics in all forms as a wilful and misguided attempt to improve natural beauty. 'Strange perfumes' are clearly inferior to the scent of roses, as we learned from 'Daphnis and Chloe'; and the force of 'paint' reminds us of Hamlet's speech to Ophelia (III, i, 148 ff.) and of the many occasions in Renaissance literature when the word is associated distinctly with harlots. The acme of absurdity is touched in the white tulip's desire for a finer complexion (l. 13), and the cosmetic comparison is worked out in an allusion to the contemporary craze for buying and breeding tulips with new colour combinations—this tulip 'learn'd to interline its cheek'. But the topical reference[43] is not the only basis for these lines: 'Its Onion root they then so high did hold,/That one was for a Meadow sold' (ll. 15–16). The inversion of values by 'Luxurious Man' is imaged by the upside-down valuation of the tulip root; and we know that no act could seem more insanely evil to Damon the Mower than to sell a meadow for a faddish trinket. Man has gone so far as to treat the earth itself as a mere object to be disposed of for his gratification. And Marvell presses the notion a bit further by speaking of 'Another World' and the 'Oceans new' discovered and searched not for themselves but for a tulip. This is the climax of the first diatribe against man's frenzied pursuit of the unnatural, but Damon moves from this point to a still more passionate denunciation of human vice. His flat 'And yet' ushers in the description of the one greater crime—that of miscegenation, both physical and moral. All these wanton expenditures might have been allowed, says Damon,

> Had he not dealt between the Bark and Tree,
> Forbidden mixtures there to see.
> No Plant now knew the Stock from which it came;
> He grafts upon the Wild the Tame.
>
> (ll. 21–24)

The passage is ostensibly about the contemporary arts of grafting, but by using the business term 'dealt' Marvell enlarges the reference so that it glances at every human act that exploits nature for personal gain; nor need the gain be material. The impulse to force nature out of its own course is characterized as an aspect of the sin of pride ('Man, that sov'raign thing and proud'), and the biblical strictures are enforced again in line 22 by the memory of the Old Testament laws against the mingling of kinds.[44] Nor is nature's course a vague abstraction for Marvell; the orderly progression from scion to stock, the continuum between generations, the uninterrupted growth of an entity toward the fulfilment of its proper ends—all these are felt to be natural. Part of this sense is caught in the diction of the poem, which relies heavily on personification. The plant in line 23 is given not only knowledge, but the ability to be bewildered by man's unnatural dealings; in this way the correspondence between Damon and the denizens of pure nature is intensified once more.[45]

The explicit topic of unlicensed grafting of plants leads naturally to an idea of the chaos that ensues from interference with the generative powers of plants or men. The lines that follow, while they remain within the scope of plant-imagery, employ epithets that expand the reference to include a universal sexual disorder.

> His green *Seraglio* has its Eunuchs too;
> Lest any Tyrant him out-doe.
> And in the Cherry he does Nature vex,
> To procreate without a Sex.[46]
>
> (ll. 27–30)

The picture of defenceless and unsophisticated natural creatures pressed into lascivious and perverted service is consistent with the opening description of the garden, into which the plants were seduced. But the greatest disgust is reserved for any act that replaces nature's processes with experiments devised by the proud and self-willed human imagination. We shall see in 'An Horatian Ode' that the political implications of the views represented here as Damon's are profound; in the light of such beliefs about the interdependence of natural growth and legitimate sovereignty it is not difficult to see why Cromwell's assumption of power presented enormously compelling and complex problems to Marvell's mind.

The final ten lines of 'The Mower against Gardens' return to the pastoral scene that has been forsaken while man's sins were catalogued. The scene itself is forsaken, and we cannot tell exactly where Damon stands as he describes for the last time the spectacle of pointless separation presented by the garden and the fields themselves.

> 'Tis all enforc'd; the Fountain and the Grot;
> While the sweet Fields do lye forgot:
> Where willing Nature does to all dispence
> A wild and fragrant Innocence.
>
> (ll. 31–34)

'Enforced', although it means primarily 'constrained', carried in the seventeenth century, as it does now, undertones of compulsion of force and even ravishment—and thus Marvell characterizes the strength of man's aberrant desires. For the fountain and the grotto are both the symbols and the objects of his enforcement. Within the garden they exist as do the polished statues of the gods; outside it they stand metonymically for the pastoral world we have come to know in 'Clorinda and Damon'. They promise soothing refreshment, as Nature is said to 'dispence/A wild and fragrant Innocence'.[47] Not only is nature personified here, but it is pictured as the nature of the Golden Age, that nurtures man and supplies him only from innate generosity and the feelings of 'kind'.[48] In keeping with the mythology of 'willing Nature' Damon then speaks of the tutelary spirits of the pastoral:

> And *Fauns* and *Faryes* do the Meadows till,
>   More by their presence then their skill.
> Their Statues polish'd by some ancient hand,
>   May to adorn the Gardens stand:
> But howso'ere the Figures do excel,
>   The *Gods* themselves with us do dwell.
>
> (ll. 35–40)

Most of the contrasts established in these lines are easy to grasp, but others, I feel, are merely suggested and left unresolved. For example, the initial point is that the pastoral gods know nothing of the cunning science of experimental agriculture; but their lack of 'skill' does not prevent them from tilling the meadows in the true sense—from making them fertile and productive simply by the influence of their purity of spirit. But '*Fauns* and *Faryes*' are natural only in a very unusual sense; they are not real, but only the effective symbols of what is best in nature—innocence, and the impulse to produce fruits without a conscious goal of profit. In this sense the fawns are 'present' in the meadows; and Marvell points up the true meaning of the pastoral deities when he compares them to the garden statuary that imitates only the outward form but can never comprehend the fruitful spirit. Damon does not contemn the garden; since he is Marvell's voice, he is careful to show an awareness of the specific beauty that statues 'polish'd by some ancient hand' can have. His only disagreement is with the attempt to replace the essential forces of nature with pieces of artifice that try, but fail, to represent what they supplant.[49] It is an attempt that calls forth the most intense application of man's imitative art, 'But howso'ere the Figures do excel,/The *Gods* themselves with us do dwell' (ll. 39–40). Mentioning the gods is consonant with the lines on the presence of the woodland deities in line 35, and all of them are open to the same ambiguities of interpretation. The pastoral convention demands that these be pagan gods, and the argument of the poem demands in its turn that they be essences of natural virtue. Within the terms of the poem there need be no contradiction. The primary intention of Damon's use of 'us' is to align him finally with the fields that 'lye forgot'.[50] The '*Gods*' are those that maintain beauty, innocence, fertility, and unsophisticated content in a natural concert. They 'dwell' within the meadows and within the souls that tend the meadows as if they were extensions of their consciousness. Obviously such a god cannot be imprisoned in the most perfectly-crafted model; artificiality is the very negation of its powers and purposes.

In 'Damon the Mower'* the threat to nature does not come from the pride or artifice of man. Death invades the meadow in many disguises, but the dominant one in this poem is the figure of Juliana. Indeed, 'Damon the Mower' purports to be an example of the pastoral love-complaint; it is replete with cruel mistress, languishing lover, and sympathetic natural setting. But as it approaches its more central, and graver, considerations Marvell comments with great humour and freedom on the genre within which he is ostensibly writing.

A good deal of this is accomplished in the first stanza. The opening couplet, a parody of the epic call-to-attention, sets the initial tone of mock-heroic and burlesque. It also begins to establish what will be a fairly complex attitude toward Damon himself, since he appears in the poem at times as its undoubted hero, at other times as its butt, and always as a figure of natural innocence betrayed to death by an unreasonable and irrelevant passion.

> Heark how the Mower *Damon* Sung,
> With love of *Juliana* stung!
> While ev'ry thing did seem to paint
> The Scene more fit for his complaint.
>
> (ll. 1–4)

This is not adhering to the convention of sympathetic nature, but analysing the convention by pretending to describe the way it works in actuality. We have noticed the ambiguous quality of 'paint' before now, and here it is used quite explicitly to direct our attention to the way nature, allegedly, falls in with the moods and critical dilemmas of its creatures by rearranging itself to suit them. The artificiality of the idea is betrayed in the word 'Scene', which we cannot help feeling refers here to the stage rather than to the natural setting. Nor should we miss the point of 'seem', a word that allows Marvell to use the convention while revealing its emptiness. The scene itself as it is constructed reveals the discrepancy between true emotion and the pastoral conventions normally used to represent it.

> Like her fair Eyes the day was fair;
> But scorching like his am'rous Care.
> Sharp like his Sythe his Sorrow was,
> And wither'd like his Hopes the Grass.

(ll. 5–8)

To be sure, Juliana's eyes are fair and Damon's passion is scorching; but notice that the two adjectives are incommensurate, and that they take the first steps towards drawing the contrast between Juliana's destructively icy detachment and Damon's equally destructive desire. The repeated use of 'like,' the insistence on the simile, drives home the hollow absurdity of the enforced comparisons between psychological and physical events. Line 7 rests on a pun that we shall examine when we come to stanza VIII, but its humour contains as well the first intimation of a possible serious connection between the real and the farcical versions of Damon's doomed love. The metre changes to accommodate the incipient change of tone. Whereas the iambic stresses fall with sure regularity on the final syllables of lines 1 through 6, the rhythm falls in 'Sharp like his Sythe his Sorrow was'. The sharp stress on 'Hopes' in line 8 weakens the final foot so that the line falls away from the strong pattern set up in the earlier part of the stanza, just as the identification of the grass and Damon's hopes hints at the fall into despair and death that is to come. The last couplet, furthermore, makes a point of identifying Damon with the scythe he uses to cut the grass, as well as finding similarities between withered nature and Damon's decaying fortunes.

Stanza II pretends, again, to be a straightforward description; it is full of homely, familiar animals, country references, pastoral conceits, and a very rich and convincing atmosphere of a burning summer's day just before the hay-harvest. But we cannot ignore the pun in the very first line, one that Marvell will use again in a richer fashion in stanza IV of 'The Garden'; nor can the portrait of the snake in lines 15–16 go unnoticed: 'Oh what unusual

Heats are here,/Which thus our Sun-burn'd Meadows sear!' (ll.
9-10). The 'Heats' of course are not only the scorching temperatures
of the day, but the contest of passions to be run by Damon and
Juliana, and above all the consuming desire of Damon himself.
Marvell will develop throughout the poem an analogy between
Damon and the sun, just as Juliana will be progressively identified
with the moon, and not only because of her icy chasteness. Thus
line 10 is a minor preparatory note for the image that will emerge
fully in stanza VIII; the sun sears the grass, but so will Damon burn
his 'Hopes' and lay them waste. Even the songs and dances of the
traditional pastoral scene disappear in the face of this extraordinary
heat ('The Grass-hopper its pipe gives ore;/And hamstring'd Frogs
can dance no more'), and the creature left unscorched is 'Only the
Snake, that kept within,/Now glitters in its second skin' (ll. 15-16).
Marvell has been praised for the precision of his observation of
nature, but surely these lines contain more than accurate vision.
The snake stands not only for duplicity and conscious evil, but here
also for the same cold detachment Juliana displays; and in its 'second
skin' there is a hint of the hypocrisy that defends itself against the
frank emotions of nature.

The third stanza would seem to invalidate what I have said about
the correspondence between Damon and the sun, but this is because
the hyperbole makes Juliana's 'scorching beams' hotter than the
sun itself; as Marvell says, her 'higher Beauty . . . makes the Sun/
Hotter then his own *Phaeton*'. In other words, both the sun and the
mower are victims of Juliana's incomparable power.[51] Damon at
least can try to flee, but his escape is frustrated in stanza IV.

> Tell me where I may pass the Fires
> Of the hot day, or hot desires.
> To what cool Cave shall I descend,
> Or to what gelid Fountain bend?
> Alas! I look for Ease in vain,
> When Remedies themselves complain.
> No moisture but my Tears do rest,
> Nor Cold but in her Icy Breast.
>
> (ll. 25-32)

The fountain and the grot of 'The Mower against Gardens' appear
once more, but here the reference includes the meanings that it had
in 'Clorinda and Damon'; this fountain is not only a source of

coolness but a hope of spiritual cleansing and salvation. But Juliana, the phantom figure who seems to be more perfectly an abstraction in the poem than a credible object of Damon's love, has not only out-shone the sun but now is seen to control the elements themselves. She has dried up all moisture and hoarded all cold; in a 'metaphysical' turn of wit Marvell tells us that the cures themselves have succumbed to the disease, and the implication is that created nature is helpless before this apparently unfeeling goddess of destruction.

Damon tries to approach her in the fifth stanza, asking why she has disdained his presents—and a curious collection they form. Roughly, they are the delightful jewels of nature as seen by a mind that does not know the very different values of the materialistic world. But they are, too, very pertinent offerings to placate a dreaded force; Damon's 'harmless Snake' is a passive mockery of the serpent of stanza II, with its fangs and venom removed.[52] The chameleon might almost be taken as the heraldic sign of Juliana, and the victor's oak-leaves that Damon brings are 'tipt with hony due', as if to mollify the rigour of Juliana's rule. But none of these has proved acceptable, and so Damon launches into the second half of the poem with an attempt to identify himself by pointing to his signal relationship with the nature that surrounds him.

> I am the Mower *Damon*, known
> Through all the Meadows I have mown.
> On me the Morn her dew distills
> Before her darling Daffadils.
> And, if at Noon my toil me heat,
> The Sun himself licks off my Sweat.

> (ll. 41–46)

At this point the ironic viewpoint established in the first stanza gives way to the naïveté of Damon's own perception. And it becomes rapidly clear that in his mind the hackneyed notions of nature's personal reactions to men are basic truths. He distinguishes himself solely by the proofs he offers of nature's concern for him; and we are made to feel his genuine conviction, even though every phenomenon he mentions can be accounted for by simple, un-interpreted fact. We are not allowed to dwell on the question of the validity of Damon's claims, however, because Marvell is at pains to create a stance of heroism that will balance the earlier pose of stylized buffoon. Unless some such balance is achieved the poem will close in pure farce, and the meaningful overtones of 'the Mower mown' will be lost.

Damon's next boast is the only unmistakable sign we have that Marvell deliberately intended an instructive shock when he chose the figure of the mower over that of the shepherd. As against the claims of wealth of those who keep sheep, Damon points to his wide possession of the land itself, another touch in the continuing development of his correspondence with the fields.[53] But the argument turns quickly from the subject of riches to the matter of personal beauty; and in stanza VIII Marvell, I think, does achieve the desired balance between the burlesque tone that mocks Damon's innocence and pretension and the genuine pastoral tone that presents him as a heroic sacrifice to Juliana's ravages.

> Nor am I so deform'd to sight,
> If in my Sithe I looked right;
> In which I see my Picture done,
> As in a crescent Moon the Sun.
>
> (ll. 57–60)

These lines contain the pun mentioned earlier, the word 'Sithe' that can mean either 'scythe' or 'sighs'.[54] The surface sense of the lines is that Damon has glanced at his reflection in the crescent-shaped mirror of the scythe, and approves what he sees. But there is also the suggestion that he refers to the distortion of his face by the signs he has mentioned in the first stanza.[55] The second couplet is obviously an image of the truncated reflection of his face in the curved blade of the scythe; but if the constant association of Damon and the sun has any weight, then there may be a suggestion of a relationship between Juliana and the moon, since she appears as very much like another Artemis—chaste, cold, ruthless to impassioned suitors. Above all, we must not miss the humour of Damon's clumsy, clownish gesture of physical vanity. Whatever the lines are meant to convey, it is obvious that nothing could be more useless as a flattering mirror than the blade of a well-worn scythe. But the mockery is softened when Damon also remembers that:

> The deathless Fairyes take me oft
> To lead them in their Danses soft;

And, when I tune my self to sing,
About me they contract their Ring.

(ll. 61–64)

This is the proof of the extent to which the gods of the field 'dwell'
with Damon; and it is significant that Marvell associates him with
the arts of music and dance (both of which have been banished from
the world by Juliana), and with an image that recalls the dance of
the Graces around Colin Clout in *FQ* VI. However, all this is
memory of the pastoral scene before the coming of Juliana. Damon
no longer sings and dances; rather,

But now I all the day complain,
Joyning my Labour to my Pain;
And with my Sythe cut down the Grass,
Yet still my Grief is where it was:
But, when the Iron blunter grows,
Sighing I whet my Sythe and Woes.

(ll. 67–72)

The pun on 'Sythe' is used more variously in this stanza, and almost
with the sole intent of being ironical about Damon's self-induced
sorrow. His sighs are strong enough to cut down the grass, yet they
do nothing to relieve his condition. But the point of the pun in the
last couplet is that Damon, to maintain the pose of the lovelorn
swain, is quite ready to spur his grief on to new laments. That is,
the 'iron' of his sorrow becomes blunt as does his scythe from
constant use.[56] The remedy is to sharpen both his tool and his
complaint with new sighs.

In the tenth stanza we return to the viewpoint of the narrator of
the opening of the poem; only such a shift will permit the climactic
action of the poem to be seen objectively, so that the figure of the
wounded Damon can be charged with symbolic meaning.

While thus he threw his Elbow round,
Depopulating all the Ground,
And, with his whistling Sythe, does cut
Each stroke between the Earth and Root,
The edged Stele by careless chance
Did into his own Ankle glance;
And there among the Grass fell down,
By his own Sythe, the Mower mown.[57]

(ll. 73–80)

It certainly is possible to view 'Damon the Mower' as essentially a funny poem; there is enough verbal wit, enough burlesque, and enough humour at the expense of the rustic Damon to justify such an attitude. But we cannot ignore, I think, the implications of the stanza, both because of their own consistency and because of their connections with other, more serious, poems of Marvell. I do not think we need go so far as Professor Kermode, who sees in line 80 an image of religious martyrdom,[58] but surely in this stanza is the first recognition that the mower's task is one that requires of him that he be the destroyer of nature as much as he is its guardian. In this respect he figures the threat of death to nature as Juliana stands as death to him; the scythe's stroke that cuts between 'the Earth and Root' slashes as wide a scar as the 'Luxurious Man' of 'The Mower against Gardens' who 'dealt between the Bark and Tree'. In each case the human hand has interrupted the natural flow of growth and sustenance; and it is to be presumed that nature will take some form of revenge. However, I do not believe that 'Damon the Mower' rises to this ultimate vision of the Mower's fate; the accident, as Miss Bradbrook points out,[59] happens by chance, and although Damon is made to suffer the same pain he inflicts on the meadows that have given him his name and honour, the incident is once again relegated to its place in the Damon-Juliana story. And here death is redefined as the only possible cure for the disease of loving Juliana, a definition that makes it both witty and less consequential.

> Only for him no Cure is found,
> Whom *Julianas* Eyes do wound.
> 'Tis death alone that this must do:
> For Death thou art a Mower too.
>
> (ll. 85-88)

Until the last line everything is in order—the convention is being maintained with perfect decorum, the darts of Juliana's eyes are called more deadly than the deepest wound. Finally, in a variation of line 30, where the cures for all earthly pains had been vitiated by Juliana, Damon decides that the only cure for this passion is death. The only note of excess is in the last line, because Marvell forces the identification of death and the mower into a much broader meaning than it should be made to hold in this poem. It is true that the Mower is a type of Death, but in what way does this follow

from the statement of line 87? The only possible explanation is
that fellow-feeling will lead Death to ease Damon's pain—but this
is weak and unsatisfactory when compared to the power of the
underlying image of the Mower swinging the destroying scythe
of Time in the meadows of the world.

'The Mower to the Glo-Worms'[60] partially abandons the brusque
effects of the mock-heroic and turns to a diction that is deceptively
light. Although it keeps carefully within the decreed limits of the
pastoral, its simplicity and, above all, its particular vocabulary
suggest that it is dealing with matters of great importance. If this is
true, then its tone is in itself a commanding irony, since the poem
pretends to describe only, once again, Damon's distracted love for
Juliana. However, of all the 'Mower' series, this poem makes it
most obvious that the destructive force within the pastoral world
is not exclusively physical lust; Juliana can stand for whatever it is
that lures man's mind away from its true communion with nature,
and from the moral ends proper to a rational being. The central
importance of these ideas in 'The Mower to the Glo-Worms' is
indicated at the outset:

> Ye living Lamps, by whose dear light
> The Nightingale does sit so late,
> And studying all the Summer-night,
> Her matchless Songs does meditate.

(ll. 1–4)

Damon does not forget that the light the glowworms shed to guide
him emanates from a living source, a creature in sympathy with
him as he wanders distractedly through the night. And when we
see that their solicitousness is futile, when Damon confesses that
he has lost his way forever, we can understand that 'dear' means
more than 'cherished'; the light becomes still another symbol of
the natural goods that are wasted because of man's recalcitrant will
to betray his nature and his best ends.

The nightingale is an image of those goods, since it stands for
music, and instinctive art in general.[61] But more than that, it is the
figure of the mind contemplating its own creations, a concept of
supreme interest for Marvell. In this poem it stands simply for the
mind functioning in accord with its own nature, unallured and
untrammeled by the baited nets of worldly ambition and passion.

The emphasis is a vital one, since the final stanza will define Damon's fall in terms of the distraction of his mind.

The ironic mode enters in stanza II where Damon's depreciation of the glowworms' significance is undercut and shown to be false in the final line.

> Ye Country Comets, that portend
> No War, nor Princes funeral,
> Shining unto no higher end
> Then to presage the Grasses fall.

(ll. 5-8)

This is perfectly in keeping with many such thoughts in other poets about the tranquillity of the pastoral scene and its distance from the dynastic events that often are man's lifelong grief.[62] But 'end' has at least the two meanings of 'purpose' and 'the end'; and if we read the latter meaning the irony is one that prevails throughout the 'Mower' poems. We do not need instruction in the idea that 'all flesh is grass' and that 'the Grasses fall' is in fact an encompassing image of human mortality. Death in the country is limited to the death of green things; but they symbolize the greater deaths of mind and body in so far as the concept of communion between man and nature is accepted seriously. If it is, then 'the Grasses fall' is the highest, the most significant, 'end' that any comet could prophesy.

But mortality is almost a comfortable, familiar idea compared to the death of the spirit that Damon has suffered. The poem moves from the image of physical death to the condition of the errant soul.

> Ye Glow-worms, whose officious Flame
> To wandring Mowers shows the way,
> That in the Night have lost their aim,
> And after foolish Fires do stray.

(ll. 9-12)

I do not think it need be insisted on that the Mowers wandering in the night are an adequate symbol for the human situation as seen by an essentially religious mind. Darkness stands always for disorder and evil; and it must be remembered that the glowworms are only nature's guides. They give off too little light to dissipate the all-embracing night of the world of temptation; and the world itself is full of 'foolish Fires', misleading parodies of the light of nature,

shining with the allure that leads only into greater darkness.[63] And
the final darkness for Damon is in the threat posed by Juliana.

> Your courteous Lights in vain you wast,
> Since *Juliana* here is come,
> For She my Mind hath so displac'd
> That I shall never find my home.   (ll. 13–16)

This is nothing like the metaphorical style we met in 'On a Drop
of Dew', although I should say that both poems are trying to
examine aspects of the same experience. Rather, 'The Mower to the
Glo-Worms' proceeds as a kind of elementally simple allegory.
The analogies are drawn, however, on the widest scale imaginable,
and we can perceive the universal reference of Damon's narrative
only if we can accept the Mower as the human type. We cannot
escape the realization that in compressing the powers of creativity
and destruction into one pastoral symbol Marvell has made a
comprehensive statement about what he believes is the inevitable
relationship between man and the natural world.

'The Mower's Song'† is partially a meditative poem, but in part
it is also an address to the meadows, since this is to be Damon's
farewell to the world that has contained his existence in all of the
four poems.

> My Mind was once the true survey
> Of all these Medows fresh and gay;
> And in the greenness of the Grass
> Did see its Hopes as in a Glass.   (ll. 1–4)

We know from the end of 'The Mower to the Glo-Worms' what
has happened to Damon's mind, but here we are taken back to the
Mower of 'The Mower against Gardens', who saw without distortion his proper relationship to the 'sweet Fields'. The pun on
'survey' is not a trivial one, since in referring both to a map and to
the act of measuring a plot of land it connotes both the active and
passive faculties of the imagination. If Damon's mind was once in
some way the image of the meadows that were his trust, it was
also the ordering principle that, in caring for nature, gave it form
and preserved its generative powers. There is a consummate irony in
the fact that Damon's guardianship involved bringing death into
the innocent world of nature; but it is precisely that irony that best
describes Marvell's sense of the place of man in relation to the rest
of creation. The identity between Damon's mind and the world is

enforced again in the second couplet, where the grass itself becomes a mirror for the Mower's imagination.[64] Thus, the mirroring activity is reciprocal, as befits the Golden Age before the advent of Juliana. To know the myriad meanings of 'green', not only in Marvell, but in scores of medieval and Renaissance writers, would not assist us very much, I think, to decipher these lines. Clearly the colour is intended here to stand for youth, love, fulfilment, growth—these are the hopes that the image of the grass could most credibly reflect for the Mower's mind. But it is enough to know that this fruitful communion was disrupted 'When *Juliana* came, and She/What I do to the Grass, does to my Thoughts and Me' (ll. 5–6).[65] The sweeping power of the refrain intensifies the metaphor beneath it, which summons up the vision of a universal cataclysm. As the grass falls beneath Damon's scythe, so does he beneath the killing touch of Juliana; here, indeed, is where the Mower is truly mown—not by his own scythe as he mimes the roles of Time and Death, but by Death herself as the woman who has 'displac'd' his mind. But even at the moment of general destruction Marvell is careful to render a distinction that is vital to the poem. Damon may see himself reunited with the meadows in their common fall, but he himself distinguishes between 'my Thoughts and Me'. It is a distinction that is responsible, in some senses, for the fatal situation he is in. The self that is the body is indeed a part of nature, obeys its laws and feels itself in eternal sympathy with its principles. But the mind is both mirror and judge of the outside world, both its shaper and its destroyer. And the contradiction is one that can never be resolved by a man imprisoned in the body, nor by a man whose mind has betrayed its responsibility by following 'foolish Fires'.[66]

Damon then reproaches the fields because they have not withered as he has under Juliana's dominion. He forgets that grass does not die, although single blades wither; and he cannot imagine that mindless natural things do not abandon their proper places for an intellectual or physical passion. But if he cannot understand what divides him from the natural world he can at least imagine what will unite him with it again.

> But what you in Compassion ought,
> Shall now by my Revenge be wrought:
> And Flow'rs, and Grass, and I and all,

Will in one common Ruine fall.
For *Juliana* comes, and She
What I do to the Grass, does to my Thoughts and Me.

(ll. 19–24)

Death is seen not only as the inevitable end to consciousness but, as in 'Damon the Mower', as surcease from the pain and bewilderment brought by Juliana. This in itself is remarkable since, although death is normally present in the pastoral world, it is usually death by accidental violence or by pining for an unrequited love. But Marvell has introduced the concept of death through disorder and separation from the bases of nature, an idea that is much more fundamentally true to the assumptions of the pastoral genre than the more conventional ones. The necessary sympathy between man and the natural world can be maintained only by the continuance of established order and the laws of generation and growth. The stoneless cherry is as mortal a threat to pastoral existence as the distracted passion for Juliana, whatever she may represent.

If the meadows cannot show compassion by joining Damon in death, then he will have his revenge, through the agency of Juliana, and pull the entire created order down in chaos and oblivion with him. The imminence of the catastrophe is signalled by the slight change in the refrain—Juliana *comes*. But the imagination must always stop short at one barrier—it can never truly represent to itself the state of not being conscious. Damon's last words allude to his own idea of immortality, and he is essentially wise in choosing the world of nature to be his lasting emblem.

And thus, ye Meadows, which have been
Companions of my thoughts more green,
Shall now the Heraldry become
With which I shall adorn my Tomb;
For *Juliana* comes, and She
What I do to the Grass, does to my Thoughts and Me.

(ll. 25–30)

Grass and flowers are now to be Damon's blazon, since in death there can be no more intimate union. Curiously, he recognizes that although his mind had once been the survey of the natural world, the world must now become his symbol, for with the cessation of consciousness comes the final rupture in the relationship that has been the definitive one for the life of the Mower.[67]

The paradox at the heart of these poems remains unresolved; it is man's imagination that makes him aware of the countless ways in which he is suited to the world that bears and nourishes him. But it is also that imagination that keeps him from an ultimate communion with nature; for the plants and meadows do not think or imagine, and there can be no greater division on earth than that between the sentient and the imaginative. The mind alone can conceive of spiritual desires, and only the mind can be misled by the temptations of the fallen world. In effect, what Marvell was trying to do in the 'Mower' poems was to rewrite the story of Eden without a reference to the supernatural. The expulsion from the garden is the punishment for the abandonment of 'willing Nature'; but nature must always be sacrificed to the demands of the insatiable imagination. And where there is no vision of redemption death must always appear as the one possible resolution of the tragic human situation, which oscillates endlessly between pure nature and pure mind.

There is, however, one other way to reconcile the opposed qualities of man's psyche—and that is to transcend the state of opposition. This is the attempt of 'The Garden'.

Notes

1 Carew, 'An Elegie upon the death of the Deane of Pauls, Dr. John Donne', ll. 63–64; *The Poems of Thomas Carew*, ed. R. Dunlap (Oxford University Press, 1949), pp. 71–74.

2 See, for example, *Elizabethan Critical Essays*, ed. G. G. Smith, I, xxx, xlvi, pp. 175, 237, 262 ff.; II, pp. 27, 39 ff., 209, 321; H. Smith, *Elizabethan Poetry* (Harvard University Press, 1952), Chapter I; Introduction and notes to *The Pastoral Elegy*, ed. T. P. Harrison (University of Texas, 1939); W. W. Greg, *Pastoral Poetry and Pastoral Drama*.

3 Cf. E. R. Curtius, *European Literature and the Latin Middle Ages*, p. 187: 'To write poetry under trees . . . on the grass, by a spring . . . this came to rank as a poetical motif in itself. But it demands a sociological framework: an occupation which obliges him who follows it to live outdoors, or at least in the country, far from towns. He must have time and occasion for composing poetry, and must possess some sort of primitive musical instrument. The shepherd has all of these at his disposition'.

4 See particularly W. Empson, *Some Versions of Pastoral*, and R. Poggioli, 'The Oaten Flute', *Harvard Library Bulletin*, XI, 2 (Spring 1957), pp. 147–184.

5 Poggioli, op. cit., p. 147.

6 For a study of the early interpretations of the myth, see A. O. Lovejoy and G. Boas, *A Documentary History of Primitivism and Related Ideas*; see above, p. 35, n. 37.

7 Professor Poggioli's viewpoint is utterly opposed to such conclusions. He says uncompromisingly (op. cit., p. 147), 'The bucolic ideal stands at the opposite pole from the Christian one'. Later in the same essay he finds that all attempts to Christianize the pastoral have failed, and that Christianity 'was able to use consistently the pastoral convention only as an allegorical travesty and satirical mask' (p. 164).

8 Margoliouth, I, pp. 22–24.

9 M. C. Bradbrook and M. G. Lloyd Thomas, 'Marvell and the Concept of Metamorphosis', *The Criterion*, XVIII, lxxi (January 1939), pp. 252, 254.

10 Bush's remark appeared in the first edition of *English Literature in the Earlier Seventeenth Century*; the revised version says only that 'implications of religious allegory, discerned by some critics in some passages, have been increasingly rejected in favour of a literal (though not simple) reading' (p. 172). Geoffrey Hartman, in the article cited above (p. 37, n. 90), while tracing some of the poem's allegorical allusiveness to the story of the Paraclete in John 14 and 16, also draws attention to the echoes of the Song of Solomon.

11 D. C. Allen, 'Marvell's "Nymph" ', *ELH*, 23, 2 (June 1956) pp. 93–111.

12 E. S. Le Comte, 'Marvell's "The Nymph complaining for the death of her Faun" ', *MP*, L, (November 1952), pp. 97–101.

13 Allen, 'Marvell's "Nymph" ', pp. 93–94.

14 R. Heath, *Clarastella* (London, 1650) includes the following lines in a poem entitled 'Dialogue between Sylvio and Mirtillo':

> For who asks doubting lest he should obtein,
> Instructs his Mistresse to a coy disdein.

The terms are commonplaces, but they may have added their minute suggestion to the complex of ideas that issued eventually as 'To his Coy Mistress'.

15 *Andrew Marvell*, pp. 56–57. Legouis cites Blake, Burns, and Wordsworth but curiously enough has no mention of Pope's pheasant.

16 M. Legouis may not be altogether misled in relating Marvell's poem to the early Romantic poets. Hazlitt describes 'The Nymph' as 'his description of a fawn', a phrase that may indicate where he thought the poem's emphasis to be (W. Hazlitt, Lecture IV 'On Dryden and Pope' in

Lectures on the English Poets, ed. W. E. Henley, 12 vols (London, 1902) V, p. 83).

17 Cf. Peacham, *Minerva Britanna*. There is an emblem of a wounded deer (Sig. C2r) whose verse reads, in part:

> The silly Hind among the thickets greene,
> While nought mistrusting did at safetie goe,
> His mortall wound receiv'd with arrow keene
> Sent singing from a Sheepeheard's secret bowe.

18 This may be the reason for the displacement of 'And Lillies' to the following line, so that 'Roses' and 'over grown' receive an unmodified stress in line 72—the enjambment does not flow smoothly because of the stress on 'grown', and so the 'Lillies' are set off by the metre.

19 D. W. Robertson, Jr., in 'The Doctrine of Charity in Mediaeval Literary Gardens', p. 29, says, 'It is well known that a combination of lilies and roses was used to show martyrdom and purity, Charity and innocence'.

20 Marvell may have been aided in the choice of examples by the 1646 text of Crashaw's 'The Weeper'. Stanza 12 of that poem reads in part: 'There is no need at all/That the Balsame-sweating bough/So coyly should let fall,/His med'cinable Teares'. In stanza 8 there is a possible reference to the Heliades: 'Not the soft Gold which/Steales from the Amber-weeping Tree'.

21 Cf. 'The Nymph', ll. 105–108; 'Thyrsis and Dorinda', ll. 31–32.

22 Margoliouth, op. cit., I, p. 46.

23 Dryden, 'A Discourse Concerning the Original and Progress of Satire'. In *Essays of John Dryden*. ed. W. P. Ker, 2 vols. (Oxford, 1926) II, p. 19.

24 Legouis, *Andrew Marvell*, p. 52.

25 Margoliouth, op. cit., I, pp. 33–36.

26 Perhaps 'glews' in line 16 supports the rejection of 'glew' as a possible reading in 'To his Coy Mistress', l. 34. It means that the compositor would have had to mistake one of two occurrences of the same word within a few pages.

27 Cf. Stanza XVII.

28 Possibly from the Greek for 'fire'?

29 Victoria Sackville-West, *Andrew Marvell* (Faber & Faber, 1929), p. 42.

30 Empson, *Some Versions of Pastoral*, p. 129.

31 'The Mower is a special variant of the stock Swain, more English and also more of a person'; Bradbrook, *Andrew Marvell*, p. 39.

32 Legouis, *André Marvell*, p. 102; *Andrew Marvell*, p. 51.

33 See particularly C. S. Lewis, *The Allegory of Love* (Oxford University Press, 1936), pp. 324–330.

34 *English Pastoral Poetry*, p. 248. All quotations from Shakespeare are

taken from *The Complete Plays and Poems of William Shakespeare*, eds.
W. A. Neilson and C. J. Hill (Cambridge, Mass., 1942).

35 George Puttenham, *The Arte of English Poesie*, in *Elizabethan Critical Essays*, II, p. 190.

36 *Elizabethan Critical Essays*, II, p. 189.

37 *Elizabethan Critical Essays*, II, pp. 190–191.

38 *Elizabethan Critical Essays*, II, pp. 191–192. Puttenham also says (p. 188): 'And the Gardiner by his arte will not onely make an herbe, or flowr, or fruite, come forth in his season without impediment, but also will embellish the same in vertue, shape ... that nature of her selfe woulde neuer haue done, as to make single gillifloure ... double ... or cherrie without a stone ... any of which things nature could not doe without mans help and arte'. J. H. Muirhead, in *The Platonic Tradition in Anglo-Saxon Philosophy* (Allen & Unwin, 1931), comments on Cudworth's *The True Intellectual System of the Universe*: ' "whereas human art acts from without, cumberously, moliminously, with tumult and hurly-burly, nature acting from within does its work easily, cleverly, and silently". Again, "whereas human artists are often to seek and at a loss, and anxiously consult, not as artists but only for want of art, nature is never to seek, nor unresolved what to do, nor doth she ever repent afterwards of what she hath done". On the other hand, nature falls behind art in that it "never intends those ends nor understands the reason of what it doth"; and further, because "it acts without express consense and consciousness and is devoid of self-perception and self-enjoyment" ', (p. 37).

39 See J. Corder, 'Marvell and Nature', *NQ*, N.S. 6, 2 (February 1959), pp. 58–61; also J. H. Summers, 'Marvell's "Nature" ', *ELH*, 20, 2 (June 1953), pp. 121–135. Summers suggests that 'occasionally Marvell used nature as an image of classical order, an artfully contrived realization of the mean which man is to imitate'.

40 F. L. Lucas, in *Authors Dead and Living* (Chatto & Windus, 1926), p. 79, describes Marvell as a 'lover of unspoilt nature ... and herald in his degree of the Romantics'. Macdonald (xxviii) quotes Cannon Beeching, writing in *The National Review* for 1901: 'in Marvell the love for natural beauty is not short of passion. Of course his love is not for wild nature ... but for the ordinary country scenes, ... and for these he brings the eye of a genuine lover'.

41 Margoliouth, op. cit., I, pp. 40–41.

42 The metre is a version of the Latin elegiac distich. See Margoliouth, op. cit., I, p. 224; Legouis, *Andrew Marvell*, p. 86. Kermode, in 'Two Notes on Marvell', *NQ*, 197, 7 (29 March 1952), pp. 136–138, suggests that Randolph's imitations of Horace's *Epodes* was Marvell's inspiration. Margoliouth and Legouis feel that Jonson is the most likely source.

Miss Wallerstein, in 'The Development of the Rhetoric and Metre of the Heroic Couplet, especially in 1625–1645', *PMLA*, L, 1 (March 1935), pp. 166–209, speculates on the development that led from the classical elegiac metre to the closed couplet of the seventeenth century. For a more comprehensive study, see Pauline Aiken, *The Influence of the Latin Elegists on English Lyric Poetry 1600–1650. University of Maine Studies*, Series 2, No. 22 (Orono, 1932).

43 See Margoliouth, op. cit., I, p. 225.

44 Legouis, *Andrew Marvell*, p. 43, cites Leviticus, 19: 19; Deuteronomy, 22: 9.

45 The opposition between 'Wild' and 'Tame' may parallel the opposed states of nature and artifice. It should be compared to the contrast in terms of sexuality in 'The Nymph', l. 34.

46 Margoliouth (I, p. 225) joins Grosart in stating that he cannot explain the reference to the cherry. Macdonald (p. 172) offers the testimony of a horticultural friend that it is and was a common practice to propagate cherries by grafting without the agency of cherry-stones. Dennis Davison, *Selected Poetry and Prose of Andrew Marvell* (Harrap, 1952), p. 219, reminds us that 'Stones' was a colloquialism for testicles. In any case, the sexual nature of the paradox is obvious, and Puttenham's remark (quoted above, n. 38) is sufficient evidence that the process itself was known in Marvell's time.

47 Curiously, the same rhyme appears in William Habington's *Castara* (1634) in a poem entitled 'To Zephirus': 'Where nature doth dispence/ Her infant wealth, a beautious innocence'; *Poems of William Habington*, ed. K. Allott (Liverpool University Press, 1948), p. 58.

48 Compare this equation of innocence and perfume or incense with 'A Dialogue Between The Resolved Soul, and Created Pleasure', ll. 29–30.

49 The inadequacy of the statues is similar to the imperfect whiteness of the alabaster figure of the fawn in 'The Nymph', ll. 119–122.

50 Cf. Cowley's 'The Spring' on the obsolescence of the pastoral deities; *Poems*, ed. A. R. Waller (Cambridge University Press, 1905), pp. 70–72.

51 Macdonald (p. 172) notes that MS. Eng. Poet. d 49 in the Bodleian Library gives 'mads' for 'made' in line 21, which seems to me a highly preferable reading.

52 There may also be an implicit sexual allusion here.

53 'Golden fleece' in line 53 is not simply a periphrasis. It recalls the legend of the Argo and, by analogy, adds a mite of heroic stature to the Mower's portrait.

54 The O.E.D. gives 'sithe' as a variant for 'sigh'. Cf. Cowley, *Pyramus and Thisbe*, l. 71; Robert Armin, *The History of the Two Maides of More-clacke*: 'Be smilefull, and expresse no griefe in sithes'; E. IV in the Tudor Facsimile Text; Marston, *What You will*, III, i: 'So I say sithing and

sithing say'. In *Minor Poets of The Caroline Period*, III, p. 214, Saintsbury has this note: 'scythe Orig. "sithe", which some great ones (including even the other Johnson) will have to be the proper spelling, and which is certainly usual in Middle English'.

55 There is also a quibble on 'looked', which can mean either 'looked at' or 'appeared'.

56 The *O.E.D.* explains that because of a mistranslation from the Hebrew in the Vulgate, in English usage 'iron' came to be understood as an expression for spiritual agony or despair. The phrase occurs in Psalms 105: 18: *ferrum pertransiit animam ejus.*

57 The 'Mower' poems seem particularly full of onomatopoeia. 'Depopulating' in line 74 recreates the crisp, popping sounds one hears when dry corn is cut.

58 'The Mower becomes even more mysterious here. . . . Just as the poet himself assumes a quasi-blasphemous martyr-pose in *Appleton House*, and the fawn is momentarily a Christ-symbol in [*The Nymph,*] so the Mower (who belongs to the unfallen world) sheds his blood for love' (*Some Versions of Pastoral*, p. 253).

59 Bradbrook, *Andrew Marvell*, p. 42.

60 Margoliouth, op. cit., I, pp. 44–45.

61 Cf. Crashaw's 'Musicks Duell'; *Poems*, pp. 149–153. Of course Marvell lightens the symbolic meaning of the nightingale by comparing it to a scholar studying late.

62 Davison (op. cit., p. 220) cites Robert Chamberlain's 'In Praise of Country Life' (1638) which reads in part:

> Matters of state, not yet domestick jars,
> Comets, portending death, nor blazing stars,
> Trouble his thoughts.

Nor does one have to seek very far for contemporary examples of civil catastrophe of which Marvell might have been thinking.

63 Although the figure is a commonplace, it is interesting to note that it appears in Dryden's 'The Hind and the Panther': 'My manhood, long misled by wandring fires,/Follow'd false lights'; *The Poems of John Dryden*, 4 vols., ed. J. Kinsley (Oxford University Press, 1958), II, p. 472. Cf. also Mildmay Fane, 'The Fallacy of the Outward Man', *Otia Sacra*, Sig. GIv.

> Have not the wanton Fairie-Elves
> Their Torch-bearers, Light as themselves,
> That with our Fancies sport and play,
> Untill they lead us quite out of the way?

And Beaumont and Fletcher, *The Faithful Shepherdess*, I, i, 'vain illusion/Draw me to wander after idle fires'.

64 R. Skelton, in 'Rowland Watkins and Andrew Marvell', *NQ* N.S. V, 12 (December 1958), pp. 531–532, points out that in 'The Holy Maid' in Watkins' *Flamma Sine Fumo* these lines occur: 'Weak man's estate, as in a glass,/Is truly seen in fading grass'. Watkins' volume was published in 1662.

65 Margoliouth (I, p. 225) remarks that it is the only use of a refrain in Marvell's work. He compares it to the motion of a scythe. One might also say that in the preceding line the phrase 'and She' lends the same motion as the lifting of a scythe before the stroke. Note that 'She' is never followed by a comma, so that the speaking stress does not drop at the end of the line.

66 See Barbara Everett, 'Marvell's "The Mower's Song" ', *Critical Quarterly*, 4 (1962), pp. 219–224; Ruth Nevo, 'Marvell's "Songs of Innocence and Experience" ', pp. 1–21.

67 Cf. Tayler, *Nature and Art in Renaissance Literature*, Chapter VI; and Toliver, *Marvell's Ironic Vision*, Chapter III.

*Margoliouth, I, pp. 41–44.

†ibid., pp. 45–46.

4

Knowledge and the World of Change

I

In an essay intended to correct the tendency to read 'The Garden' as if it were a collection of neoplatonic commonplaces,[1] Professor Frank Kermode has argued that it is in fact an 'anti-genre' poem, written in reply to and in criticism of the *libertin* garden poems of sensual indulgence associated with Saint-Amant, Thomas Randolph, Thomas Stanley, and other contemporaries. We have seen that Marvell is given to evaluating a literary form by writing his own version of it, thereby exploiting it and criticizing it at the same time. But Kermode's idea is slightly more radical than that; although he acknowledges the existence of a genre of seventeenth-century garden poetry whose distinctive feature was the exaltation of the contemplative life over the life of action, he feels that Marvell aimed 'The Garden' specifically at the poets of the *jouissance*, and that matters of diction, metre, symbol, and convention can and should be referred to the dominating idea of criticizing the assumptions of the *libertin* genre. Kermode has received support from an unexpected quarter; in conscientious pursuit of a major theme of Horatian poetry through the seventeenth, eighteenth, and nineteenth centuries in English poetry, Miss Maren-Sofie Røstvig has written two lengthy and well-documented volumes on what she calls the '*beatus-ille* theme'.[2] She demonstrates that during the seventeenth century, poems about the pleasures of retirement and the excellences of the contemplative life are so numerous that they appear to be a genre in themselves. Miss Røstvig makes clear the relationships of this genre not only to Horace's *Odes* but also to Stoic philosophy in general; she recognizes the sources of the genre in Christian literature and the importance for its symbolism of neoplatonic philosophy. And she does not ignore the political and social significances of the poetry she is writing about; she considers 'the poem of the happy country life the most typical expression of the Royalist and Anglican spirit of the seventeenth century'.[3] As this quotation makes clear, her work is devoted particularly to the poetry of rural retirement,[4] a theme which appears to have grown tremendously in importance during the mid-seventeenth century, perhaps in response to the galling pressure of public events, but which we may certainly see as a limb sprung from the pastoral tree. The rejection of the life of affairs had always been an implicit tenet of pastoral poetry; in Horace the preference for simplicity and ease in country life is raised to the level where it becomes a commanding ethical viewpoint. Naturally enough such a view is easily connected with Stoic ethics; for English poetry it was fortunate that some of the forms of Stoicism were absorbed as fully and congenially into Christian ideas of morality as were more rarefied Platonic metaphysical doctrines.

However valuable the work of Kermode and Røstvig may be in keeping us from reading Marvell's octosyllabic couplets as if they were versified *Enneads*, it would be unwise to allow their emphasis on genre to obscure the importance of Marvell's originality of treatment. Rather than devote his energies to discovering novel and witty ways to express familiar pastoral themes, Marvell chose to invent the figure of the Mower, and to use him to probe the meaning of man's relation to nature. In the earlier poems, such as 'Young Love' and 'The Gallery', Marvell used a common form in order to subject it to uncommon scrutiny—and to suggest the complicated questions the forms created but did not attempt to answer. I think it likely, therefore, that 'The Garden' represents an enterprise similar to these others. Marvell is quite obviously writing a poem whose type would seem thoroughly familiar to his audience (especially if this audience were made up of Lord Fairfax, Lord Westmorland, and their friends—that is, if 'The Garden' was written and circulated during Marvell's stay at Nunappleton, which seems very probable). But further, with typical ingenuity and the integrity of a mind that cannot relax before it has seen the farthest possible reach of a problem, he is forcing the garden poem to absorb and contain all the meanings that he saw the genre to possess potentially.

A year before the publication of their *Andrew Marvell*, Miss Bradbrook and Miss Lloyd Thomas collaborated on an article entitled 'Marvell and the Concept of Metamorphosis'.[5] They suggested there that 'the concept of Metamorphosis, the basis of the poem, fuses the modern psychological idea of sublimation and the modern theological idea of transcendence into something more delicate'.[6] I am not sure that this fusion really occurs in 'The Garden' or that the idea of metamorphosis in the poem is 'the poetical answer to the problem of Time and the decay of beauty'.[7] But it can be shown very convincingly that not only the separate events of the poem but also many individual images, puns, exempla, and analogies are related and held in their respective places by the omnipresent poetical mode of transmutation. 'The Garden' is full of plants, gods, men, and words that change from one thing into another and are seen at times as one thing, at times as another, and sometimes as both. The effect is to insist on the reality of both states of a metamorphosed entity, but more clearly to delineate the reality of the process itself of change. 'The Garden' is 'about' mutability only in so far as it uses the phenomenon of change as its universal metaphor—as a key signature, as it were.

The first two lines of 'The Garden' exhibit the characteristics of symbolic reference, pure punning, and ironic statement that will pervade the entire poem: 'How vainly men themselves amaze/ To win the Palm, the Oke, or Bayes' (ll. 1–2). To notice that 'vainly' means 'in vain' and 'from vanity' at once and with equal force is to enter into the fictive viewpoint of the speaker of the poem. The two meanings constitute something more than a pun, for they represent two kinds of judgment. The second (from vanity) is that of a man assessing the behaviour of other men according to standards he has learned in the world he has quitted for the Garden. The first (in vain) implies a knowledge superior to that world, a knowledge that creates a vantage-point from which all human activities can be viewed in comparison with all *possible* forms of action, not just those that experience provides. Both judgments are important, but it is the latter that is to set the tone for the poem, for it justifies the transition from a mocking portrait of men's actual pursuits to the praise of the way men *should* choose, in the light of the Garden's lesson.

The pun on 'amaze' is of a different quality but it, too, is related to both of the viewpoints we have just described. Its first set of meanings refers to the effects ambition and purposeful activity have on the men who suffer from them—'to amaze' meant 'to bewilder', 'to infatuate', 'to drive oneself stupid'. When all these senses are understood in apposition to the meanings we have just observed for 'vainly' the impression of hectic futility is deepened and begins to appear pathetic. And that sense is reinforced by the other meaning of 'amaze', which is 'to trap oneself in a maze'. This is the life of action seen from the Garden; and there is a sort of grace note in our realization that a maze would normally have been a proud part of any formal garden. How much less harmful, we are made to feel, is the maze of box-hedges than the endless and meandering prisons of greed and striving.

The first mention of the objects of all this futile strife raises the criticism from the level of contemporary society to a consideration of the life of action as a constant type in human history. 'The Palm, the Oke, or Bayes' are respectively, the classical (and therefore classic) reward for military victory,[8] the civic crown for valour,[9] and the traditional prize of the poet. It becomes clear immediately that Marvell is not criticizing courage or poetry but the ways in which men seek to outdo each other to win an honour that is symbolized by the leaves or fronds of a tree. The witty stance of the poem will be to pretend that the honour is truly *in* the leaves, that they are no so much the symbol as the reality; the joke is, of course, that men could much more easily and more satisfactorily 'win' what they compete for by retiring to the Garden and consorting with the trees themselves. The brief catalogue of trees not only establishes a background of classical reference for the poem but presents its claim to be able to judge men not only as they follow the ignoble pursuits of business and litigation but the admired callings of warfare and the arts.[10] In either case, it is the desire to excel that is shown to be vain, or perhaps just the intensity of any desire. For it will be demonstrated that the plants offer rewards when no effort has been made to win them; and often they reward effort with a prize it has not sought (as in Marvell's revision of the myths of Apollo and Pan). The task of the first stanza is to make it apparent that the usual criteria of human achievement are irrelevant in the Garden, and indeed that achievement must be redefined in the terms insisted on by the contemplative paradise. The futility of human endeavour is underlined in the second couplet: 'And their uncessant Labours see/Crown'd from some single Herb or Tree' (ll. 3-4). To sacrifice all other human and supernatural values for a symbol that is more beautiful, intrinsically, than the thing it symbolizes is the best measure of man's inspired stupidity. Not only is the crown of leaves either inadequate or far too rich for the dreams of ambitious mankind, but it is made from a tree 'Whose short and narrow verged Shade/Does prudently their Toyles upbraid' (ll. 5-6). The point is that the economy and simplicity of the trees (as evinced in the small circle of their shade) is an implicit criticism of the excesses and hectic activities of the men of 'uncessant Labours'.[11] Marvell follows this with an image of the activity that the trees oppose to the weaving of crowns and chaplets for the heroes of the world: 'While all Flow'rs and all Trees do close/To weave the Garlands of repose' (ll. 7-8). The amazing thing about these lines is that they set up with magnificent economy and with absolute nonchalance the contrasted values that will be forced into conflict in the first three stanzas of the poem, only to be transcended by the mythological allusions in stanza IV. Moreover, they show a tactful awareness of Kermode's 'anti-genre', since the central image is one that can be duplicated in several *libertin* poems.

It is obvious that 'repose' is introduced as the state preferred by trees and preferred by the mind of contemplative man to the active life of field and city. As Justus Lipsius declared in a book of widespread popularity in the seventeenth century, gardens 'be ordained, not for the body, but for the mind: and to recreate it, not to besot it with idlenesse: only as a wholsome withdrawing place from the cares and troubles of this world'.[12] One could multiply instances of this thought, from Sir William Temple's *Upon the Gardens of Epicurus*, Sir Thomas Browne's *Garden of Cyrus*, and from uncounted poets and essayists of the century who looked to the green and ordered garden for a symbol of the natural, contemplative life. Here Marvell is proposing that the life of rational retirement seeks and finds its own 'crowns' in the 'inter-wreathed bay'[13] formed by the instinctive motions of the trees, the 'closing' of their vegetable loves. The important thing to note is that these are not rewards for effort, but gratuitous gifts given because of the very nature of trees, which is to grow into garlands for the contemplative life—or so at least the poem pretends.

But we must also notice that in weaving 'the Garlands of repose' the trees behave as they do in, for example, Thomas Randolph's 'A Pastorall Courtship', in which

> The lofty *Pine* deignes to descend,
> And sturdy *Oaks* doe gently bend.
> One with another subt'ly weaves
> Into one loom their various leaves;
> As all ambitious were to be
> Mine and my *Phyllis* canopie![14]

The difference is sufficiently marked in the last couplet; but perhaps a more representative example of the vigorously amorous landscapes drawn by the naturalist poets is this, from Thomas Stanley's 'Loves Innocence':

> See how this Ivy strives to twine
> Her wanton arms about the Vine,
> And her coy lover thus restrains,
> Entangled in her amorous chains,
> See how these neighb'ring Palms do bend
> Their heads, and mutual murmurs send.[15]

In Randolph and Stanley, and in Saint-Amant from whom Stanley took so much, the need was often to create a landscape that in its natural ardour would match and incite the passions of the lovers who inhabited it. The pretence was that all was natural, therefore all was permitted; trees and flowers can hardly be accused of sin, and if man in the Golden Age was a innocent as the trees the analogy must hold for human sexuality. Such, at least, was the half-joking, half-serious, philosophy that lay behind lines such as these from Saint-Amant's 'La Jouyssance':

> Sous un climat où la nature
> Monter à nud toutes ses beautez
> Et nourrit les yeux enchantez
> Des plus doux traits de la peinture,
> Nous voyons briller sur les fleurs
> Plustost des perles .... [16]

Again, in 'La Metamorphose de Lyrian et de Sylvie', Saint-Amant's Ovidian tale of the elm and the ivy, we find:

> Et son corps s'attachant à l'arbre qu'il contemple
> Se change en mille bras tournoyans a l'entour,
> Dont il acquit le nom de symbole d'amour;
> Bref, ce fidelle amant n'est plus qu'un beau lierre,

Qui, sur la tige aimée, en s'elevant de terre,
Cherche en sa passion, qu'il tasche d'appaiser,
La place où fut la bouche, afin de la baiser.[17]

A recent French critic of the *libertin* and *précieux* poets defines, as a distinctive trait of Saint-Amant, Théophile de Viau, and others, 'the interplay of amorous and sensuous delights in woman's beauty with those in nature, so that the naiad's serenade in her crystal dwelling, the caressing waters, the fluid hair of a woman, the whiteness of hands . . . the games of love and those of fancy are all made of the same delicate and transparent substance'.[18] Randolph and Stanley may have learned a great deal from this technique; and it is clear that Marvell knew it well and, in 'The Garden', was exploiting it only to turn the tables on the entire convention in order to celebrate the delights of natural beauty at the expense of female beauty.

Because this is not the exclusive aim of the poem the second stanza relinquishes the subject (to take it up again in stanza III) in favour of the exploration of the mythology of the Garden itself.

Fair quiet, have I found thee here,
And Innocence thy Sister dear!
Mistaken long, I sought you then
In busie Companies of Men.
Your sacred Plants, if here below,
Only among the Plants will grow.
Society is all but rude,
To this delicious Solitude.

(ll. 9–16)

The joint goddesses of pastoral contemplation[19] are discovered in the Garden, 'Ther wher noe thronging multituds/Disturbe with noyse'[20] and where innocence is defined by the lack of worldly ambition.[21] The active and acquisitive life is remembered and judged in the word 'then'; and the 'busie Companies of Men' refers both to tumultuous crowds and perhaps to the business 'companies' that were an important economic phenomenon before and during the Civil War period. In the first stanza Marvell made fun of human passion in so far as it was misdirected; in the third stanza he will consider both the physical realities of lust and its highly artificial manners. In stanza II, then, he creates a kind of parodic version of his

own love-affair with the trees, which partakes of many of the characteristic traits of human lovers, but which the poem must pretend is
saner and more exalted. 'Delicious' casts an ironic light back upon
the earlier part of the stanza, since the speaker relishes the supposedly
pure delights of quiet and innocence with quite as much sensuous
fervour as the 'Fond Lovers' of stanza III. In 'The Garden', I think,
this is meant to be understood as a piece of self-conscious humour,
but the personification of virtues as beloved creatures was taken
seriously by other poets, as in Drummond's

> Deare Wood, and you sweet solitarie Place,
> Where from the vulgare I estranged liue,
> Contented more with what your Shades mee giue,
> Than if I had what *Thetis* doth embrace;[22]

or, even more passionately,

> I hugg my Quiet and alone
> Take thee for my Companion,
> And deem in doing so, I've all
> I can true Conversation call,

from Fane's 'To Retiredness', where 'Conversation' carries quite
definite sexual overtones. This is not to say that Fane and
Drummond were not aware of the joke implicit in the hyperbole;
but Marvell is alone in turning the joke against the point of view
his poem is trying to establish, and making the pursuit of innocence
as passionate as any of the more earthy quests he is criticizing.

The notion of plants that grow on earth as living emblems of gods
who have left it because it has grown corrupt is venerably founded
in classical tradition. But Marvell converts the idea to his own uses
by deliberately confounding the abstract values of Quiet and
Innocence with their vegetable insignia; in the Garden, he implies,
trees and what they represent are once again united harmoniously.[23]
Lord Fairfax had a different explanation for the peculiar affinity of
the pastoral gods for gardens:

> Times past Fawnes Satyrs Demy-Gods
> Hither retird to seeke for Aide
> When Heaven with Earth was soe att odds
> As Jupiter in rage had laide
> O're all a Deluge these high woods
> Preseru'd them from the sweling floods.[24]

In both poets the mythology serves the idea that informs the closing lines of 'The Mower against Gardens'; the gods of peace and fertility have abandoned the 'busie Companies of Men' and lend their influence only to the calm and ordered pastoral of the country garden.

The same point is made once more in the last couplet of the stanza, but in a way that permits Marvell to comment wittily on the pretensions of 'civilization'. As we have seen, it was at least a continuing debate in the seventeenth century whether primitive societies were indeed replicas of the Golden Age or mere rough conglomerations of ignorant and vicious savages. The heroic visions of the sixteenth century were gradually giving way before the accumulation of factual evidence brought back by wide-ranging exploration; and the view that society was the means to progressive civilizing of human instincts was gaining ground. But Marvell, by taking solitariness as the standard of individual and moral value, can turn and call society 'rude' with infinite aplomb and with a full awareness of the point of his paradox.[25] It is the final blow to the 'Companies of Men', and he can now attend to the phantoms of courtly lovers that still haunt the paradisiacal Garden.

> No white nor red was ever seen
> So am'rous as this lovely green.
> Fond Lovers, cruel as their Flame,
> Cut in these Trees their Mistress name.
> Little, Alas, they know, or heed,
> How far these Beauties Hers exceed!
>
> (ll. 17–22)

We do not have to know much Petrarch, or Donne, or Carew, to realize that 'white nor red' stands for all the worlds, both real and conventionally literary, of passionate lovers. And the synecdoche itself implies a judgment on these worlds in so far as they can be reduced so easily to their trivial components of white and red. In contrast, the 'am'rous . . . green' is extended and made to seem meaningful by the addition of its adjective; the phrase also functions as a corrective to the view that fails to see true passion and fruitful love in the plants of the Garden rather than in the painted mistresses of the world outside.[26] The corrective is applied in terms that blend mockery with stern disapproval; we know that 'Fond' can mean both 'loving' and 'foolish', but this kind of foolishness is drawn for us as callous brutality to the sensitive and animate trees. The pun on 'Flame' helps to describe the lovers and their inane situation since it refers both to the passion of love that 'burns' those in love, and the mistress herself (as in our rather dated use of 'flame') who is traditionally cruel in her denial and disdain of the posturing suitor. The word-play, then, characterizes the lovers as dupes caught in the hopeless toils of an elaborate and pointless game, but dupes who compound their guilt by revenging their pains upon innocent nature, and by the same tortures they have undergone. The custom of cutting names, initials, and entwined hearts into trees has not yet disappeared, but the basis of Marvell's objection to the practice is not simply that of the conservationist. He is also pointing to the greater stupidity that thinks to preserve and celebrate a name in this fashion when it is only performing an act of desecration against a tree whose 'name' is infinitely more significant than any human name can be.[27] The lovers' mistake is announced quite bluntly in lines 21–22; but the justification for the superior beauty of the trees must be found in the preceding and the following stanzas. In stanza III Marvell is content to display his speaker's feelings as he promises, 'Fair Trees! where s'eer your barkes I wound,/No Name shall but your own be found' (ll. 23–24). Of course this is meant to be a joke, but, as we have just seen, the concept that lies behind the joke is a serious one. Marvell is conscious of the fact that wounding the 'barkes' is in some ways akin to dealing 'between the Bark and Tree'; no matter how pure the passion that inspires it, it is still an interference with nature. He tries to redeem the act by swearing that *this* lover will carve only the trees' own name. The idea must be seen as part of the parody, since nothing could be more irrelevant to the pure love of nature than behaviour modelled on the deeds of fleshly lovers. Even so, the only name that may properly be graven into bark is the name of the thing itself, a recognition that the tree transcends the categories applied to it by the mind distracted by passion of any sort.[28]

Marvell will not have done with these trees, and in stanza IV goes on to the most important instances in history and mythology that reveal the true nature of the relation between passion and trees. Here the pun is raised to a level well above simple word-play; it begins to assume the proportions of a symbolic analogy, and the various puns in the stanza are the primary means whereby Marvell converts the traditional myths into evidence for his metaphor of metamorphosis:[29] 'When we have run our Passions heat,/Love hither makes his best retreat' (ll. 25–26). In 'The Garden' the puns are marshalled to give the sense of physical passion driving the lover through the exhausting flames of desire, while at the same time the lover drives himself through the predestined course of lust and frustration. The result is the 'retreat' of 'Love' to the Garden; and it is intended that 'Love' be understood both as a generic word and as the personification. The mention of the God of Love will provide the transition to the following lines and their mythological innovations. Miss Bradbrook and King have commented on the meanings of 'retreat' and have shown that the predominant sense is that of retiring gratefully from the field of amatory combat.[30] Marvell follows the image with a catalogue of the gods who thus abandoned an initial desire for the higher satisfactions of the Garden: 'The *Gods*, that mortal Beauty chase,/Still in a Tree did end their race' (ll. 27–28). As Miss Bradbrook points out, '*Race* is a pun on *contest*, and *family*, *seed*'.[31] The pun refers to the myths of Apollo and Pan retold in lines 29–32 and the '*Gods*' are the Olympians who were notoriously fond of earthly maidens.

Marvell's argument is taken from Ovid; and rarely has the phenomenon of change been interpreted with more purposeful wit.

> *Apollo* hunted *Daphne* so,
> Only that She might Laurel grow.
> And *Pan* did after *Syrinx* speed,
> Not as a Nymph, but for a Reed.
>
> (ll. 29–32)

To begin with, King makes it perfectly clear that 'Only' and 'for' have the force of 'for no other end or purpose than', as is shown in *Hortus*.[32] Marvell takes up the Ovidian paradox in the form that Randolph gives it in: 'Love Laurell gives: *Phoebus* as much can say,/Had not he lov'd, there had not been the Bay'[33], and changes it into another and different paradox by asserting that Apollo pursued Daphne just so that she might become the laurel tree. Miss Bradbrook interprets this to mean that Marvell 'finds, as the gods find, that the only lasting satisfaction for the instincts is an activity which does not employ them for their original purpose. Apollo hunted Daphne for the laurel crown of Poetry and Pan sped after Syrinx to capture Music. Desire is only to be quieted in the permanence of Art'[34]. King offers a slight objection when he says, 'Apollo and Pan do not see in the laurel and reed objects of natural contemplation. Apollo, god of poets, is interested in laurel wreaths, the reward of poets; an interest condemned in the first stanza of the poem. And Pan wants the reed as a musical instrument'.[35] I think Miss Bradbrook is closer to the truth, and primarily because the rest of 'The Garden' will make it clear that the mind and the soul (which are meant to take precedence over the passions according to the pagan and Christian traditions, and according to the ethic of Marvell's pastoral as well) attain their highest and happiest states when contemplating the creations of their own faculties. In this sense the most perfect meaning of 'Apollo' is the abstract idea of 'poetry', and of 'Pan', 'music'. It is difficult to avoid the conclusion that, among many other concerns, Marvell is thinking of the nature of his own art in 'The Garden', and the gods of poetry and music might be expected to have a prominent part in its symbolism.

Moreover, I think King is mistaken in taking his readings of 'Only' and 'for' too literally; that is, he assumes that the ambiguous words refer to the intentions, felt as such, of Apollo and Pan. Yet surely the prevailingly ironic mode of the poem makes it easier to believe that the passions of the gods have been frustrated and then redirected by the intelligible order of the universe, or whatever power governs the Garden and makes trees more beautiful and more valuable than human beauties. The main point of the stanza is that the gods 'that mortal Beauty chase' are destined to have their folly reproved by the truths embodied in nature. The order that enforces this ironic teaching is the same one, presumably, that decides, in Miss Bradbrook's words, 'that the only lasting satisfaction for the instincts is an activity which does not employ them for their original purpose'. Hers is the more cautious statement, but I cannot help feeling that the meaningful metamorphoses described in this stanza are meant to reveal a governing concept in the worlds of the gods and of men. The lusts of Apollo and Pan are rewarded with the emblems of art, and the implication is that every kind of passion directed toward objects lower in the scale of values than the perfectly abstract forms of contemplation will be purified in the Garden. For, besides the underlying allusions to the Garden of Eden and to all the gardens that appear in Western literature as the types of pristine innocence and perfection, there is in 'The Garden' a continuing reference, I believe, to the garden as a symbol of *sapientia*, or wisdom, as opposed to *scientia*, which is merely worldly wisdom or knowledge.[36] It is important to notice now that the linking of contemplation and gardens is not gratuitous; the fact that the mind is so often said to achieve pure perception in the natural setting of the garden is simply the other side of the truth that the garden itself is not only conducive to contemplation, but is the very *place* where contemplation can attain wisdom.[37]

The first four stanzas have brought us through the snares of the active life[38] and the more deceptive lures of passionate love. Marvell's *persona* has shown us the nature of his conversion to the worship of the quiet and innocence of the Garden, and what remains is to trace the stages of his refinement from knowledge of the senses to the pure apprehensions of the intellect. With due regard for the decorum of this Platonic ascent, stanza V is devoted to portraying the life of the senses in the setting of the Garden, where carnality does not obtain.

> What wond'rous Life in* this I lead!
> Ripe Apples drop about my head;
> The Luscious Clusters of the Vine
> Upon my Mouth do crush their Wine;
> The Nectaren, and curious Peach,
> Into my hands themselves do reach;
> Stumbling on Melons, as I pass,
> Insnar'd with Flow'rs, I fall on Grass.
>
> (ll. 33–40)

Before attending to details, we must notice that the basic metaphor for Nature in this passage is the one that distinguished the pastoral settings of the Golden Age; it is a Nature that gives of herself freely and bounteously, in recognition of her sympathetic ties with the human creatures who live by her bounty. In 'Bermudas' island fruits behave with the same passionate benevolence, but there is a distinction: 'He makes the Figs our mouths to meet;/And throws the Melons at our feet' (ll. 21–22). 'Bermudas' differs from 'The Garden' in that sustaining nature in that poem is directed and inspired by the will of God. In 'The Garden' the various fruits are rendered animate so that they can express the projected attitudes of natural things toward the innocent contemplative, one who has shown his faith and renounced the world of carnal desire and material greed. His reward is to be nourished lavishly while he remains utterly passive, the grapes crushing their wine against his mouth and the peaches putting themselves into his hands. It is made to appear that nature is as possessive of her true lovers as human mistresses can be. And this, of course, is part of the point of the stanza; for the poem will grow more complicated and more profound as we move away from this idyllic, but mindless and unproductive, scene.

Legouis is the only critic to notice that almost all the fruits mentioned in stanza V were grown in England only through careful cultivation;[39] Damon the Mower would have called them the products of vicious artifice rather than of 'willing Nature' (a phrase that, nevertheless, describes this stanza impeccably). The point is that the Garden is not the epitome of simple, pastoral nature; it is the achievement of Nature working with all her skills as creator, and is designed according to the principles of order that man tries only to imitate. It is as superior to the ornate garden of 'The Mower against Gardens' as it is to the chaotic society of the 'busie Companies of Men'. But the fruits of this Garden are as sophisticated as they are animate, and we may assume that Marvell meant to convey certain meanings by his choice of particular plants. The apples in stanza V are, of course, impressive in that they do not wait to be plucked by disobedient man or woman; they fall of their own will, and therefore they precipitate no 'fall' in the theological sense. The grapes do not entice man to drunkenness, nor are they related to Dionysiac worship. Their wine is given as the free gift of a joyous and vivid nature, delighting in its ability to enamour its human suitor. The nectarine and the peach as well convey themselves into his eager hands, as if to feed a hunger of which he has not yet grown aware.[40]

The only difficulty in the stanza arises in the last couplet, where Empson's remark that 'Melon, again, is the Greek for apple',[41] is misleading in that it suggests that the apple here is the cause of another, if less guilty, fall: 'Stumbling on Melons, as I pass,/ Insnar'd with Flow'rs, I fall on Grass' (ll. 39–40). Marvell may indeed be playing on the Greek etymology, but the Christian idea is badly suited to the meaning of the couplet as I interpret it. He might rather have in mind the legend of Atalanta and Hippomenes, for Marvell has the habit of remembering all the examples of the symbolic event he is describing. But when L. W. Hyman follows Empson's interpretation, even to the point of repeating the derivation of 'Melon', and says 'when he stumbles on melons . . . he is falling into carnal sin',[42] some disagreement is called for. Hyman later modifies this statement, but nowhere does he say, as I think one must say, that this fall on grass is entirely without sin, as that word is understood in any of the ethical or theological systems Marvell would have known.

The 'Grass', we know, is flesh, and as such it again signals the inherent identification between created nature and the man, at least, who is still part of nature by choice and by instinctive sympathy. The speaker in 'The Garden' falls on grass—that is, relapses into a passive, vegetative dependence upon the loving nurture of earth. Neither disobedience to God's commandment nor a fall into lustful sexuality is involved here; indeed, heterosexual passion has been banished from the Garden from the moment the lover offered up his devotion to the trees. They return his love, and so the imagery of stanza V is redolent of sensual indulgence. The point is that it is a conscious parody of the love-relationship between man and woman; and the humorous innocence of the last line can be understood only if the element of parody is appreciated. This fall is an innocent piece of mimicry; just as the grass cushions the fall and keeps both man and the world from shock,[43] so the human figure falls not from immortality to mortality, as Adam did, but from ordinary mortality into a form of mortal life raised to the heights of passive sensitivity and supine enjoyment. It is the apotheosis of life in the flesh, but there is nothing sinful about it. The only problem is the flowers that entangle the passing feet of the poem's 'I'. Empson says that the flowers are 'the snakes in it [the grass] that stopped Eurydice',[44] but I think we need not more but fewer mythological allusions if we want to clarify the poem. If the grass is the fundamental element in man and in nature, and the fruits are the active, animate nutrients that sustain the human-natural relationship, then the flowers are the signs of the outward beauties of the natural world, the lures that attract only the purified senses. In a passage in 'The Mower's Song' the flowers appear as the heraldic emblems of the meadows themselves: 'That not one Blade of Grass you spy'd,/But had a Flower on either side' (ll. 9–10); and we have seen how in 'The Coronet' Marvell made a clear and careful distinction between fruit and flowers (l. 6), with the implication that fruits are the substantial products of creative genius, and flowers merely the decorative and substanceless shadows of these fruits. If this is indeed a consistent concept in Marvell, then to call them the 'snares' in this earthly paradise is thoroughly justified. The speaker has been overcome by the passionate court-ship of the Garden, and he has succumbed most easily to the temptations of the eye; his susceptibility has its antecedents in the Spenserian pastoral and in Christian doctrine as well. Though Marvell seems to be describing a snare that catches at the feet of the speaker and brings him to the ground, it would be well within the limits of intelligibility and decorum for a metaphysical poet to speak of eyes entrapped in flowery snares. Thus the stanza con-cludes with a vision of man as a sensuous creature abandoning his will, his freedom, and even his consciousness to the blandishments of a supremely beautiful nature. It is the high point of earthly perception; but the next step on the ladder leads up to the level of the rational intellect, and that is indeed where stanza VI begins.

The diction of these eight lines proceeds with a degree of am-biguity unusual in Marvell, while the concepts the stanza deals in both explicitly and implicitly are delicate and elusive in their own right. The trouble starts with the very first line: 'Mean while the Mind, from pleasure less,/Withdraws into its happiness' (ll. 41–42). Following as it does the lush and riotous terms of concrete description in stanza V, the phrase 'pleasure less' carries an air of cool, un-questioning dismissal that minimizes the impression made upon us by that paean to the senses. If it is only 'pleasure less', we feel, then the mind must indeed have resources immense beyond imagining. We note, too, that pleasure is tacitly contrasted with happiness, as if the latter state were somehow more exalted and more real than pleasure, which begins to appear as simple indulgence. A similar idea of the mind's happiness is expressed by Henry More:

> But senses objects soon do glut the soul,
> Or rather weary with their emptinesse;
> So I, all heedlesse how the waters roll
> And mindlesse of the mirth the birds expresse,
> Into myself, 'gin softly to retire
> After hid heavenly pleasures to enquire.[45]

And in Cudworth we can find yet another definition of happiness that also sheds light on the development of the ideas of 'The Garden' through this and the following stanza:

Now our onely way to recover God & happines again, is
not to soar up with our Understandings, but to destroy this
Self-will of ours: and then we shall find our wings to grow
again, our plumes fairly spread, & our selves raised aloft
into the free Aire of perfect Liberty, which is perfect
Happinesse.[46]

But Marvell is not so strictly doctrinal as this; nor does he leave us
long in doubt about the nature of the happiness the mind seeks.[47]
To understand its 'withdrawal'[48] we must know something of the
character of the mind itself, and Marvell gives us this information
in the parenthetical—'The Mind, that Ocean where each kind/
Does streight its own resemblance find' (ll. 43-44). The idea that
the seas contained exact replicas of all the animals to be found on
land was, as many editors have remarked, a commonplace of
medieval and Renaissance natural philosophy.[49] But Marvell is
using the comparison to reveal the mind's power to create a mental
reality as complete and consistent as the reality of the physical
world. It is important that we be made to feel that the world of
the mind's images (if that is what it is stocked with) is as complex
and alive as the world of real creatures. Of course 'kind' meant,
primarily, a genus; but the word was used commonly to refer to
the different genres of poetry and drama; and since, presumably,
the abstract kinds of poetry would be as real in the mind as the more
concrete kinds of animals, it is possible that Marvell intends a
general statement about the correspondence between the structure
of the mind and the nature of all universal concepts. For we must
be careful to remember that the metaphor of the mind as an ocean
simply names an analogy; it does not insist that we think of the
mind as an enormous underwater menagerie. The mind contains
the kinds in *its* way as the ocean allegedly contains the kinds in *its*.
It is equally important to notice that the emphasis is put on 'kinds'
rather than creatures; the ocean shelters *typical examples* and the
mind too deals in ideas rather than specific parts of experience.
But the implications of the couplet carry further; the 'kinds' of
earth, after all, are material in so far as they are embodied in
individual creatures. For the mind's abstract mental forms to have
a 'resemblance' to individuals requires another act of metamorphosis.
The mind must transmute the essence of the earthly kind into an
idea that retains that essence yet strips it of its material qualities.

Yet it creates, transcending these,
Far other Worlds, and other Seas;
Annihilating all that's made
To a green Thought in a green Shade.[50]

(ll. 45–48)

The mind is pictured here as a creator, and the analogy to Divine creation is unavoidable. But the mind is also, it seems, uncircumscribed by the actual creation of God as we have seen it on land and in the seas in lines 43–44. It creates its own 'garden of the kinds', a new earth and a new ocean to contain the creatures of its mental generation. 'Transcending' can mean both 'to overpass' and 'to exceed', as Miss Bradbrook points out,[51] but I am not sure that she is right in saying that it does not also carry the theological sense of going beyond normal human experience. It is true that the events of 'The Garden' are intelligible entirely within the terms of the Christian universe; even the symbolism of stanza VII is not truly mystical in character. Nevertheless, the mind as it is described in stanza VI appears to be capable of unlimited creation. The only admissible qualification is that it does, in fact, create 'other Worlds, and other Seas', as if its imaginings are, or must be, modelled on the created universe whose shape and essence have been impressed upon the mind by the senses. In other poets the imprisonment within the senses was indeed the key to the mind's freedom of imagining. Benlowes, for example, says:

Man may confine the body, but the mind
(Like Nature's miracles, the wind
And dreams) does, though secur'd,
    a free enjoyment find.

Rays drawn in to a point more vig'rous beam;
Joys more to saints, engoal'd, did stream;
Linnets their cage to be a grove, bars
    boughs esteem.[52]

In any case, the poets and philosophers who accepted the assumptions of Christian Platonism were at one in believing that the mind (or the soul) could achieve its proper end and function only by turning from the distractions of sense. They were aware, nevertheless, that the mind's powers of imagination can operate only upon the qualities and meanings of 'events' they have met in real experience. There is some uncertainty about whether the mind is meant to contemplate only the ideal truths communicated to it through its resemblance to the Divine Mind, or whether it imitates the Divine by contemplating its own creations. The problem of knowledge, as it affected the relations between knowing intellect and known object, absorbed the best thinkers of the seventeenth century; the habit of analogical thinking was strong enough even in the late Renaissance for platonic philosophers to find a solution to the problem in the literal identification of knower and known. Others thought the mind affected its objects in such a way that it might almost be said to create the things it contemplated. For example, in J. Hall's elegy for Lord Hastings, which appeared with Marvell's in 1649, Hall speaks of the quality of Hastings' intellect:

> as if that every Thing,
> Stript of its outward dross, and all refin'd
> Into a Form, lay open to his Minde:
> Or if his pure Minde could suddenly disperse
> It self all ways, and th'row all Objects pierce.[53]

To be sure, this is hyperbole dictated by the occasion and the need for high-flown terms of praise; but in a sober and encyclopedic treatise, *The True Intellectual System of the Universe*, we find Cudworth discussing the apprehension of 'secondary attributes' in very similar terms:

> But sensible things themselves (as for example light and colours) are not known or understood either by the passion or the fancy of sense, nor by anything merely foreign and adventitious, but by intelligible ideas exerted from the mind itself, that is, by something native and domestic to it.[54]

Marvell would have heard many similar opinions at Cambridge during his stay there, for although the Cambridge Platonists did not form so cohesive a school as many histories of philosophy pretend, they held a good many epistemological and ethical ideas in common. And Cudworth's concept of the powers of the mind to affect objects outside it would lend itself to the interpretation of the 'annihilation' of created things of which Marvell speaks in line 47.

It should be remembered that none of this contradicts the picture of the mind as 'withdrawing' from the world of sense. The latter was a necessary act, as we can learn from Henry More:

> For they will be in the flaring light or life of the body as the starres in the beams of the Sunne scarce to be seen, unlesse we withdraw our selves out of the flush vigour of that light, into the profundity of our own souls, as into some deep pit. ... Thus being quit of passion, they have upon any occasion a clear though still and quiet representation of every thing in their minds, upon which pure bright sydereall phantasms unprejudiced reason may safely work, and clearly discern what is true or probable.[55]

But this withdrawal did not hamper the mind's abilities to judge and create; on the contrary, it provided precisely the same atmosphere of retirement and freedom from temptation that the Garden provides for man seen as a complete entity. In this state of freedom, the mind can perform its dual function of 'creating' forms for the world of sense, and understanding the forms of the ideal universe.[56] But at this point in 'The Garden' Marvell is not yet concerned with the mind as the intermediary between ideal perfection and the less perfect world of creatures.[57] Stanza VI concentrates on the mind's 'Annihilating all that's made/To a green Thought in a green Shade' (ll. 47–48). There are both ambiguities and contradictions within this couplet; the contradiction is in the use of 'annihilate' to describe what is essentially another act of metamorphosis. 'All that's made' is reduced (or simply changed) to a green thought; it is not destroyed and turned into nothingness. I think it is unlikely that Marvell meant 'Annihilating' to carry the impression of 'obliterating'. For one thing, the idea of not-being was noxious to the Platonic philosophy that dominates the poem; and it was equally untenable within a Christian context. And, finally, 'a green Thought' is very far from nothingness to the mind in the Garden. Rather, Marvell seems to have used the term to parallel in force and audacity the previous word, 'transcending'. Extraordinary powers are thus predicated of the mind, powers that appear to equate it with the faculties of the Divine Mind. And it is possible that the lines constitute a deliberate use of hyperbole, whose irony will be revealed in the next stanza when the soul attains a higher state of apprehension than the mind does in stanza

VI. The point is that even when 'all that 's made' has been transformed into the peculiar idiom of the mind's ideas, there is yet
another way of perception and understanding, yet another avenue
open to the solitary contemplator.

The ambiguity is in the phrase 'all that 's made', since we do
not know whether this refers to the Creation itself or to the
'other Worlds, and other Seas' whose progenitor is the mind.
As we have noted, the ambiguity is clearly intended; it is an
instance of Marvell's typical desire to express a complicated
concept by rendering it in all its complexity and refusing to
resolve it for the sake of a clarity that would be untrue to the
lines of the question itself. The mind has already transcended the
'kinds' of earth and sea; it would not be difficult to accept the
assertion that it has changed the material creation into purely
mental phenomena. But the syntax will allow us also to believe
that lines 47–48 mark a second step in a process only begun in
lines 45–46, and that the mind is now performing its function of
transmutation on the very worlds and seas with which it originally
passed beyond the limits of actual experience. This time it abandons
altogether the categories of 'Worlds', 'Seas', and even 'kinds'; in
contemplating its own creations it has reached the point where
it must impose its own categories of apprehension upon them. Thus
all that the *mind* has made becomes 'a green Thought in a green
Shade'.

I doubt that it would be profitable to speculate too freely on the
meanings that attach to 'green' in this line. The 'green Shade'
obviously looks back to the reproving shade cast by the evergreen
trees of the Garden down on the inanities of the 'busie Companies
of Men'; but this time it is neither 'short' nor 'narrow verged'. It
has so widened its scope under the pressure of the mind's creative
impulse that it now overshadows all that is and all that the
imagination can call into being. The symbolism of the colour in
this line is clearly delimited; this green shade does not shelter ideas
of fickleness, or even of hope, and it seems to have little to do with
love of any kind, even the pure and unassertive love of the trees
that cast the shade (in the mind's eye). By the same token, 'a green
Thought' can have little to do with any of these significations;
it must have some reference to the symbolic value of green as the
sign of growth and the essence of naturalness. Thus the correspondence between the mind and the principles of order represented

by the trees is driven home by a metaphor of metamorphosis that makes its point by using unexpected epithets. The mind, in transforming nature into intellectual phenomena, has paralleled the trees' transformation of human passions into fruitful attitudes toward nature. It is thus like the trees in several important ways, and can therefore be said to put its 'green Thought' in the 'green Shade' that inspired it at first. But the following stanza makes it clear that the 'green Shade' is still but the furthest reach of the powers of the natural reason; its enclosing coloured shadow is unilluminated by the intelligible truths through whose reflected light the soul shines. In an article to which I have referred before, D. W. Robertson Jr. mentions that both the trees in the Garden of Eden and their shadows had perfectly recognizable connotations, and that the Tree of the Knowledge of Good and Evil (which by definition is the symbol of mortal, or human, knowledge) 'is frequently associated with *scientia* (as opposed to *sapientia*) for worldly wisdom is conducive to a false sense of security'.[58] It is my contention that the tree that shelters the winged soul in stanza VII is the tree of *sapientia* (the Tree of Life).[59] It is to this higher, this ultimate, form of wisdom that Marvell turns in the climactic passage of 'The Garden'.

The sensuous life of stanza V was depicted with intense particularity of place and object, but the intellectual metamorphosis of stanza VI took place only within the mind, while we lost contact with the realities of the Garden itself. The very first word of stanza VII redirects our attention forcefully to the *place* in which this experience occurs, as if to remind us that the symbols and metaphors are all along rooted in the basic figure of an actual garden, and also as if to enforce the paradoxical connections between physical acts and their philosophical significances: 'Here at the Fountains sliding foot,/Or at some Fruit-trees mossy root' (ll. 49-50).

The exact spot Marvell specifies for the transformation of the soul that is about to take place is a fine example of his talent for choosing particulars that will also be expressive of a wide range of meanings. The fountain and the fruit tree are familiar landmarks of the pastoral landscape; but they are, as well, Christian symbols of spiritual regeneration and the site of man's lapse from grace. The soul is obviously on the point of entering into divine wisdom, as contrasted to the purely intellectual apprehension of stanza VI. Furthermore, as Robertson remarks, 'a well or fountain appears often beneath the Tree of Life'; and, finally, the association of sin with the Tree of Knowledge is clearly absent from this scene—the soul is purified both of the clay of the flesh and of the lesser understanding of the unaided intellect, and has passed beyond knowledge to the edge of wisdom. As evidence that the presence of the Tree of Life in a garden signified the ultimate separation of the soul from worldly bonds we may adduce the following, from Walter Mountague's *Miscellanea Spiritualia* (1648):

> They then who live in this holy Garden of Speculation, may be said to be already under the shady leaves of the Tree of Life; this state of separation from the world, seeming to be in such an order and relation to the supreme beatitude, as *Adams Paradice* was to Heaven, as it is in a maner of integrity of ease, and passeth away out of this life by a kinde of translation to glory.[60]

In contrast, Cowley gives the attributes of the Tree of Knowledge thus:

> The sacred *Tree* midst the fair *Orchard* grew;
> The *Phoenix Truth* did on it rest,
> And built his perfum'd Nest.
> That right *Porphyrian Tree* which did true *Logick* shew,
> Each *Leaf* did learned *Notions* give,
> And th'*Apples* were *Demonstrative*
> So clear their *Colour* and divine,
> The very *shade* they cast did other *Lights* out-shine.[61]

But Marvell's allusions to the biblical tree are part of an attempt to increase the drama of the final metamorphosis of the speaker.

> Casting the Bodies Vest aside,
> My Soul into the boughs does glide:
> There like a Bird it sits, and sings,
> Then whets, and combs its silver Wings.
>
> (ll. 51–54)

We need not comment again on the image of the soul as having wings or even as being a bird;[62] nor, perhaps, does the concept of shedding the body's restrictive covering need further elucidation.[63] But it is suggestive that the bird of the soul sings; for it is fair to say that this is a reference, once more, to the art of poetry. To a

Renaissance poet 'song' always meant 'poem'. Furthermore, one suggestion inherent in the 'longer flight' of line 55 is that this refers as much to this different kind of poetry (the kind that Marvell implies he has not written in 'The Coronet') as it does to the final flight of the soul to its reunion with God.[64]

The final couplet, 'And, till prepar'd for longer flight,/Waves in its Plumes the various Light' (ll. 55–56), leaves no doubt that the naturalistic description of the bird has been subsumed in the Christian (and, in this case, Platonic and Plotinian) image of the soul shining with the reflected light of God. In this convention, as we have seen in 'On a Drop of Dew', Divine Light is always single, pure, white; while its reflections in the phenomena of the world are many-coloured, as they are less perfect than their source.[65] Thus the religious tone of the stanza is maintained and brought to its complete expression; it is no less important to recognize that the soul is left in the world of phenomena. The 'various light' signifies the earth; and its illumination of the soul's 'Plumes' indicates that the soul still contemplates the creation that surrounds it. Perhaps the waving of the plumes is a very refined symbol of the act of writing poetry; but at the very least it suggests that the preparation required for 'longer flight' will be both long and demanding. For Marvell this would be true of both the apprenticeship to poetry and the life of spiritual education that leads to salvation.

The transition in the final stanza of 'The Garden' from the world of speculation we entered in stanza IV back to the imagined garden of the opening is not so abrupt as the exclamation that begins the penultimate eight lines.

> Such was that happy Garden-state,
> While Man there walk'd without a Mate:
> After a Place so pure, and sweet,
> What other Help could yet be meet!

(ll. 57–60)

We have returned, with a jolt, to the speaker's voice and to the detached, ironic viewpoint of the first three stanzas of the poem. The view is over the entire experience we have passed through in the Garden, from sense to intellect to the soul's perception; and as yet we are not sure to what condition of knowledge we are meant to have attained. We find that it is a sort of worldly wisdom, but wisdom informed with the sense of what is possible to human faculties. Nevertheless, the tone is nostalgic, for we have emerged from the vision of pure apprehension into the world of natural beauty. And to reinforce the nostalgia Marvell picks up again the rather subdued allusions to Eden in stanza V and recalls the myth of Adam in almost literalist fashion. The contemplative Garden we have just left is characterized as Eden before the creation of Eve, apparently to allow the poem's wit to modulate back again into the mode of the rejection of erotic love. But it is interesting that the absence of a 'Mate' is rejoiced in; there is no mention of a 'Mistress', something we might expect if Marvell is merely making fun again of the 'Fond Lovers' of stanza III. The implication is, rather, that the introduction of Eve into the Garden disturbed the delicate balance and sympathy that existed between man and the living nature of the Garden in the central part of the poem. But the implied statement is not followed by a lament for lost innocence and quiet; rather, it provides an excuse for the most forthright bit of word-play in the entire poem—'What other Help could yet be meet!'

> But 'twas beyond a Mortal's share
> To wander solitary there:
> Two Paradises 'twere in one
> To live in Paradise alone.   (ll. 61–64)

This can be called an elegant form of misogyny—or even misanthropy—but it is not so intent on deprecating Woman that it ignores the opportunity to probe the idea a bit with more puns. It was indeed 'beyond a Mortal's share' to wander in Paradise; or at least it proved to be once Eve's sin had made Adam mortal. And 'one' in line 63 may be taken to mean Adam as well as the Garden of Eden; the joy of possession of the Garden might well have been doubled if it had not been shared—the mathematics is fairly simple.

Nevertheless, there is undoubtedly a sense of sorrowing yearning after the eternally lost world of innocence and natural sympathy that pervades this stanza. It is almost desperate, as we realize when it attempts to revise one of the Christian world's basic myths; the wit is in the expression of the attempt, not in the wish itself. 'To live in Paradise alone', aside from being the direct antithesis of the world's usual vision of eternal bliss, is a state that can be achieved only in the imagination; neither the mythical nor the real world will accommodate this kind of solitude.

It is this recognition that governs the strangely complicated conceits of the ninth, and final, stanza. The floral sundial has bewildered many readers, not only because of the puns and ambiguities that go to make up its description, but because of its ostensibly emblematic position in 'The Garden'.[66] It certainly represents a return to the actual garden created by human skill, and we shall see that the structure and meaning of the dial are both indicative of a newly-discovered relationship between art and nature. This 'Gardner' has nothing in common with the 'Luxurious Man' who distorted nature to abet his illicit desires. The sundial is a work of the imaginative intellect in that it imposes an order on nature that becomes symbolic of the meanings that creatures alone cannot express. Not only the flowers but the bee as well contribute to the emblematic function of the sundial, and together they assume a degree of control over time itself: 'How well the skilful Gardner drew/Of flow'rs and herbes this Dial new' (ll. 65–66). As Miss Bradbrook mentions, 'well' implies both that the work was done skilfully and that the gardener was right to undertake it.[67] In both senses there is no irony in the praise for the gardener and for the dial. It is made of decorative emblems ('flow'rs') and useful, even medicinal, herbs—so that it combines beauty and utility, the twin shibboleths of Renaissance poetic. But the point of a sundial is that it measures the passing of time, even if such measurement is taken by living creatures who are the mortal subjects of time: 'Where from above the milder Sun/Does through a fragrant Zodiack run' (ll. 67–68). King's article is indispensable to an understanding of the puns in this couplet, in that they are based quite clearly on the parallel passage in *Hortus*, as most of 'The Garden' is not. He explains that *Sol ibi candidior fragrantia Signa pererrat* 'shows that *milder* means less dazzling than up in the sky . . . and that *fragrant* must be stressed, meaning that the zodiac up there is not fragrant'.[68] And since the sundial measures hours, the comparison to the zodiac is one between the lesser and the greater, where both are scales to judge the passing of time. For the flowers to pretend to measure the passage of the months is daring enough, but Marvell then turns to 'th' industrious Bee' who, 'as it works . . ./Computes its time as well as we'. King points out the pun on 'time' and 'thyme',[69] but the important thing to note is that the bee is as busy here as were the 'busie . . . Men' who were repudiated early in the poem; yet nothing in the bee's industry is found false to nature or to the values of the Garden. The conclusion must be that this is the proper and natural use of time, and that the living creatures can subject time to their measurement. In the comparative 'Computes its time as well as we' the pun is vital, since the two terms of the comparison are the bee's collecting nectar from the thyme blossoms and man's measuring out his time under the influence of nature. Both are natural creatures and both have learned how to deal most profitably with the forces that rule them: 'How could such sweet and wholsome Hours/ Be reckon'd but with herbs and flow'rs!' (ll. 71–72). Time is no longer a threat, but a reality that is always, in the Garden, qualified by the epithets 'sweet and wholsome'. And the herbs and flowers have proved themselves to be not only the proper setting for contemplation and the approach to wisdom, but a real means of conquering time through natural beauty. The final couplet suggests that the floral sundial is the only *possible* means to measure time, as if the phenomena of aging and decay could not be understood—perhaps would not exist—without the intermediary influence of nature and its creations.

From stanza to stanza the poem proceeds by a series of free variations on the theme of change and transmutation; and many of the individual metaphors and puns are based on the trope of calling something by another name, or on viewing a common tradition from an uncommon viewpoint. The most important example, of course, is the series of transmutations the speaker goes through during the poem. He rehearses the life of man as it would have been understood by Plato, and he ends his saga with strong intimations of Christian salvation. The poem leaves him, and us, with a corrected view of the meanings implicit in nature; for we have come far from the conventional treatment of the garden as the setting for contemplative and rural retirement. Rather, that is only Marvell's starting point; as we saw in the 'Mower' poems, he is more concerned to understand the relationship between the inevitably abstract mind and the recalcitrant materialism of the world of the senses. The analogies he finds and the sympathetic correspondences on which he bases his metaphoric diction are both supported by his perception of the underlying 'naturalness' of man. But that perception is only the beginning of the problems that are raised and dealt with in the 'The Garden'. The paradoxical outcome is that man must transcend his natural faculties if he is ever to understand nature correctly and live harmoniously with her.

'To his Coy Mistress', 'The Definition of Love', and 'The Picture of little T.C. in a Prospect of Flowers' are like 'The Garden' in that they are all very much concerned with the irresolvable conflict between imagination and mortality, although each one dramatizes the battle differently. Each poem moves toward a statement of resolution that will signal a victory won over inevitable decline and death; and in each poem this victory is won by different forces and with different tactics. All deal with the life of earth against a background of abstract and ideal values; none relies either for its logic or for its moral sanctions on recognizable Christian doctrines.

The subject of 'The Picture of little T.C. in a Prospect of Flowers' is a young girl;[70] but the last stanza of Marvell's poem turns it from the path of courtly praise to a consideration of both the power and the evanescence of physical loveliness. Nor is it a conventional treatment of those themes, which would identify it more closely with the 'persuasion to love', a genre which would be, by definition, inappropriate to this subject (but which was applied, nonetheless, to children by several of the Cavalier poets). Rather, Marvell's animadversions are addressed to the imagined mature powers of the beautiful child; she is warned to be kind to nature lest nature destroy her prematurely. The warning is given less with anxiety than with knowing playful, sternness.

It is clear from the first stanza that the sight, or the imagined 'picture', of little T.C. summons up in Marvell associations and ideas we have met before, in 'Young Love' and in the portrait of the shepherdess in 'The Gallery'. Here is the 'Infant Love' of the early poems incarnate, innocent of lustful passion and enjoying her command over nature without any clear sense as yet of the extent of her dominion. Her days are 'golden', 'In the green Grass she loves to lie', and she is explicitly called a 'Nimph'. And Marvell uses the word as precisely here as he did in 'The Nymph complaining for the death of her Faun', as we see in stanza II where he refers to the 'chaster Laws' that T.C. will one day enforce to break the rule of 'wanton Love'. Beauty, youth, and chastity are combined once again as the formula for the proper human relationship to the beauties of the natural world. And T.C., like Damon the Mower, is pictured as not only the ruler but the very shaper of her surround-

ings; her role as destroyer is only previsioned, and comes into the
poem only in the climactic stanza of warning.

> And there with her fair Aspect tames
> The Wilder flow'rs, and gives them names:
> But only with the Roses playes;
> And them does tell
> What Colour best becomes them, and what Smell.
>
> (ll. 4–8)

T.C. here is very much like Mary Fairfax in the concluding section
of 'Upon Appleton House' as her beauty changes into the power
to order nature.[71] But 'The Picture of little T.C.', as is evident from
these few lines alone, is in some ways a tissue of ideas and images
developed in other poems. There is the emphasis on taming 'wild'
nature, and this act is almost equated with the gesture of giving
names to plants—as if this were the only way man can establish a
connection with created nature, since a name is an abstraction
applied by the mind—a mind that is in other respects a part of
nature itself. This is a concept whose importance is clear in 'The
Garden', but which is referred to only in passing in this poem. The
roses, of course, are as usual a symbol of the perfection of fleshly
beauty; but the point of the stanza is that T.C. controls the qualities
of even the rose, so that its symbolic value is malleable in her hands.

In consonance with the decorum of courtly compliment, Marvell
moves from the pastoral vision of the first stanza to the extended
military metaphor of stanzas II and III. Here T.C. is described as the
all-conquering mistress whose lineaments and gestures are familiar
to us from all too many poems that elaborate the trope of love as
an armed conflict. Of course the innovation in 'Little T.C.' is that
the young goddess triumphs over Cupid himself, or at least the
particular Cupid who guards and abets erotic love. Marvell casts
his metaphor even a bit higher, making T.C. appear to be something of a divinely inspired scourge of God: 'Who can foretel for
what high cause/This Darling of the Gods was born!'[72] (ll. 9–10).
This is the language of prophecy, of epic, even of Scripture—yet
Marvell does not hesitate to apply it to the figure of a little girl
playing among the roses of her garden. One might be tempted to
conclude that he is under the influence of some such vision of youthful purity and wisdom as informs some of Wordsworth's poems;
but the point very obviously is not that this child is to be the origin

of the mature adult, nor is she the creator of 'natural piety'. Her infant innocence will give way before the conquering force of her adult, chaste beauty; and Marvell clearly feels the change is inevitable. The final exhortation is not to try to retain the purity of youth, but to avoid trespassing against that nature which was once her nurturing companion and willing subject.

The military metaphor is sustained by words such as 'compound', 'parly', 'force', 'wound', 'Triumph', and 'Glories', but the last lines of stanza III introduce another consideration while continuing the complimentary tone: 'Let me be laid,/Where I may see thy Glories from some shade' (ll. 23–24). The major point of these lines is, clearly, that T.C.'s 'Glories' will be, after her triumph over Love and lovers, too blazing bright to be seen with impunity by mortal eyes. But Marvell is also carrying on the battlefield diction by pretending to be a wounded, if not slaughtered, lover; and the phrase suggests that the 'shade' in which he asks to be laid may indeed be the grave, presumably the only place where he can be ultimately safe from the scorching beauty of the adult T.C.[73] The solution is the same that Damon found to protect himself finally from the destructive force of his passion for Juliana. But this hint of death's intrusion into a scene that has hitherto been one of conventional praise is enough to change the course of the poem momentarily, before it is returned to in the final stanza. Marvell goes back to T.C. amid the flowers, as if to fix the vision once more firmly; but this time he attempts to teach T.C.'s youthful innocence a lesson in its own use. There is a note of haste and an implicit recognition of futility as he asks that, before she assumes the armour of the all-conquering female beauty, T.C.

> Reform the errours of the Spring;
> Make that the Tulips may have share
> Of sweetness, seeing they are fair;
> And Roses of their thorns disarm:
> But most procure
> That Violets may a longer Age endure.

> (ll. 27–32)

The tone may appear light and graceful, but it barely conceals a concern with questions that in their seriousness reach to the heart of Marvell's poetry. The nature that bows before T.C.'s sovereignty of beauty is not taken as the criterion of excellence in preference to the artistic skills of man; the Spring is capable of 'errours'. But the significance of what Marvell is asking T.C. to do is ambiguous. She must cleanse nature of its impurities, correct the inevitable propensity of roses to have thorns, and of tulips to lack scent. Yet she can do this only by, in effect, dealing 'between the Bark and Tree', by changing the 'kinds' and interposing her human powers in the processes of nature. It is impossible to believe that Marvell was not aware of the intelligent pathos of this catalogue of labours; for the violet, epitome of transience, to endure a longer age would be to violate its nature and be no longer a violet, nor beautiful in its particular way. And by implication the same thing is true of the 'picture' of T.C. Marvell can see in her omnipotent beauty only the guarantee that it will change into something else, and that to forestall that change would be to alter the beauty unrecognizably. The protest against the decay of earthly beauty is no strange theme to English poetry; but Marvell shapes it to his own purposes by creating an image of a Golden Age for beauty itself, and marking the decline from that perfection as a descent into the adult world of bodily beauty that is the norm for other poets who treat the same theme. But this is not done through sentimentality about innocence, or children, or anything else. Rather, it stems from the perception that all change must be away from perfection when the perfect state is understood to be the time when man is in natural sympathy with created nature. The development of consciousness, or reason, of the power to abstract and to imagine the self—all of these threaten the instinctive relationship with nature. And, since Marvell is pre-eminently a poet of the Renaissance, the perfection of that primal state is equated easily with beauty, or brightness, or innocence, or the shape of the sphere —all the common symbols of perfection whether moral or physical.

The T.C. we have seen once again among the flowers in stanza IV is now warned to:

> Gather the Flow'rs, but spare the Buds;
> Lest *Flora* angry at thy crime,
> To kill her Infants in their prime,
> Do quickly make th' Example Yours;
> And, ere we see,
> Nip in the blossome all our hopes and Thee.

(ll. 35–40)

Decorum requires that 'all our hopes' be concerned with T.C.'s prospects for the 'Glories' of her future; but the syntax will allow us to see that Marvell's 'hopes' are as strongly for the green and natural 'Buds' as they are for the young girl. And this is true despite the fact that the stanza depends on an underlying sense of correspondence between the buds and the girl; they are both youthful shoots of growing nature, but the vital difference between them is that the human creature has the power to kill as well as the power to order and cultivate. The rather shocking point of the lines is to imagine nature taking retribution for the wanton destruction of innocent flowers; Marvell thus gives a dramatic reinterpretation of the familiar argument that beauty is inevitably cut off by devouring time. Here the 'necessary end' is seen as an act of vengeance by nature against destructive man; the relationship that begins in elemental sympathy ends in mortal opposition. The vital point is that nature's hostility is awakened by interference with youth, with the buds symbolic of the principles of growth and generation. And yet such interference may be part of the act of ordering and purifying that Marvell advises T.C. to perform. Furthermore, nature can be said to interfere with the budding potentialities of T.C., since it is inevitable maturing that will change her from innocent empress to cruel mistress. Both nature and the girl despoil each other unwittingly and by obeying their instinctive forces; there can thus be no reconciliation, and Marvell sees each threatening the other with death and ravage because of the unbridgeable divorce between the conscious mind and the material world. The distinction is one that will be characterized in a more purely intellectualized fashion in 'The Definition of Love'.[74]

In *Elizabethan and Metaphysical Imagery* Miss Tuve included Marvell's poem in the genre of 'the definition' that she believed to govern many poems of the late sixteenth and early seventeenth centuries that were related to the widespread interest in logic, and in Ramist logic in particular.[75] Frank Kermode claims that the genre, if there was one, was different from that described by Miss Tuve, and that Marvell's 'Definition' bears no relation to any type of logical, descriptive poem.[76] Kermode discerns no logical structure in the poem, and judges finally that 'the best that can be said for Marvell's title is that the poem offers a hostile analysis of the commonplace, sublunary kind of love by bringing it into comparison with the specially pure variety (hence all the imagery of the incorruptible heavens) that it celebrates'.[77] Now Marvell's 'Definition' is neither particularly concerned with attacking 'sublunary' love, nor with 'defining' love by the method Miss Tuve ascribes to the genre—that of collecting parallel phrases and epithets that accumulate to create, almost by deprivation, the portrait of the thing being described. Marvell's 'Definition' is not made up of such instances of illustrative periphrasis, but is in fact a description of a passion given in terms drawn from geometry, geography, astronomy, and astrology. The joke is in speaking of passionate love in a vocabulary germane to abstract science. But the joke also contains part of the poem's meaning, which is that *this* love shares the attributes of the heavenly bodies, not only in being uncircumscribed by the limitations of lovers in the flesh, but also in being capable of abstraction and geometric expression. I hope it is not necessary at this point to state that although the basic stance of the poem is a witty one, it does not in any way preclude its dealing with an intensely serious theme, the contradictions between passion and fate.

It is hard to know exactly what Kermode means by calling this poem a 'celebration of despair in love', unless he is in fact referring to the paradox Marvell insists on in the opening stanza, that his love has sprung from circumstances that are its perfect antinomies.

> My Love is of a birth as rare
> As 'tis for object strange and high:
> It was begotten by despair
> Upon Impossibility.[78]

(ll. 1–4)

L. Hyman has an ingenious explanation for some of the puzzles in this stanza,[79] but it needs little penetration to see that the personified states present at this begetting are meant to stand for the greatest possible discouragement an earthly lover can suffer. The convention of the love-vow would now necessarily turn to the lover's undying hopes, but Marvell forestalls those by pushing his paradox still further:

> Magnanimous Despair alone
> Could show me so divine a thing,
> Where feeble Hope could ne'r have flown
> But vainly flapt its Tinsel Wing.

(ll. 5-8)

This may have some relation to Cowley's arguments against Crashaw in 'On Hope', since Cowley mentions hope's 'weake being'; but Marvell is not engaged in verse-debate. He is more daring in rejecting one of the cardinal virtues in favour of despair, one of the cardinal sins. The ease with which the Renaissance poet could alternate between sacred and profane terminology assists him here, so that 'Magnanimous Despair' is linked with divinity, and the latter word carries both religious associations and those of the hyperbolic style of love poetry. The cruel mistress is often called 'divine', but here the very hopelessness of physical love is elevated to become a spiritual value.

But the physical is not ignored; the next stanza quickly disposes of the possibility of carnal consummation. The lover's 'extended Soul'[80] is presumably 'fixt' on the object of his love, and the word can mean both 'directed at' and 'adhering to'. In either case, it is 'Fate' that 'crouds it self betwixt' and prevents the desired union; it will not let 'Two perfect Loves . . . close'.[81] Indeed, Fate's 'Decrees of Steel' part them to the extreme edges of the imagined universe.[82]

> And therefore her Decrees of Steel
> Us as the distant Poles have plac'd,
> (Though Loves whole World on us doth wheel)
> Not by themselves to be embrac'd.
>
> (ll. 17–20)

The image is that of a globe or of the spherical universe of Ptolemaic astronomy; the lovers are at opposite poles, joined by the circumference that in its circularity represents the perfection of their love, but separated by the entire Creation. The poles themselves are described as lovers ('Not by themselves to be embrac'd') in a way that emphasizes their paradoxical state of separation and connection.[83] The only possibility of their joining is if 'giddy Heaven' should fall, or if 'some new Convulsion' should make the world collapse and 'Be cramp'd into a *Planisphere*'. The point about the planisphere, of course, is that it was a representation of the globe as it would appear in two dimensions, with the poles brought together on one plane. The figure serves Marvell both as an accurate visual image of the 'meeting' of the two lovers, and also as a gauge of the impossibility of overcoming the disjunction of his imagined lovers. Heaven and earth must be wrenched out of their accustomed shapes and courses to achieve this union; and this, in fact, would destroy the very basis of their love since it would (on the realistic level) conquer despair and defeat Fate, and (on the symbolic level) flatten the perfect sphere.

The next conceit is derived from geometry, and changes one term of the comparison from the material world to what Kermode calls 'sublunary' love; values are assigned to different kinds of lines and angles in the same way that Renaissance philosophers found greater and less value in circles and ellipses.

> As Lines so Loves *oblique* may well
> Themselves in every Angle greet:
> But ours so truly *Paralel,*
> Though infinite can never meet.
>
> (ll. 25–28)

'*Oblique*' describes the lines that intersect at any angle, and their obliquity is equated with the physical contact of lesser lovers than Marvell. But the perfect loves are parallel in their spiritual quality, and their parallelism, reverting to the geometrical figure, forbids them to join at any place in the same plane. The point is, of course, that they exist on a different, and higher, plane than the physical; and this truth is symbolized by their infinite extension. The very fact that they transcend the limitations of 'sublunary' lovers is what makes them perfect and what keeps them from the ordinary satisfactions of mere desire. But Marvell was also fond of the proposition that a line infinitely extended will eventually become a circle and return to its point of origin.[84] Thus we return to the figure of the perfect circle, and this time it is shown to have transcended even infinity by enclosing it within the infinite parallel lines. The lines are those that circle the sphere imagined in stanza V, and the correspondence between the two gives the entire conceit consistency and point.[85]

The notion of the sphere and its faculty of joining points that are separated to the extremes is recalled in the final stanza, where Marvell again alters the conceit, this time to include concepts drawn from astrology, almost as if the 'Definition' were a catalogue of the symbolic modes of seventeenth-century science and pseudo-science.

> Therefore the Love which us doth bind.
> But Fate so enviously debarrs,

> Is the Conjunction of the Mind,
> And Opposition of the Stars.

(ll. 29–32)

Margoliouth (I, p. 224) rightly cites Cowley's 'Impossibilities' as a suggestive comparison for Marvell's figure:

> As *stars* (not powerful else) when they *conjoin*,
>   Change, as they please, the Worlds estate;
> So thy *Heart* in *Conjunction* with mine,
>   Shall our own fortunes regulate;
> And to our *Stars themselves* prescribe a *Fate.*[83]

Both poets are thinking of the astrological dictum that says that two stars (or planets) have the power to affect human destiny when they are in conjunction (in a straight line when seen from 'here below'). But Cowley claims that the joining of the lovers' hearts will give them control over their destinies; Marvell's lovers do not so much conquer material Fate as move beyond its sovereignty. They are as stars only in so far as their polar position places them in opposition; but the 'conjunction of the Mind' obviates their fatal separation and unites them in the sphere of perfection that transcends mere accident and the limitations of the flesh. Indeed, he insists on the difference between the love of the mind and the passions that are controlled by Fate, by making it clear that this love is the 'Opposition of the Stars'. The stars rule man's destiny, but these lovers defy their apparently hopeless state by discovering the infinite power of the 'Conjunction of the Mind'. Thus the scientific and mathematical metaphors lead ultimately to a statement of transcendence over mortality. The same end will be achieved in 'To his Coy Mistress', but by means entirely different.

Although recent critism has done much to reveal the careful logical structure of 'To his Coy Mistress', the poem strikes us immediately as an example of the *carpe diem*, and only later do we begin to appreciate its intense rationality. That the logical argument should be so evident in what pretends to be a persuasion to love is a sign that Marvell has assessed the genre thoughtfully and found that beneath the passionate rhetoric of the form there lay commonly a rather bald attempt to muster plausible reasons for the satisfaction of desire.[87] Thus the very extravagance of some of the figures in Marvell's 'Coy Mistress' is a comment on the enormous emotional distance that lies between the ostensible cool suasions and the nature of their conscious intent.

Henry King's 'The Exequy' has been suggested as a poem that parallels Marvell's in tone and in its major metaphorical modes;[88] and it is true that King, in trying to express the incomprehensible distinctions between eternity and human time, stretches his imagination to the widest possible conceptions. Indeed, the 'Coy Mistress' gains in intensity because the exaggeration of the first twenty lines underlines the impossibility of ignoring the menace of death while it mocks the conventional hyperbole of *carpe diem* poetry. Not only is there not enough time (as measured in the ordinary days of earthly lovers), but there is not enough 'World'—it will wear out or decay, the speaker pretends, before the Lady's beauties can be praised adequately. And as if to give a halting measure of the expanse that would be needed for the task, the world is spanned from India to England and the scale of time is stretched from 'ten years before the Flood' to the day of Judgment.[89] The 'vegetable Love' that would grow 'vaster then Empires' has been explained as a cabbage[90] and as a cedar of Lebanon,[91] but it seems obvious that Marvell is only playing secondarily on the idea of some monstrous plant that will expand indefinitely so long as it has 'World enough, and Time'. The primary reference must be to the concept of the 'vegetative soul' which in Aristotelian psychology is said to govern pure animal sensation, and is peculiarly the source of the power of growth.

The enumeration of the years and ages that should be devoted to the appreciation of the mistress's several charms is thoroughly conventional;[92] but Marvell's underlying bantering tone shows through;

> But thirty thousand to the rest.
> An Age at least to every part,
> And the last Age should show your Heart.
> For Lady you deserve this State;
> Nor would I love at lower rate.

(ll. 16–20)

That 'thirty thousand' is spoken by the spendthrift who can be lavish with his offers of time since he knows they are meaningless—there is never enough time. But there is also some iron beneath the lightly-held cynic pose. The absurdity of the enterprise he has been

describing justifies the promise, 'the last Age should show your
Heart', since the last age will indeed reveal the true nature of all
hearts. At the 'Conversion of the Jews' the lady's heart will be
anatomized in all its disdainful emptiness. By the same token, I
find an ironical tone in the last couplet; this 'State' is exactly what
the lady deserves, since it is as extravagant and as pointless as her
'coyness'.[93]

The bitterness is transformed into a solemn, but acid, warning at
the sound of 'Times winged Charriot' in line 22. The sound of
death is behind, the prospect of arid and endless unfulfilment
before; the lovers are caught and balanced on the point between
the two, and Marvell's exhortation has all the urgency of their
precarious position.[94] But this urgency is combined with a relent-
lessly clear-sighted vision of the inevitable fate of 'coyness' fallen
victim to the effects of time. The taste for grave-humour in lines
25–32 is not precisely Donne's, because Marvell is not speculating
curiously on the inappropriate union of death and passionate flesh.
Rather, he is destroying the pretence of chastity constructed by the
rules of worldly hypocrisy; worms shall 'try' the lady's virginity
and her 'Honour' will turn to dust. The terms are colloquial and
precise, and the ideas are neither morbid nor metaphysical in
their single-minded probing of the realities of death and decay
that cannot be softened by pose, pretence, or eloquence. The
gesture in the direction of the fastidious lady, and the equally
determined gesture toward the *memento mori* he would have her
observe are combined in: 'The Grave's a fine and private place,/
But none I think do there embrace' (ll. 31–32). In the grave the
lady will indeed be safe from his importunities; and her monument
may be made of marble with suitable elegance. But the speaker's
point is simply that all 'fineness', while satisfied by the privacy of
the grave, becomes ultimately irrelevant beside the brute fact that
death, like 'coyness', shuts out passion and consummation.

Having established the nature of the necessary end, the poet turns
with a demonstrative 'Now therefore' to the final act of persuasion,
which receives its impetus from the horror inspired by the vision
of encroaching death. Thus far Marvell has diverged from the
conventions of the genre in not including any precise description
of his mistress's beauty. And even here her portrait is given only in
images that convey her readiness and her eagerness for love; we
know nothing of her features.

Now therefore, while the youthful hew
Sits on thy skin like morning dew,
And while thy willing Soul transpires
At every pore with instant Fires,
Now let us sport us while we may.[95]

(ll. 33–37)

The lines provide us with an image of burning appetite, and also with the most famous textual crux in Marvell.[96] From this point the imagined surrender of the lady and the consummation of their love is not rendered in the familiar terms of pastoral dalliance or courtly compliment. Rather, the images and conceits are harsh and vigorous, as if in recognition of the struggle that must be waged if time is to be defeated.

And now, like am'rous birds of prey,
Rather at once our Time devour,
Than languish in his slow-chapt pow'r.

(ll. 38–40)

This is utterly uncompromising, and there can be no difficulty in understanding its 'metaphysical' diction; the lovers become predators as they turn on the enemy, Time, and destroy him with his own weapons. But the energy of 'devour' is contrasted implicitly with the creeping destruction of Time's 'slow-chapt pow'r';[97] and some of that energy derives from the unspoken allusion to the sexual act that dominates the final nine lines of the poem. Margoliouth (I, xiii–xiv) sees lines 38–44 as explicitly sexual, especially the reference to the Danube straits in line 44; but I think such a belief limits the poem arbitrarily. Surely Marvell's mind is not on the act of sexual consummation, but rather on the symbolic force of the physical union between the lovers. For example, Margoliouth explains that 'Let us roll all our Strength, and all/ Our sweetness, up into one Ball' (ll. 41–42), is an image of the pomander; yet even if this is true, the more important meaning, as he also points out, is that of the union of the opposite but complementary qualities in the male and female, strength and sweetness. The ball is also the sphere of perfection, even while it may carry the suggestion of the cannon ball that will crash through the gates in line 44.[98] In any case, the violence of consummation is certainly suggested by the succeeding couplet: 'And tear our Pleasures with rough strife,/

Thorough the Iron gates of Life' (ll. 43–44). But the image is too complex to mean simply the physical act of sex, whatever the configuration of the Danube straits. This pleasure cannot be attained without 'rough strife'; and here Marvell has raised a commonplace bawdy paradox into a perception of the nature of physical pleasure. Furthermore, 'the Iron gates of Life' is an unusual phrase in that it has no antecedents that I can discover, but it obviously is an inverse echo of the very familiar 'iron gates of Death'.[99] Perhaps the point is that when passion reaches its perfect state and renders Time powerless, the way that normally leads to death opens up unimaginable prospects of life—life lived so intensely in the moment that it seems to subsume eternity itself within a point of time.[100] And this conquest of time is characterized climactically in the last two lines: 'Thus, though we cannot make our Sun/Stand still, yet we will make him run' (ll. 45–46). The stress on 'Sun' holds up the flow of the enjambment and the Joshua-like idea is reflected in the verse rhythm. But the idea itself is slightly difficult to paraphrase even though its intent is clear.[101] Marvell's hyperbole will not extend to the point of falsifying the facts of existence; the consummation of physical passion cannot do away with Time or eternity, but it can create a world of its own where passion is the only sovereign force. And in this world life and death change their meanings (even including the bawdy colloquial ones) so that the lovers seem to arrest their own decline by the timeless perfection of their union.[102] If this is an illusion, Marvell makes it seem more real than the crude realities of the grave because all the 'World, and Time' are compacted in the 'Ball' of love. The stress on 'Thus' and the caesura that follows it have the force of a triumphant 'Q.E.D.', as if the arguments he has adduced are convincing beyond debate; the poem has sought a way to find more world and time than either the World or Time will provide for the consummation of love, and the answer has been found in consummation itself. The answer alone is unusual in Marvell's poetry, but the attempt to transcend the limits of life in the flesh by seeking the perfection of passion in abstract concepts is of Marvell's very essence.

Notes

1 F. Kermode, 'The Argument of Marvell's "Garden" ', *EC*, II, 3 (July 1952), pp. 225–241.

2 The pertinent volume for students of Marvell is: *The Happy Man: Studies in the Metamorphoses of a classical ideal. 1600–1700, Oslo Studies in English;* 2. *Publications of the British Institute in the University of Oslo* (Oslo, 1954).

3 Røstvig, *The Happy Man*, p. 22.

4 Cf. M. C. Bradbrook, 'Marvell and the Poetry of Rural Solitude', *RES*, XVII, 65 (January 1941), pp. 37–46.

5 'Marvell and the Concept of Metamorphosis', pp. 236–254.

6 ibid., p. 243.

7 ibid., p. 243.

8 Henry Hawkins in *Partheneia Sacra* says that 'if the Pine be higher, it is the weaker; if the Oak be stronger, it is nothing neer so high; and therefore with Antiquitie it was the Symbol of constancie and victorie' (p. 154).

9 Margoliouth, I, p. 226.

10 The tree catalogue has as venerable an ancestry as the flower catalogue of the pastoral poem. Miss Rosemary Freeman, in *English Emblem Books* (Chatto & Windus, 1948), p. 44, refers to 'the classical tradition of the tree lists which came down from Vergil and Ovid and made their way to England in the fourteenth century. There is one in the *Parliament of Foules* as well as that at the burial of Arcite: they appear again in *The Faerie Queene*, in Drayton's *Endymion and Phoebe*, in Matthew Royden's *Elegy on Sidney*, and there is a last remnant of the same tradition in Dyer's *Grongar Hill*'.

11 The lines in *Hortus* that parallel these do not quite clarify the image; rather, they give a more concrete explanation: *Arbor ut indomitos ornet vix una labores;/Tempora nec foliis praecingat tota malignis.* As A. H. King points out in 'Some Notes on Andrew Marvell's Garden', *English Studies*, XX, 3 (June 1938), pp. 118–121, the Latin 'suggests that the *shade* is *short* because the wreath does not go all the way round the head'. But the lines in 'The Garden' are not explicitly humorous as those in *Hortus*; they certainly do not suggest that a single tree is inadequate to the celebration of man's achievements.

12 Justus Lipsius, *Two Bookes of Constancie* (Englished by Sir John Stradling), ed. R. Kirk (*Rutgers University Studies in English*; No. 2) (Rutgers University Press, 1939), p. 135.

13 Eldred Revett, *Poems* (London, 1657), Sig. A6ʳ.

14 *The |Poems of Thomas Randolph*, ed. G. Thorn-Drury (Etchells & Macdonald, 1929), p. 109.

15 *The Poems and Translations of Thomas Stanley*, ed. G. M. Crump (Oxford University Press, 1962), p. 26.

16 *Oeuvres Poétiques de Saint-Amant*, ed. L. Vérane (Paris, 1930), p. 41. Stanley translates this rather freely in 'The Enjoyment': 'Now in

some place where Nature showes/Her naked Beauty we repose;/ Where she allures the wandring eye/With colours, which faint Art out-vye;/Pearls scatter'd by the weeping Morn,/Each where the glitt'ring Flowres adorn' (*Poems and Translations*, p. 23).

17 Vérane, op. cit., p. 32.

18 Odette de Mourgues, *Metaphysical Baroque and Précieux Poetry* (Clarendon Press, 1953), p. 98.

19 A. H. King, 'Some Notes on Andrew Marvell's Garden', p. 119, says that 'Marvell is thinking of the "favourable" as well as "beautiful" sense of *Fair*', as shown by *Alma Quies* in *Hortus*, l. 7.

20 Thomas, Lord Fairfax, 'The Recreations of my Solitude', in *The Poems of Thomas, Third Lord Fairfax*, ed. E. B. Reed. *Transactions of the Connecticut Academy of Arts and Sciences*, XIV, pp. 237–290: (New Haven, 1909), p. 263.

21 Cf. Mildmay Fane, 'My Happy Life, to a Friend':

> I settle to a Countrey life;
> And in sweet retirement there,
> Cherish all Hopes, but banish fear,
> Offending none; so for defence
> Arm'd Capapee with Innocence,

Otia Sacra (London, 1648) Sig. S1^r.

22 William Drummond, *Poems* (Edinburgh, 1616), Sig. E4^v.

23 Kermode's remark in 'The Argument of Marvell's "Garden" ', p. 233, is very persuasive: 'The joke here is to give Quiet and her sister plant-emblems like those of the active life, and to clash the emblematic and the vegetable plants together'.

24 Fairfax, *Poems*, p. 263.

25 Cf. Katherine Philips, writing some years later, in 'A Country-life': 'What blessings doth this World afford/To tempt or bribe desire?/Her courtship is all fire and sword,/Who would not then retire?/Then welcome, dearest Solitude,/My great felicity;/Though some are pleas'd to call thee rude,/Thou art not so, but we' (Saintsbury, I, p. 558).

26 In 'Marvell and the Concept of Metamorphosis', p. 238, Miss Bradbrook says: 'The adjectives of the second line are enough to show that the state of being a lover is not forgone, even if the heraldic use of colours . . . did not make this clear'. I presume she refers to a commonplace of colour symbolism, *viz*: 'Green indeed is the colour of lovers' (*Love's Labour's Lost*, I, ii, 90). But 'green' also was known to symbolize youth, inexperience, fickleness, hope and even lust. (See D. C. Allen, 'Symbolic Colour in the Literature of the English Renaissance', *PQ*, XV, i (January 1936), pp. 81–92). My feeling is that the deliberate characterization of the speaker as a lover of trees is intended to produce

an ironical impression that will be resolved as the problem of passion is resolved in the new myths of stanza IV. Each successive movement in the poem will mark a further step toward transcendence of all limiting passions. I cannot agree, therefore, that this early in the poem 'the passions are looked at without preconception or bias; in the strictest sense, from a metaphysical point of view' ('Marvell and the Concept of Metamorphosis', p. 237). The entire passage seems to me framed in a very conscious irony.

27 Marvell may be thinking of Adam's naming of the trees in Eden. The belief in an innate correspondence between essence and name was important in our period, especially in neoplatonic thought. Adam's uncorrupted intelligence could perceive the only possible name for each plant and animal because he could understand their essences. It is this kind of knowledge toward which the soul reaches, as in stanza VI.

28 A more usual treatment of the relation of love-tokens and trees is this, in Herrick's 'To Groves': 'Yee silent shades, whose each tree here/ Some Relique of a Saint doth weare:/Who for some sweet-hearts sake, did prove/The fire, and martyrdome of love./Here is the Legend of those Saints/That di'd for love; and their complaints:/Their wounded hearts; and names we find/Encarv'd upon the Leaves and Rind'; *The Poetical Works of Robert Herrick*, ed. L. C. Martin (Oxford, 1956), p. 169.

29 It is hardly necessary to mention that the obvious source for the stories of Apollo and Pan is Ovid's *Metamorphoses*. The two tales appear very close to each other in Book I.

30 King, 'Some Notes on Andrew Marvell's Garden', p. 119: '*Hortus* enables us to see in *retreat* a metaphor of the cloister ... (*Hic Amor, exutis crepidatus inambulat alis* 32) and of the field, the soldier giving up (*Enerves arcus & stridula tela reponens* 33)'. Miss Bradbrook says merely: '*Retreat:* not primarily in the military sense' ('Metamorphosis', p. 238).

31 'Marvell and the Concept of Metamorphosis', p. 239.

32 'Some Notes on Andrew Marvell's Garden', pp. 119–120.

33 'A complaint against Cupid that he never made him in Love', *Poems*, pp. 35–40. Cf. also Waller, 'The Story of Phoebus and Daphne, Applied', where he sums up the myth's import: 'Like Phoebus thus, acquiring unsought praise,/He catched at love, and filled his arms with bays', *The Poems of Edmund Waller*, ed. G. Thorn Drury (London, 1893), p. 52.

34 'Marvell and the Concept of Metamorphosis', p. 239.

35 'Some Notes on Andrew Marvell's Garden', p. 120.

36 Cf. Robertson, 'The Doctrine of Charity in Mediaeval Literary Gardens', p. 26.

37 Cf. Hawkins' catalogue of famous gardens in *Partheneia Sacra*, p. 11:

'I Speake not heer of the *Covent-Garden*, the garden of the *Temple*, nor that of the *Charter-House*, or of *Grayes-Inne Walkes*, to be had and enjoyed at home; nor of the *Garden* of *Padua*, or of *Mountpelier*, so illustrious for Simples. I speake not of the Garden of *Hesperides*, where grew the golden Apples, nor yet of *Tempe*, or the *Elizian fields*. I speake not of *Eden*, the Earthlie Paradice, nor of the *Garden* of Gethsemany . . . but . . . of Thee, that GARDEN so knowne by the name of HORTUS CONCLUSUS'.

38 For a very different view of the virtues of the contemplative's garden, see Henry Peacham's *Compleat Gentleman* (1634), p. 2: 'For since all Vertue consisteth in Action, and no man is borne for himself, we adde, beneficiall and usefull to his Country: for hardly they are to be admitted for Noble, who . . . consume their light, as in a darke Lanthorne in contemplation, and a Stoicall retirednesse' (quoted in Freeman, *English Emblem Books*, p. 72).

39 Legouis, *Andrew Marvell*, p. 45.

40 Empson's note (*Some Versions of Pastoral*, p. 132) is convincing: '*Curious* could mean "rich and strange (nature), improved by care" (art) or "inquisitive" (feeling towards me, since nature is a mirror, as I do towards her)'. Only the last suggestion is perhaps over-ingenious. The 'feeling toward' is amply conveyed by 'reach', and other meanings are more germane to the sense of artifice in the fruit, and to the speaker's wondering reception of the plants' advance.

41 *Some Versions of Pastoral*, p. 132.

42 'Marvell's "Garden" ', *ELH*, 25, 1 (March 1958), pp. 13–22.

43 Cf. *Paradise Lost*, IX, ll. 782–784.

44 *Some Versions of Pastoral*, p. 132.

45 Henry More, 'Cupids Conflict', in *Philosophical Poems of Henry More*, ed. G. Bullough (*Publications of the University of Manchester*. No. CCIX, English Series No. XX. Manchester University Press, 1931), p. 110.

46 Ralph Cudworth, *A Sermon Preached before the Honourable House o, Commons* (Cambridge, 1647) Sig. D2ᵛ.

47 Although the metre is apparently a normal iambic, I think there should be a stress on 'its' to indicate the distinction between the pleasures of mind and of the senses.

48 See Empson's idea (*Some Versions of Pastoral*, p. 125) that the work is part of the metaphor of the mind as a sea, and refers to the ebbing of the tide. I think Marvell means to imply a more animate and willed act, with little of the cyclical passivity of ocean tides.

49 Margoliouth (I, p. 226) cites Sir Thomas Browne, *Pseudodoxia Epidemica*, III, xxiv. But Browne is far from accepting the received opinion uncritically. He says 'that all Animals of the Land, are in their kind in the Sea . . . is a tenent very questionable, and will admit of

restraint'. Browne's objection is that in believing the 'tenent' we 'restrain the hand of God, and abridge the variety of the creation'. (*The Works of Sir Thomas Browne*, ed. G. Keynes, 4 vols. (Faber & Faber 1964), II, pp. 242–244.) However, Henry Hawkins in *Partheneia Sacra* repeats the traditional idea as evidence of the fertility of God's creation: 'They [the seas] are another world in themselves, wherin GOD hath plunged and drencht the diversities hath its like in the *Sea* also' (pp. 236, 246). Legouis (*André Marvell*, p. 125) cites Cleveland, 'On the Memory of Mr. Edward King', ll. 33–34; and Butler, *Hudibras*, Part II, Canto II, ll. 241–244.

50 Margoliouth (I, p. 226) offers as the two possible readings of these lines; 'reducing the whole material world to nothing material' or 'considering the whole material world as of no value compared to a green thought'. Empson (*Some Versions of Pastoral*, pp. 119–120) accepts these, but goes on to the 'seventh Buddhist state of enlightenment'. However, I think he goes even farther afield when he likens Margoliouth's second reading to 'the unconscious animal nature'. How this can be predicated of the obviously creative mind is impossible to see. But he does point out that 'made' in line 47 may refer to the creations of God or of the mind. As my discussion will show, this is a true ambiguity, but the major reference is to the mind's activity.

51 'Marvell and the Concept of Metamorphosis', p. 240.

52 *Theophila*, Canto XIII (The Pleasure of Retirement), stanzas LXIX, LXX (Saintsbury, I, p. 459).

53 *Lachrymae Musarum*, Sig. D2^v.

54 *The True Intellectual System of the Universe*, III, p. 62. Cf. Cassirer, *The Platonic Renaissance in England*, p. 64: 'whatever is perceived, is assimilated to the soul not so much by the powers and properties of that which is perceived as by the activity and agency of the perceiving subject. The mind cannot stand in relation to any object or pass judgment on it, without indirectly expressing its own essence and revealing its original nature. For the mind all objective knowledge is also an act of self-knowledge'.

55 Preface to 'Antipsychopannychia' in *Philosophicall Poems* (Cambridge, 1647), Sig. R6^r.

56 Cf. Cassirer, *The Platonic Renaissance in England*, p. 27.

57 Cf. Plotinus: 'Since the sense world is an animal which embraces all animals, since it derives both its existence and its manner of existence from a reality different from itself, a reality which in turn is derived from Intelligence, it is Intelligence that must contain all archetypes and be that intelligible world which Plato calls "the truly real animal" ' (*The Philosophy of Plotinus*, ed. J. Katz, p. 37); 'The self-knower knows himself by Divine Mind with which he becomes identical,—knows

himself as no longer man but as a being that has become something other through and through; he has thrown himself over into the superior order, taking with him only that better part of the soul which alone is winged for the intellectual Act and gives the man, once There, the power to garner what he has seen' (*The Essence of Plotinus*, ed. G. H. Turnbull (New York, 1934), p. 160).

58 'The Doctrine of Charity in Mediaeval Literary Gardens', p. 26.

59 Robertson, op. cit., p. 25.

60 Quoted in Røstvig, *The Happy Man*, p. 121.

60 Cowley, 'The Tree of Knowledge', ll. 1–8, *Poems*, pp. 45–46.

62 Cf. the Elder Brother's speech in *Comus*, ll. 375–380, where Wisdom herself, accompanied by Contemplation, appears as a bird; *Complete Poems*, p. 99.

63 Cf. Lord Herbert, 'A Meditation upon his Wax-Candle burning out':

> Or if as cloid upon this earthly stage,
> Which represents nothing but change or age,
> Our Souls would all their burdens here devest,
> They singly may that glorious state acquire,
> Which fills alone their infinite desire
> To be of perfect happiness possest.
> (ll. 49–54; *Poems*, pp. 83–85)

William Hammond in 'The World' has two couplets that combine this image with one that foreshadows ll. 55–56 of 'The Garden':

> Stript of the flesh, in the clear spring
> Of truth she bathes her soaring wing,
> On whom do all ideas shine,
> Reflected from the glass divine.
> (Saintsbury, II, p. 508)

64 A very slight bit of evidence may be this, from Fane's 'My Happy Life, to a Friend', in *Otia Sacra*, where the shade and the birds' song are connected externally with religious poetry:

> a well-grown Tree;
> Under whose Shades I may reherse
> The holy Layes of Sacred Verse;
> Whilst in the Branches pearched higher,
> The wing'd Crew sit as in a quier.

65 This is another symbol that hardly needs supporting references since there are so many examples in the poetry and prose literature of the period. But cf. Fane, 'Annus annulus, etc. Diminutione largimur', stanza 2, *Otia Sacra*, Sig. CI^r; and the following, from Henry More's *Psychozoia*, (*Philosophical Poems*, pp. 15–18):

And this I wot is the Souls excellence,
That from the hint of every painted glance
Of shadows sensible, she doth from hence
Her radiant life, and lovely hue advance
To higher pitch, and by good governance
May wained be from love of fading light
In outward forms, having true Cognizance,
That those vain shows are not the beauty bright
That takes men so, but what they cause in human spright.

(Canto, I, st. 12)

For who can it unfold, and reade aright
The divers colours, and the tinctures fair,
Which in this various vesture changes write
Of light, of duskishnesse, of thick, of rare
Consistencies: ever new changes marre
Former impressions. The dubious shine
Of changeable silk stuffs, this passeth farre,
Farre more variety, and farre more fine,
Then interwoven silk with gold or silver twine.

(Canto I, st. 22)

The 'various light' is often used to symbolize the rainbow of God's Covenant, but the context does not seem to admit that as a primary meaning in 'The Garden'.

66 In his edition of Marvell, Grosart (I, p. 64) gives examples of actual floral sundials, including the hourly schedules of the flowers' opening and closing.

67 *Andrew Marvell*, p. 64.

68 'Some Notes on Andrew Marvell's Garden', p. 121. Bradbrook (*Andrew Marvell*, p. 64) adds 'Marvell's Latin has a kind of pun in *fragrantia signa*; they would normally be *flagrantia*, burning'.

69 'Some Notes on Andrew Marvell's Garden', p. 121: '*Hortus thymo* shows that the English has a pun on *time*—"time" and "thyme".... The pun requires a wider sense than "calculate" for *Compute*; but such a wide sense existed in the 17th century—"take into consideration" O.E.D. Compute v. i. d. And that Marvell is in the punning mood just here is shown by the *Hortus Signare*, which he spells with a capital letter in order to bring out the punning references to *Signa*, the signs of the zodiac'.

70 Margoliouth (I, p. 224) conjectures that Theophila Cornewall, daughter of William Skinner, was meant.

71 Cf. Robert Heath, 'On Clarastella walking in her Garden' (*Clarastella*, Sigs. B9ᵛ–B10ʳ); William Hammond, 'The Walk' (Saintsbury, II, pp. 489–490).

72 Margoliouth (I, p. 224) compares Carew, 'Upon the King's sicknesse', l. 37, for the phrase 'Darling of the Gods'; but it would seem to be a commonplace.

73 Cf. Summers, 'Marvell's Nature', p. 134.

74 Margoliouth, I, pp. 36–37.

75 See especially pp. 302–303.

76 F. Kermode, 'Definitions of Love', *RES*, N.S. VII, 26 (April 1956), pp. 183–185; 'The only poem I have come across that bears any relation to Marvell's enormous celebration of despair in love is Desportes' "Le mal qui me rend miserable" '.

77 Kermode, 'Definitions of Love', p. 184.

78 Cf. Heath, 'The Quare: What is Love?', in *Clarastella*, Sig. B6ᵛ: "'Tis a child of Phansies getting,/Brought up between *Hope* and *Fear*'. In the same volume, in 'To one blaming my high-minded love', Heath writes: 'Love makes equality; nor wil admit/Finites should bound an Infinite' (Sig. B7ʳ).

79 *Andrew Marvell*, pp. 56–57: 'In the seventeenth century, "strange," besides its meanings of "unaccountable" and "surprising", meant "coyness ... unwillingness to accede to a request or a desire," (OED). The qualities "strange" and "rare" are given geometrical form in the parallel lines: "strange", because they never meet; "rare," because one, and only one, line can be drawn through a given point parallel to a given line.'

80 The phrase is deliberately paradoxical, and plays on the contemporary theories (especially Descartes') of the differences between the metaphysical categories of thought and extension. They were held to be mutually exclusive; Marvell's 'soul' can represent either soul or body.

81 Cf. 'The Garden', l. 7.

82 Cf. Henry King, 'The Boy's answere to the Blackmore', *The Poems of Henry King*, ed. M. Crum (Oxford University Press, 1965), p. 151.

83 In 'The Search', ll. 43–46, George Herbert characterizes the distance between Divine and human will by saying that, by comparison, 'the poles do kisse'; (*Works*, pp. 162–163).

84 'And as a straight line continued grows a circle, he had given them so infinite a power, that it was extended unto impotency'; *The Rehearsal Transpros'd* (Grosart, III, p. 146).

85 For a different example of the use of theories from physical science, cf. Carew, 'Incommunicabilitie of Love', *Poems*, p. 62; Herrick, 'Upon Love': 'Love is a Circle, and an Endlesse Sphere', *Poetical Works*, p. 274.

86 'Impossibilities', ll. 9–13, in *The Mistress*, included in *Poems*, p. 130.

87 The 'coy' mistress, to begin with, was a commonplace; cf. Cowley, 'The Request', *Poems*, pp. 65–67; Randolph, 'A complaint against

Cupid that he never made him in Love', *Poems*, pp. 35–40. Examples could be multiplied.

88 See E. E. Duncan-Jones, 'Notes on Marvell's Poems' *NQ*, 198 (October 1953), pp. 430–431.

89 The 'conversion of the Jews' was to precede the establishment of Christ's kingdom on earth; at least this was the interpretation put upon passages in Revelation, Daniel, Isaiah, and other prophetic books by Puritan sectaries. At mid-century the Fifth Monarchists were pre-eminent among many millennarian groups preaching the imminence of the Second Coming. See Christopher Hill, *Intellectual Origins of the English Revolution* (Oxford University Press, 1965), pp. 269–270; *Puritanism and Revolution* (Secker & Warburg, 1964), pp. 323–324; see also Ernest Lee Tuveson, *Millennium and Utopia* (Harper & Row, 1964), pp. 76–78 & 85–86.

90 See J. V. Cunningham's comments in 'Logic and Lyric', *MP*, LI, 1 (August, 1953) pp. 33–41.

91 This is Pierre Legouis' suggestion in 'Marvell and the New Critics', *RES*, N.S. VIII (November 1957), pp. 382–389. He rejects the Aristotelian hypothesis because Marvell's term is an 'abstraction'. Yet surely the point of the conceit is to associate the qualities of an abstract concept of the soul with the real passion of the lover. The wit lies precisely in saying that his love will grow with the same relentless insistence that describes the development of the 'vegetable soul' of plants. Dennis Davison in 'Notes on Marvell's "To His Coy Mistress" ', *NQ*, N.S. 5 (December 1958), p. 521, compares this from Lord Herbert's 'Sonnet' 'You well compacted Groves . . .': 'A self-renewing vegetable bliss?' But Herbert refers specifically to the imagined emotions of the trees he is addressing.

92 Cf. Carew, 'To A. L. Perswasions to love', ll. 55–58, *Poems*. pp. 4–6; Cowley, 'My Dyet', stanza 3, *Poems*, p. 89.

93 Cf. Herrick's 'Upon a delaying Lady': 'I scorne to be/A slave to state:/And since I'm free,/I will not wait,/Henceforth at such a rate,/For needy Fate', *Poetical Works*, p. 137.

94 Margoliouth suggested first in 'Marvell and Cowley', *The Saturday Review*, CXXVII, 3319 (7 June 1919), pp. 550–551, that 'Desarts of vast Eternity' is an echo of 'And all beyond is vast *Eternity*' in Cowley's 'My Dyet'. But he did not point out that the poem immediately preceding 'My Dyet' in *The Mistress*, 'The Wish', contains the line 'In *desarts Solitude*', which makes the possible source complete. 'Vast Eternitie' appears in Herrick's 'Eternitie', and 'Vast Eternity' in Benlowes' *Theophila*, V, xii. In a poem by J. Cave in *Lachrymae Musarum* we find: 'Whose every Marble page as vast doth look/As th'immense Volume of Eternity'.

95 Cf. Crashaw, 'To the Name above every name, the Name of Jesus':
'What did Their weapons but with wider pores/Inlarge thy flaming-
brested Lovers/More freely to transpire/That impatient Fire', *Poetical
Works*, pp. 239–245.

96 The Folio gives 'glew' in line 34. Margoliouth's original conjecture
was that 'the 1681 printer repeated the "g" at the end of *morning*'. He
gives examples of the use of 'lew' to mean 'warmth' (1st ed, I, p. 224).
In the revised edition of Marvell's poems (1952) Margoliouth returns
to Cooke's reading (1726), 'dew'. Macdonald (p. 168) points out that
Bodleian MS. Eng. poet d. 49 has 'glew' and 'dew' as the rhyme-
words in ll. 33–34. 'Dew' certainly seems to be the preferable reading
for line 34.

97 Cf. Fairfax, 'The Recreations of my Solitude': 'By teeth of all
devouring time', *Poems*, p. 267.

98 For another significance, cf. Lovelace, 'Paris's Second Judgement':
'What pity the whole World is but one Ball', *Poems*, p. 179.

99 Sometimes these are the 'brazen Gates of Death', as in Henry More's
'An Hymn Upon the Resurrection of Christ'. The image comes
originally from the legend of Christ's harrowing of Hell; in the
Gospel of Nicodemus the gates of Hell are of iron. Biblical sources may
be found in Psalms 107:16 and 9:13. Only in Matthew 7:13 is there a
suggestion of Marvell's use, in the well-known 'strait is the gate . . .
which leadeth unto life'. For a Marxist interpretation of these lines,
see C. Hill, *Puritanism and Revolution* (Secker & Warburg, 1958),
pp. 337–366. Speaking of the 'Coy Mistress' as a whole, Hill says 'the
laxity and ease of the *rentier* ruling class are contrasted with the effort,
asceticism, concentration typical of Puritanism and commercialism.
And . . . iron symbolizes the harshness and impersonality of this world
which we *must* accept'. Mr Hill seems to forget that sweetness is
combined with strength in Marvell's image; more important, he
seems to forget what the poem is about.

100 Although Mr Hyman (*Andrew Marvell*, p. 62) recognizes that the iron
gates are the traditional guardians of Hell, he insists that 'The intensity
of the sexual union, therefore, leads to death in both senses of the
word'. This is riding one's hobby-horse unmercifully. Marvell is
probably alluding to the slang meaning of 'death', but the point of the
couplet is that *these* gates open to life, that *this* consummation is not
subject to the usual metaphor of death. The point is supported by
the poem's final couplet.

101 Miss Bradbrook (*Andrew Marvell*, p. 44) explains that: 'The final paradox
suggests that though the lovers cannot control Time, yet *a fortiori* it
is their energy alone that supplies the motive power of existence
whereby Time is created'.

102 Cf. the 'Song' in Jasper Mayne's *The Amorous Warre* (1648): 'Let us imploy its treasure,/And make shade pleasure;/Let's number out the Houres by Blisses,/And count the Minutes by our Kisses./Let the Heavens new Motions feel;/And by our Imbraces wheele./And whil'st we try theWay,/By which Love doth convey/Soule into Soule;/And mingling so,/Makes them such Raptures know,/As makes them entranced lye/In mutuall Extasy:/Let the Harmonious Spheares in Musicke rowle' (Sig. H2^r); Cf. John Hall, 'The Lure': 'we'll now essay/ To piece the scant'ness of the day,/We'll pluck the wheels from th' chariot of the sun,/That he may give,/Us time to live/Till our scene be done' (Saintsbury, II, 195).

*Professor Kermode, in *The Selected Poetry of Andrew Marvell* (New English Library Limited, 1967), p. 108, reads 'is' for the 'in' of the Folio; although it is an emendation one would like to follow, he gives neither authority nor reason for it.

5

The Country House Pastoral

Few of Marvell's poems can be dated with even relative certainty, but 'Upon the Hill and Grove at Bill-borow' and 'Upon Appleton House, to my Lord Fairfax' were written in all probability during the two years, 1651–1653, that Marvell spent as tutor to Mary Fairfax, the Lord General's daughter, at Nunappleton in Yorkshire.[1] Fairfax resigned his commission as commander of the Parliamentary armies in 1650, at the age of thirty-eight, in protest against carrying on the war with Scotland, and retired to his family estate at Nunappleton. Presumably he brought Marvell with him from London, and the poet left Fairfax's household only to seek office under the Protectorate, and with the sponsorship of Milton.[2] At the time of his retirement Fairfax's was the best-known military name in Europe, and both complimentary poems that Marvell wrote display a full awareness of the true height of eminence from which Fairfax had chosen to descend. The Lord General is reputed to have been immensely fond of the countryside and especially of his ancestral lands,[3] and we can see in his few amateurish poems a sincere taste for rural solitude and for the religious, contemplative life.[4] It is hard to imagine a household that could have been more congenial to Marvell at this period in his life than this of the grave, devout, well-read, and battle-proved Lord General Fairfax. And the poems Marvell wrote partially in his honour not only reflect his typical interests in pastoral scenes and the virtues of rustic simplicity, but go far into the problems raised by Fairfax's career itself. They consider the different kinds of courage that his own life and the public stage demand of a man, and weigh the relative excellences of a life of action against the life of inner meditation and individual pursuit of good. The debate between the active and the contemplative life had been carried on since the beginnings of

Greek philosophy, but Marvell's poetry seems to resume the entire course of its dialectic, again without reaching a clear resolution. This debate is very much present beneath the show of other concerns in 'Bill-borow' and 'Upon Appleton House'; and, as we shall see, it forms the true core of 'An Horatian Ode', which must have been written not long before the Fairfax poems.

The two poems to Fairfax are connected as well with the genre that G. R. Hibbard has named the 'country house poem'.[5] If we exclude Horace's descriptions of his Sabine farm (because they lack the characteristic moralized description and are addressed to other purposes than personal compliment) the genre's history runs from Jonson's 'To Penshurst' through Carew's 'To Saxham' and Herrick's 'A Country-life' to its late development in Pope's Epistle 'To Burlington', the fourth of the *Moral Essays*. Denham's *Cooper's Hill* shares some of the methods and aims of the genre in so far as Denham uses features of landscape and architecture as illustrations of his historical and moral arguments; but it does not show the same intimate relation to a specific society and its *mores* that distinguishes the 'country house poem' proper. In discussing 'Upon Appleton House' I shall try to demonstrate what force Marvell draws from this form of socially conservative compliment and where it is that his poem differs significantly from Jonson's or Carew's. But I shall be better able to isolate the elements of this peculiar blend of flattery, natural detail, and architectural theorizing if we look first at 'Upon the Hill and Grove at Bill-borow. To the Lord Fairfax'.[6]

As Sir Clements Markham tells us,[7] Bilborough Hill is a few miles north and west of Nunappleton; it rises 145 feet above sea-level, and what we know of the hill fails to correspond to several things Marvell says about it.[8] But there are two facts which Marvell omits to mention that are more important for understanding the poem than the details about which he is so inaccurate. One is that Bilborough, aside from Nunappleton, was Fairfax's favourite place in the entire countryside to walk and contemplate. The other is that if Marvell had been looking for a grander and more conspicuous eminence with which to symbolize Fairfax's relinquished glory, he could have found several close by. To the south Hambleton Hough and Brayton Barf both stand much higher than Bilborough; and in the distance to the west the hills of Yorkshire present a formidable, almost mountainous, appearance. But Marvell's perception of meaning within the forms of nature is far removed from the concepts and poetic techniques of the Romanticists. He is not creating a natural symbolism to express human thoughts and emotions, nor to replace the outworn figures of classical mythology. Rather, he finds in the ordered English countryside itself the expression of the moral values he is celebrating in Fairfax. It is almost impossible to say whether this order is truly discovered or whether it is imposed by the poet's mind, that perceives correspondence and pattern throughout the joint realm of nature and man. The case is simpler when he deals with a formal garden or, as in 'Upon Appleton House', with a building; for there the metaphors must be consistent with the nature of a setting that has been fashioned by conscious art. But in the Bilborough poem we can observe the technique of the *paysage moralisé* in comparative purity, since the object to be interpreted and personified is completely natural, and yet is as expressive of the poet's meanings as the floral dial of 'The Garden'.

'Upon the Hill and Grove at Bill-borow' begins, indeed, with precisely this argument, as if to make clear to the reader that the question of the morality of man's shaping of nature is not at issue here:

> See how the arched Earth does here
> Rise in a perfect Hemisphere!
> The stiffest Compass could not strike
> A Line more circular and like;
> Nor softest Pensel draw a Brow
> So equal as this Hill does bow.
> It seems as for a Model laid,
> And that the World by it was made.
>
> (ll. 1–8)

The poem will characterize the moral perfection of Fairfax's retirement from the battles and political disagreements of the Civil War; if the hill is to be taken as the natural scene and counterpart of his retreat to the country, then it, too, must be shown to be perfect in its own fashion. Legouis (*Andrew Marvell*, p. 58), in trying to analyse this technique, says of Marvell's brain that 'out of its object it abstracts the essential quality, which it substitutes for the object and on which it works, making it live and shine anew by dint of unexpected metaphors and of comparisons that suddenly bring to light unsuspected analogies'. We can accept this only with the qualification that 'the essential quality' need not be in the object described, but may come from the larger subject of the poem, or indeed from the poet's argument to which the objects themselves are only illustrations. Legouis goes on in this passage to compare the Fairfax poems to Donne's 'The Storme' and 'The Calme', since he feels that Marvell learned from Donne the method of viewing nature only with an eye to extracting ideological significances. The statement cannot quite be reconciled with the remarks of many of Marvell's critics about the poet's great sensitivity to natural scenes, and his distinction among his contemporaries for the precise observation of the details of flora and fauna. A more meaningful comparison with Donne might have been made on the basis of the obvious impulse in 'Upon the Hill and Grove at Bill-borow' to express an encompassing moral idea by means of a specific image, or by a figure that reverses the roles of macrocosm and microcosm. Thus, the trope that Marvell and Donne share most typically is not exactly synecdoche, but the pretence of understanding a synecdoche literally. The hyperbolic statement of lines 7–8 is a good illustration; in 'A Valediction: of weeping' the famous image of the globe works by Donne's insistence that a plain ball becomes '*All*' by the skill of the map-maker. The idea gains its force only by our agreeing to understand '*All*' as both the world itself and the entire universe of material and intellectual creation. Marvell's trope is much less ambitious, but just as radical in its implications. The hill, in its hemispherical perfection, seems to be a model rather than a natural occurrence; to carry the notion one step further is to see that the hill must have served for the model upon which the world itself was made, which is to reverse the usual order of taking the world as the archetypal sphere. What the trope accomplishes in the poem is merely to add another dimension to the imagined 'perfection' of the hill, but also it concentrates our interest on this particular plot of ground, a concentration that is necessary to our later agreement that Fairfax was right to abandon the great sphere of the world in favour of this smaller, but more perfect, model.

The first stanza also manages, almost in passing, to create an incipient scale of values to govern the rest of the poem. We are told that nature here has outdone both science and art in drawing a hemisphere; the compass is surpassed and the 'Pensel' cannot hope to equal nature's instinctive skill. It is possible that the 'Brow' that is not so 'equal' as Bilborough Hill could be found in many of the portraits of aristocratic ladies Marvell remembered at the court of Charles. Those brows represented the painted arts of both the cosmetician and the portraitist, and both are unequal to the unthinking beauty of natural form.

Nevertheless, these are petty targets compared with the graver moral concerns Marvell means to touch. The mountains that must have been within sight as he stood on Bilborough provide the next instance of visual support for his argument:

> Here learn ye Mountains more unjust,
> Which to abrupter greatness thrust,
> That do with your hook-shoulder'd height
> The Earth deform and Heaven fright,
> For whose excrescence ill design'd,
> Nature must a new Center find,
> Learn here those humble steps to tread,
> Which to securer Glory lead.
>
> (ll. 9–16)

In a poem in praise of a man who has given up the most powerful position in an army that has triumphed over one of the world's most stable monarchies we must expect some attack on worldly ambition, especially since 'modest contentment' is the indispensable theme of both pastoral verse and the literature devoted to the virtues of contemplation and religious solitude. But in so far as Marvell shared these sentiments with Fairfax, it is all the more important to remember this passage and others like it in 'Upon Appleton House' when we come to consider 'An Horatian Ode'. Apparently Marvell was willing to grant that man's own mind could conceive of the necessity for abandoning the world of warfare and competition, but could find in Cromwell's irresistible drive to power the evident hand of God. Although the two Fairfax poems are filled with symbolic references to a universe of absolute values, there is no explicit mention of the religious inspiration of the Lord General's surrender of power.

As if in deference to the large metaphor on which the stanza is constructed, the word-play is neither obtrusive nor very complicated; it maintains only the dual reference to visual shape and to moral quality. Thus, the mountains are 'unjust' in that they show brute ambition, but also in that they are out of proportion; in the same way they are 'ill design'd'—as if drawn by a poor crafts-man, but also as if they reveal their sinister purposes in their very shape. Nor is Marvell modest about the predictable consequences of mountainous ambition; the idea of Nature searching for a 'new Center' may owe something to the rudimentary science of geology, or to astronomy, but as we have seen in 'A Dialogue Between The Resolved Soul, and Created Pleasure', the earth's centre was the material symbol for the stability of the universe itself.

The 'humble steps' that describe the slope of Bilborough may suggest something of the life of religious humility, as indeed may 'securer Glory'; but the latter phrase seems to be a pun on the meanings 'safe' and 'without care' of 'secure'. Furthermore, this is no doubt an honest view of the fact that Fairfax is now out of danger of actual combat, and the poem goes on to accentuate the gentleness of the hill as a sign of the true 'way of the conqueror'.

> See then how courteous it ascends,
> And all the way it rises bends;
> Nor for it self the height does gain,
> But only strives to raise the Plain.
>
> (ll. 21–24)

A rhetorician's handbook would define this as personification, but this is not the *prosopopoeia* whose importance Miss Tuve has demonstrated in Marvell's pastoral poems and his versions of the débat.[9] To speak of the hill as 'courteous' is perhaps to animate it in a fairly circumscribed way, but it also serves to sketch in a picture of true courtesy, which for the seventeenth century was not defined by court manners but especially by its handling of responsibilities toward lesser beings.[10] Thus Fairfax's rejection of personal ambition is tempered by his due recognition of what he yet owes to his country because of the talents and the position with which he has been graced. Whether he can fulfil these obligations in some other way than by leading the Parliamentary armies is one of the questions to which 'Bill-borow' is addressed. The suggestion that his magnificence is directed only toward elevating the general state of England (ll. 23–24) should be considered in relation to the criticism of the Levellers in 'Upon Appleton House', LVII, where Marvell charges them with wanting to cut society down to the lowest level of spurious equality rather than lead it to the heights of civilization that can be marked out only by the extraordinary personality. Clearly Marvell's thoughts on democratic government took into account the same factors of instability in English society that forced Cromwell eventually to assume ruling powers he would have much preferred not to need. Although enlightenment is superior to divine right as the sanction of sovereignty, there is no doubt that someone must rule.

The point is made when the poem shifts from observing the humble ascent of the hill to describing its pre-eminent stature in the surrounding countryside.

> Yet thus it all the field commands,
> And in unenvy'd Greatness stands . . .
>
> How glad the weary Seamen hast
> When they salute it from the Mast!
> By Night the Northern Star their way
> Directs, and this no less by Day.
>
> (ll. 25–26, 29–32)

The initial metaphor is quite obviously drawn from Fairfax's military career, but we may think that 'unenvy'd' is either predictive or wishful rather than an accurate adjective. The absence of envy, like the absence of ambition that generates it, is an essential part of the landscape of pastoral retirement; but Marvell has never shown himself unaware that the lack of ambition deserves no great credit for not being envied. For the moment it is sufficient to his purpose to suggest that the hill, like Fairfax, stands as a solid and reliable guide to wandering sailors; it is possible that we are meant to feel the barely worked out allusion to the 'ship-of-state' metaphor. The emphasis is on constancy, as the reference to the Pole Star shows, and its purpose is to show that Fairfax has adhered to unchanging principles of public and private conduct despite the undeniable change in his chosen course.

The existence of the grove of oaks mentioned in stanza V may be open to question,[11] but Marvell's purpose in calling attention to it is clear. Not only is the oak a symbol of civic achievement,[12] but the mention of the 'sacred Shade' gives to the passage the support of a meaningful classical allusion. Greek literature in particular is full of references to sanctified groves that were never touched by hostile invaders;[13] and Marvell's allusion manages to relate the sanctity of the trees to the martial and dedicated spirit of Fairfax, who there assumes the role of the tutelary deity of Bilborough Hill. Thus Marvell ennobles Fairfax's actual preference for this particular plot of earth. And, since part of the intent of the poem is to celebrate the house of Fairfax as well as its most famous scion, the following stanza brings in the Vere family by mentioning the Lord General's wife, Anne. The union of the Veres and the Fairfaxes will be of greater importance in 'Upon Appleton House'; in this poem it is used to expand the portrait of Fairfax himself.

> *Vera* the *Nymph* that him inspir'd,
> To whom he often here retir'd,
> And on these Okes ingrav'd her Name;
> Such Wounds alone these Woods became:
> But ere he well the Barks could part
> 'Twas writ already in their Heart.[14]

(ll. 43–48)

Fairfax's action is regarded as innocent and decorous, since within the terms of the compliment Anne Vere's name is of a worth to match the excellence of the venerable oaks; her name is as fit to be carved as were the trees' own names in 'The Garden'. Marvell carries the idea one step further by saying that the trees had readily taken the letters of her name into their hearts; and the trope would have been recognized as an oblique comment on the love-conventions that we observed in 'The Gallery' and Donne's 'The Dampe'. Apparently the Bilborough oaks are as fervent admirers of Anne as is Fairfax himself.

In a true *prosopopoeia* Marvell goes on to attribute to the sacred oaks not only the power to love but also the feelings of due reverence for the noble house whose essence they symbolize. The identification between the trees and the Fairfaxes is made more comprehensive by an explicit allusion to the role of the Lord General as the local deity of Bilborough Hill.

> And underneath the Courser Rind
> The *Genius* of the house do bind.
> Hence they successes seem to know,
> And in their *Lord's* advancement grow;
> But in no Memory were seen
> As under this so streight and green.

(ll. 51–56)

The literature of the age of royal patronage under Elizabeth and James I is full of such images of courtiers 'growing' as do their masters;[15] here the metaphor is turned upon itself by characterizing the trees as such courtiers. Marvell uses the significantly altered trope only to reinforce the argument that is to end the poem, that Fairfax has acquired more and 'securer' glory in retirement than he had achieved in the most responsible and conspicuous public offices. Other members of the house of Fairfax had distinguished themselves on the battlefields, but the Bilborough oaks have never grown so 'streight and green' as under the tutelage of this supremely modest and conscientious Lord.

This, at least, is the point of view Marvell proposes; but the concluding three stanzas of the poem reveal, I think, if not a full-fledged ambivalence toward the demands of public fame, then a mild note of regret for the greater field of command that Fairfax has left.

> Yet now no further strive to shoot,
> Contented if they fix their Root.
> Nor to the winds uncertain gust,
> Their prudent Heads too far intrust.
> Onely sometimes a flutt'ring Breez
> Discourses with the breathing Trees;
> Which in their modest Whispers name
> Those Acts that swell'd the Cheek of Fame.
>
> (ll. 57–64)

Marvell was as much concerned with the 'rootedness' of a society as was Yeats or Burke; yet, as we shall see in 'An Horatian Ode', the 'shooting' of a meteoric personality into the constellations of heroism was a phenomenon that fascinated as much as it appalled him. In the ordered beauty of Nunappleton, and in the constant presence of a man of Fairfax's nobility, it was easy for Marvell to see the events and intrigues of Parliamentary politics as 'winds uncertain'; and the sharp poignancy of the mention of 'prudent Heads' is increased when we think of Fairfax's resolute opposition to the execution of Charles I.[16] In the last years of the 1640s the strong principles that had guided the leaders of the Revolution appeared to be crumbling before the exigencies of internal dissension between the Parliament and the Army; it was a time, indeed, of 'uncertain winds', and although Fairfax had removed himself from the theatre of temptation, he had salvaged his principles at the expense of his power to give them sway. Marvell looks hard at this truth, and it is the message that the 'flutt'ring Breez' exchanges with the 'breathing Trees.'

> Much other Groves, say they, then these
> And other Hills him once did please.
> Through Groves of Pikes he thunder'd then,
> And Mountains rais'd of dying Men.
> For all the *Civick Garlands* due
> To him our Branches are but few.
> Nor are our Trunks enow to bear
> The *Trophees* of one fertile Year.
>
> (ll. 65–72)

The 'Groves of Pikes'[17] and the 'Mountains . . . of dying Men' resume the moralized imagery of the poem's opening, and sharpen the contrast by referring metaphorically to the objects that had *then* symbolized Fairfax's most famous qualities. The present grove, the oaks themselves, complain that all their leaves are inadequate to honour the past military deeds of Fairfax. And it is the poet's voice that interrupts the colloquy to instruct the trees in the new and more satisfying philosophy of modest retirement.

> 'Tis true, ye Trees nor ever spoke
> More certain *Oracles* in Oak.
> But Peace (if you his favour prize)
> That Courage its own Praises flies.
> Therefore to your obscurer Seats
> From his own Brightness he retreats:
> Nor he the Hills without the Groves,
> Nor Height but with Retirement loves.
>
> (ll. 73–80)

The rebuke is given in the softest admonitory terms, and not without an allusion to the oracle of Dodona[18] that implies the speaker's respect for the oaks as symbols and as the favourites of Fairfax. But notice that the answer contains no suggestion that Fairfax has rejected the arts of warfare and public policy *per se*, even though the historical record makes it perfectly clear that his reasons for giving over his military command were those of very high policy indeed. Marvell will not diminish the achievements of Fairfax even to the extent of admitting that the Lord General had found them less rewarding than the simple solitude he sought at Nunappleton. Rather, the poet explains that the hero's natural embarrassment at the reputation he has won will not permit him to listen to the praises of the oak grove. This courage, unlike the epic bravery that flourishes under legitimate praise, flees modestly from flattery as it never did before the 'Groves of Pikes'; and the only retreat Fairfax has been guilty of is that from 'his own Brightness'. Now Marvell more than many of his contemporaries was drawn to the paradoxical relationships between the mind and its creations. He could not have ignored the overt paradox of the hero disclaiming the effulgent glory he had earned through his proper actions. It cannot be explained; but it can be turned into, in a poem limited as this is to the praise of a public figure who has negated the very qualities that have created him, the logical basis for praise. This is the ingenious method of 'Upon the Hill and Grove at Bill-borow', and we shall see Marvell attempting to do something similar in 'An Horatian Ode'. He sums up his pseudo-logical demonstration by the deliberately paradoxical lines: 'Nor he the Hills without the Groves,/Nor Height but with Retirement loves' (ll. 79–80), which is not quite the same thing as rejecting the life of fame wholly for the life of contemplative integrity. The implication is strong that Fairfax cannot altogether erase the character that had led him to military supremacy; but Marvell begs the question by transferring the emphasis in the couplet back to the local description that has been present throughout the poem, to be used at any given moment for precise and varying purposes. Here the hill's prominence is said to be of no greater importance than its isolation, and its commanding summit no more significant than the trees that crown it, with a special provision for the natural retreat that Fairfax is said to love. The focus has shifted, rightly, from the hill itself to the character of the Lord General, since the major work of fixing in our minds the correspondence between the two has been done. But we have come far from the original thought of the hill serving as the model for the spherical world; the concluding concept is that Fairfax's principled modesty has imposed its qualities on the landscape. And this is a theme that will be of very great importance in 'Upon Appleton House'.

II

The study of a poetic genre can often reveal more than variations in the techniques and interests of the authors who have practised it. The development of the 'country house poem' from Jonson to Pope can tell us a great deal about such apparently unrelated matters as the changing opinion of the use of wealth in a capitalist state, the relationships between poets and patrons, the ways in which architectural styles reflect the *mores* of a social group, and even the kind of activities that a civilization feels to be most favourably representative of itself. Our view is limited, however, by the fact that all the major writers within the genre of the 'country house poem' are evidently sympathetic with the values represented by the landed gentry of England. The homes and the patrons that people these poems are not in all cases of the nobility, but they are all eminent examples of the English reliance on the land itself as the basic, stable, indispensable form of property that maintains a nation no matter what political, social, or religious convulsions may disrupt the constitutional order. The point of view shared by Jonson, Carew, Marvell, and Pope is in many ways related to the picture of the world I have characterized as 'pastoral'. Simplicity is the ultimate value in manners, artistic style, even in eating and drinking; and the reluctance to compete with the court and the city in pursuit of novelty and extravagance is equally essential in the world of old mansions and bountiful squires. Very often the apparent democracy of the manners of the 'great hall' is deceptive; it is really only a vivid demonstration of the meaning of *noblesse oblige*, and none of our poets would have understood the modern, pejorative meaning of 'condescension'. The rural gentry of England took very seriously their responsibilities toward their tenants; in this case the dictates of political economy coincided very happily with the Christian teachings of the parson's homilies. Indeed, the lordly owners of the great estates understood the mingled privileges and obligations of 'divine right' almost as clearly as Charles I. To shun ostentation became nearly as urgent a duty as to care for the welfare of the families under the lord's jurisdiction. In this sense the art of government was seen to mirror both the state of the soul and the condition of his earthly estate.

Nevertheless, certain significant changes can be observed in the century-long development of the 'country house poem' between

Jonson and Pope. The great houses of the sixteenth century had been centred on the great hall, where most of the family lived and most of the estate's business was done. The life was communal and crude in its amenities; and its relation to the traditions of the Anglo-Saxon moot-halls was strong. Beginning with the late years of James I's reign and extending well into Caroline times, the country house became more and more a showplace, dependent upon the talents of architects imported from France and Italy, and dedicated to progressively more elaborate displays and celebrations of state occasions. Decoration grew more independent of utility, and the appointments, the entertainment, and the food and drink became sumptuous to the point of uncontrolled luxury. By 1731 Pope could write of his emblematic villa of Timon:

> To compass this, his building is a Town,
> His pond an Ocean, his parterre a Down.
>
> (ll. 105–106)

> Is this a dinner? this a Genial room?
> No, 'tis a Temple, and a Hecatomb.
> A solemn Sacrifice, perform'd in state,
> You drink by measure, and to minutes eat.
>
> (ll. 155–158)

One of the main points in Jonson's 'To Penshurst' and Carew's 'To Saxham' had been the measure and proportion that governed the tables of Sidney and Crofts—the 'good sense' that Pope celebrates in 'To Burlington'. But the earlier poets had also made a point of describing the entertainments at Penshurst and Saxham in terms of the rural feast, replete with capons, nuts, apples, and 'rurall cake'.[19] The tenant farmer was as welcome as an unexpected visit from the King, and 'no man tells my cups; nor, standing by,/A waiter, doth my gluttony envy'.[20] Thus moderation is enlivened by freedom and good-fellowship, and the excesses of exotic gluttony and social pretension do not mar the simple warmth of the great country houses of this Golden Age of English hospitality. It is not difficult to see many connections between Jonson's and Carew's visions of the ideal state of social man and the dominant concepts of the pastoral tradition. The facts of social hierarchy are softened by the inherent democracy of the rustic world, and the philosophy of moderation is constantly exemplified in the very material furnishings of the lord's hall and board. Where there is no cramping desire for superior place there can be no envy to warp and wizen the traditional structure of country society. And it is important to the overt assumptions of the 'country house poem' that the buildings themselves were often mere renovations of the original manor-houses of the distant ancestors of the family. Not until later in the century did the fad for new and architecturally elaborate country houses make itself fully felt. The older buildings, which in their solidity and square simplicity seemed to the conservative poets easily available symbols of the virtues of their owners, were replaced by structures that bore witness only to the ephemeral artifice of man, and had no visual relation to either the site or to the civilization that had called them into being. This had not been true in the great days of Elizabethan and Jacobean domestic architecture, which had created a style that expressed both unmistakable Englishness and also the growing prosperity of a country in transition between its agricultural past and its future economic predominance in Western Europe. Foreign architects and craftsmen were brought in to introduce to the English the latest styles of cultures that had developed their artistic tastes at the top of a very steep pyramid of social position. And the advocates of the historical English virtues realized, or thought they realized, that the ornate French and Italian styles could never represent faithfully the spirit of a landed society that entertained, as a matter of course, farmers and villagers in the squire's hall. Much of this feeling may have been the kind of nostalgic chauvinism that does not hesitate to misrepresent historical fact, and to which England was especially subject in the late days of Elizabeth's reign and in the more troubled portions of James I's. But Jonson, Carew, Drayton, Daniel and others were, in a way, creating a national mythology for England, a mythology in which the supreme virtues were those of modesty and generosity. We can see it at work in Jonson's climactic compliment to Penshurst.

> Now, *Penshurst*, they that will proportion thee
> With other edifices, when they see
> Those proud, ambitious heaps, and nothing else,
> May say, their lords have built, but thy lord dwells.[21]

(ll. 99–102)

Marvell's poem takes account of at least two aspects of the idea

Jonson puts forward. The first stanza of 'Upon Appleton House' begins a discussion of the moral significance of the proportions of a noble building. And in stanza IX, while referring to a poem written by Fairfax himself to stand at the entrance to Appleton House,[22] Marvell alludes to the religious view that sees man only as a temporary sojourner on earth.

> The House was built upon the Place
> Only as for *a Mark of Grace*;
> And for an *Inn* to entertain
> Its *Lord* a while, but not remain.

(ll. 69–72)

The Protestant ethic had rejuvenated the belief that material wealth was given by God in 'stewardship' to its possessors on earth, and it was this idea that helped to support the tenets by which men like Fairfax guided their actions as landowners and great lords. Like the king himself, they had been granted by Divine Providence possessions and privileges that yet carried with them important responsibilities toward their dependents. Furthermore, the Protestant belief that each man rehearsed in some measure the life of Christ was also implicit in the image of the world as an inn; and Fairfax's poem makes it clear that in calling Appleton House an inn he was also referring to the world in which man lived so short a part of his eternal life.

But Marvell's poem is never overburdened by religious reference; the 'country house poem' was essentially a secular form, even though the social values it encompassed were usually related to a particular religious world-view. Again we observe how intimately the two sets of ideas were associated in Renaissance England. As Miss Røstvig points out,[23] the inspiration for the genre came originally from Roman poets, and particularly from Martial (*Epigrams*, III, 58) and Horace (*Epodes*, II). Within the classical tradition, the praise of country life was based on the wholesome moderation of rural living, the possibility of contentment with a small, choice acquaintance, and on the continuation of familial and cultural traditions in a place and in a manner untouched by the shifting fads of the city. All this is incorporated into the seventeenth-century genre, but its scope is enlarged by the addition of Christian concepts of the virtue of contemplative retirement and the rejection of worldly temptations. The latter is no longer the pleasant duty of the man of intelligence and taste, but a duty enjoined upon him by God.

'Upon Appleton House', however, goes beyond these typical concerns into various digressions that are more pertinently related to the recurrent problems and ideas of all Marvell's poetry. It is for this that it has often been criticized for lack of coherent structure, and even for lacking the appearance of any internal principle of organization.[24] Indeed, it would be hazardous to suggest one theme, one motif, or one dominant idea that can be described as central to 'Upon Appleton House'. The poem is divided, roughly, into six parts of varying length: the introduction on Appleton House itself; the story of Isabella Thwaites and William Fairfax; the description of Lord Fairfax's garden; the descent into the meadows; the poet's retreat into the woods; and the final address to Mary Fairfax, daughter of the Lord General and Marvell's pupil. There is no narrative or rhetorical device that holds these sections together in any very obvious way; but as the poet's mind and eye turn from one object of concentration to another, we shall see that the meanings he draws from what he sees and what he remembers *are* related, and that they constitute an inventory of most of his characteristic poetic subjects. In particular, the process and the concept of metamorphosis will assume great importance in this very long poem.

The introductory passage on Appleton House consists of the first ten stanzas, but even within this section there is a division between the conceited characterization of the home of the Fairfaxes and the initial note of the poem, outrage with man's presumption and with his wanton extravagances. Indeed the opening stanza recalls several earlier poems in which Marvell had touched on the problem of man's right to interfere with or alter the procedures of nature.

> Within this sober Frame expect
> Work of no Forrain *Architect*;
> That unto Caves the Quarries drew,
> And Forrests did to Pastures hew;
> Who of his great Design in pain
> Did for a Model vault his Brain,
> Whose Columnes should so high be rais'd
> To arch the Brows that on them gaz'd.

> (ll. 1–8)

Notice that no mention is made at first of the constructive achievements of the 'Forrain *Architect*'; his typical act, in Marvell, is to
deplete nature's 'store' by turning abundance into flat or hollow
emptiness. Here the poet speaks with the pained indignation of
Created Pleasure in the dialogue, and with the outraged sympathies
of Damon the Mower—and the fact that the lines also include a
topical allusion to the contemporary craze for continental architects
does not diminish their expressive power. The jokes in lines 5–8
at the expense of the architect are aimed at his pretensions and the
extravagance of his favourite forms, not at the innate skill of the
craftsman in general. We are reminded by the mirror-image of
the arched columns and the raised eyebrows of the 'Brow' of
Bilborough Hill, so 'equal' that it could never be guilty of trying to
amaze simply for the sake of creating a sensation. Marvell would
have a man's home be as responsive to his inner nature as the shape
of Bilborough is to the nature of its rural setting.

Thus the attack on human pretension in stanza II is mounted in
terms of comparison with the artless creatures of nature.

> Why should of all things Man unrul'd
> Such unproportion'd dwellings build?
> The Beasts are by their Denns exprest:
> And Birds contrive an equal Nest;
> The low roof'd Tortoises do dwell
> In cases fit of Tortoise-shell:
> No Creature loves an empty space;
> Their Bodies measure out their Place.

(ll. 9–16)

The emphasis on proportion is one that will need justification as
Marvell goes on to expand the conceit, for the initial point is that
animals take only so much room for their homes as their bodies need.
But to 'express' a man is not quite so simple a task, unless humility
decrees that man shall humble his spirit so that it does not demand to
be represented by material symbols. In one sense man, as an animal,
should require no more 'place' than his body can 'measure out'.
But as a thinking and imagining creature, ambitions he can scarcely
understand drive him to try to transcend his natural limitations.
Marvell's answer is given in tones of mocking scorn:

> But He, superfluously spread,
> Demands more room alive then dead.

And in his hollow Palace goes
Where Winds as he themselves may lose.
What need of all this Marble Crust
T'impark the wanton Mote of Dust,
That thinks by Breadth the World t'unite
Though the first Builders fail'd in Height?

(ll. 17-24)

It has been observed often that Marvell's later satirical poems are precocious examples of a style that would flourish finally in Pope and the earlier Augustans; yet, considering the inherent limits of versification in the octosyllabic couplet, the first two lines of this stanza nevertheless display the ability to characterize and judge in the same phrase, a technique that is vital to Augustan satirical poetry. Indeed, Marvell's judgment is overt to the point of being blatant, as we feel in the indignation of 'Crust', 'impark', 'wanton', and 'Mote'.[25] The tone of outrage in the last couplet carries the verse almost to the edge of obscurity, although the reference to the tower of Babel is clear enough. But the phrase, 'the World t'unite' seems to be not so much a specific conceit as a symbol for the uncircumscribed aspirations of prideful man. The target of the attack is the architect's mistaken assumption that material empires can be represented by sheer magnificence, without regard to the spiritual dimensions of human life.

The corrective vision is the substance of stanzas IV through X; Marvell has his eye on the physical appearance of Appleton House,[26] but in a passage that exhibits both the lessons of Donne and the consequences of 'Clevelandizing' he interprets that appearance to conform to the heroic portrait he continues to draw of Lord General Fairfax.

But all things are composed here
Like Nature, orderly and near:
In which we the Dimensions find
Of that more sober Age and Mind,
When larger sized Men did stoop
To enter at a narrow loop;
As practising, in doors so strait,
To strain themselves through *Heavens Gate*.

(ll. 25-32)

We shall find that 'Nature' is not 'orderly and near' throughout the poem, although Fairfax's famous garden will indeed prove to be a perfectly worked-out symbol of the intelligible order of the natural world. But the events of the meadows and the woods, the 'wild' nature that surrounds Nunappleton, will yield different meanings. At this point Marvell is examining the symbol of the ideal conformity between man and his setting, and the design of Appleton House shows the same respect for innate principles that Bilborough Hill did. The 'more sober Age' that the poet looks back to may be simply an English version of the Golden Age, before the Civil War, before the country was torn by the kind of dissension that reveals the ultimate irreconcilability of the elements of modern society. Then, it may be a reference to an imagined age of purer faith, as the Scriptural allusion would suggest.[27] Marvell is conscious of the religious significance of his image, since in the next stanza he changes the conceit in Donnean fashion to imply that Appleton House will one day be the site of sacred pilgrimages in memory of Fairfax and his wife. And the pilgrims will wonder at the modesty of the building that housed a man of such eminence; it would be blasphemous to permit an allusion to an actual shrine, so Marvell departs from the religious tenor of the conceit to refer to the legendary birthplace of Romulus (l. 40). The comparison is not gratuitous, however, since it does equate Fairfax with a heroic, almost mythic, founder of a great civilization.

Stanza VI takes the suggestion offered by Romulus' 'Bee-like Cell' and transmutes it into a brief discourse on the powers of humility.

> *Humility* alone designs
> Those short but admirable Lines,
> By which, ungirt and unconstrain'd,
> Things greater are in less contain'd.
> Let others vainly strive t'immure
> The *Circle* in the *Quadrature*!
> These *holy Mathematicks* can
> In ev'ry Figure equal Man.

> (ll. 41–48)

Humility, whose symbolic description we have had in 'Upon the Hill and Grove at Bill-borow', becomes in this highly 'metaphysical' passage not only the master architect but a mathematician who can outstrip the most devoted scientists or even cabalists. The paradoxes show that Marvell intended some of his absurd claims to be taken lightly; we can see this in the pun on 'immure', but much more clearly by the fact that in the very next stanza Appleton House itself disproves Marvell's argument that only vain science occupies itself with useless, abstract problems such as the squaring of the circle. The 'laden House', on Fairfax's arrival, strains itself so to honour him properly that 'the *Square* grows *Spherical*' (l. 52). This is indeed 'immuring' the circle in the square, yet it also is a clear and amusing way to describe the cupola atop Appleton House which consisted of a hemisphere set on a flat-sided tower.

The contrast between the 'sweating' house that changes its shape in an effort to accommodate its master's fame and the '*holy Mathematicks*' of humility is informative because the conceit involving the house is one that Dr. Johnson might well have used to illustrate the excesses of the metaphysical imagination, while the latter is a fine example of Marvell's use of abstractions for morally didactic purposes. The difference between the two modes is a sign of the incoherence in 'Upon Appleton House' that draws the criticism of so many readers. Marvell's use of personification does not usually succumb to the temptations of such naive animism; and the house that sweats is, even in this poem, a deviation from the norm of symbolic diction. The stanza that follows returns to the moral preoccupations of the genre, and Marvell, typically, chooses to express them in paradoxes:

> Height with a certain Grace does bend,
> But low Things clownishly ascend.
> And yet what needs there here Excuse,
> Where ev'ry Thing does answer Use?
>
> (ll. 59–62)

The first couplet gives a mocking reprimand to the misguided efforts of the 'swelling Hall'; and it is tempting to believe that Pope might have remembered the second when he wrote: ''Tis Use alone that sanctifies Expence'.[28] But the decorum of the complimentary poem demands that didacticism be more than balanced by detailed, recognizable descriptions; stanza IX returns to the conceited style in order to give us some idea of the place Appleton House assumes in the society around it. Country ways have changed somewhat since the robust democracy of the Sidneys at

Penshurst, but the weight of custom is still felt strongly enough so that Marvell must indicate the scope of Fairfax's responsibilities by referring to both ends of the social scale.

> A Stately *Frontispice of Poor*
> Adorns without the open Door:
> Nor less the Rooms within commends
> Daily new *Furniture of Friends*.
>
> (ll. 65–58)

If we can assume that the italics mean anything definite, we may also assume that Marvell was more pleased with the cleverness of his metaphors than we are likely to be. Nevertheless, it is interesting to note that the tropes work by reversing the normal process of Marvell's figurative verse; here the animate is rendered inanimate and even artificially decorative. And if the device succeeds at all, it is in reinforcing the idea that at Appleton House man, nature, and artifacts are brought into an harmonious whole by the guiding spirit of Fairfax himself, whose modesty and ability leave an impress on the very buildings and lands that bear his name.

Marvell adheres to the conventions of the 'country house poem' by mentioning other localities and places connected by history and by choice with the Fairfax family—Bishop's Hill, Denton, and Bilborough—but he quickly makes it evident that his concern in the poem is not solely with praise of his patron, nor with topography, nor yet with traditional anatomies of the life of pastoral retirement. There is a certain naïveté, apparent nowhere else in his poetry, in his saying: 'But Nature here hath been so free/As if she said leave this to me' (ll. 75–76). The lines that follow, however, are more obviously reminiscent of the arguments put forward in the 'Mower' poems:

> Art would more neatly have defac'd
> What she [Nature] had laid so sweetly wast;
> In fragrant Gardens, shaddy Woods,
> Deep Meadows, and transparent Floods.
>
> (ll. 77–80)

In the light of Marvell's pastoral poems these lines may seem to be an instance of conventional elements he has created for himself, or at least made particularly his own. But this is not simply a casual listing of the elements of 'Nature' that he finds most congenial; the garden, the wood, the meadow, and the flood will be described and interpreted in roughly that order in the later parts of 'Upon Appleton House'.

Before Marvell can examine the natural scene that encloses the little world of the Fairfax home and family, he must give due attention to another requirement of the 'country house poem'— the genealogy of the hero. The convention has clear, if slight, connections with similar elements in the epic; but it is especially fitting in a poem dedicated to Fairfax. For one thing he himself was intensely interested in family history; and for another, the consciousness of personal tradition is an important part of the sense of legitimacy that supports the governance and ethos of the landed gentry. Marvell was obviously attracted by any idea or institution that promised a reasoned stability to any human system; one of the great problems he faced in writing 'An Horatian Ode' was the morality and wisom of destroying 'the great Work of Time'. The recounting of the hero's ancestry in 'Upon Appleton House', especially since it was a history of such public and military distinction, was vital to the purpose of establishing Fairfax as a figure who might serve as a model to a warring and chaotic nation.

But the question remains why Marvell should have devoted so much of his poem—twenty-five stanzas, or almost one quarter of the whole—to the story of Isabella Thwaites and Fairfax's great-great-grandfather. In his compliment to Sir Robert Sidney, Jonson managed to pay homage to his most distinguished relation simply by referring to 'That taller tree, which of a nut was set,/At his great birth, where all the *Muses* met';[29] and Herrick's 'A Panegerick to Sir Lewis Pemberton' takes in several generations in these complimentary lines:

> Thou do'st redeeme those times; and what was lost
> > Of antient honesty, may boast
> It keeps a growth in thee; and so will runne
> > A course in thy Fames-pledge, *thy Sonne*.

> (ll. 41–44)

But Marvell goes back to an incident of the early sixteenth century and relates it with a wealth of detail and a seriousness of dramatic organization that challenge us to explain why so much effort has been spent on what should be an incidental allusion in the body of the poem.

I am not sure that there is a completely satisfactory answer to that challenge, or that Marvell was not, simply, fascinated with the story and unable to refrain from treating it at length. But it is never wise to assume easily that Marvell was not in full, conscious control of his material. By virtue of no great subtlety, we can realize that the story of the virgin imprisoned by nuns and rescued from her captors by the bold and forceful William Fairfax rehearses the situation of Lord General Fairfax himself, retired to the delights of his garden from the dangers and brute realities of the world of the Civil War and Parliamentary strife. And this is puzzling only if we believe that Marvell's attack upon the luxury and Jesuitical subtlety of the Abbess is completely single-minded.[30] For if the basic idea of retirement is being criticized in this long passage, then surely Fairfax's retreat to Nunappleton must be open to some part of that criticism. I think we shall see, rather, that Marvell's treatment of the persuasions of the Abbess reveals the same kind of ambiguity of intent, due to his integrity of vision, that we met in 'A Dialogue between the Soul and Body'. Nor is it beyond Marvell's intellectual powers to discriminate between the unworldly seclusion of a Catholic religious and the consciously chosen retirement of a great man of affairs who had seen his principles betrayed by comrades-in-arms and had perhaps seen that his continuing in office would have led to further dissension within his own party.

That Marvell's attitude toward the story of Isabella's captivity[31] is a complicated one is indicated by the paradox with which he begins the narration:

> We opportunly may relate
> The Progress of this Houses Fate.
> A *Nunnery* first gave it birth.
> For *Virgin Buildings* oft brought forth.

> (ll. 83–86)

In one way this is a glance at typical anti-Catholic beliefs about the behaviour of nuns; but, more important, it is a joke that also includes a truth of English social history. Many of the great estates of England were formed with wealth and land acquired at the dissolution of the monasteries under Henry VIII, and Nunappleton was one of these. Whatever the convent may represent in the poem, it is always the actual foundation upon which the Fairfax house was established and grew. There is an implication that the significance of Fairfax's retirement is somehow related to the values symbolized by the convent, and this is brought out in the first words of the wheedling nun:

> 'Within this holy leisure we
> 'Live innocently as you see.
> 'These Walls restrain the World without,
> 'But hedge our Liberty about.
> 'These Bars inclose that wider Den
> 'Of those wild Creatures, called Men.
> 'The Cloyster outward shuts its Gates,
> 'And, from us, locks on them the Grates.
>
> (ll. 97–104)

Although Marvell will declare later, with a gloating humour that seventeenth-century Protestants were not loath to use toward the defeated Catholics, "Twas no *Religious House* till now' (l. 280), the passage might describe Fairfax's own situation, were it not for the feminine fastidiousness about the 'wild Creatures', men. But 'leisure' and 'innocence' are of the very essence of Nunappleton, nor is the outside world ever forgotten in this sanctuary where the master constructs a garden-fort to protect his citadel against 'ev'ry Sense' (l. 288). However, if Marvell is aware that the nuns' rule of solitude is in some ways comparable to the 'choice of life' made by the Lord General, he is also alive to the double-edged significance of every kind of wall and bar; they may shut out the menacing or deluded world, but they also limit the inmates' own freedom very compellingly.

Once the imagination is drawn within the narrow circle of the convent walls, however, the nun's speech takes on the power of persuasive rhetoric, convincing sensuous detail, and a curiously Marvellian turn of figurative diction. For example, in speaking about the nuns' custom of embroidering saints' lives, the nun interrupts herself to add:

> 'But what the Linnen can't receive
> 'They in their Lives do interweave.
> 'This Work the *Saints* best represents;
> 'That serves for *Altar's Ornaments*.
>
> (ll. 125–128)

The interpenetration of art and life, and the grammatical chiasmus in the last couplet, are typical of Marvell's qualifying wit. But there emerges from her conceited diction a genuine portrait of a clever and determined woman whose piety is at the service of her cunning; the speech of the nun is probably Marvell's most successful attempt at creating a truly dramatic character.

Her appeal to Isabella is not only in the name of the sweetness and sanctity of the nun's life; she also offers her the equivalent of temporal power, and her flattery is addressed to the idea that Isabella's virtues will provide a model for the nuns themselves. Once again, in propounding this argument she uses a phrase that reminds us not only of the sacred plants in 'The Garden' but also of Marvell's frequent allusions to a metamorphosis in which an object becomes its own essence: '"Those Virtues to us all so dear,/ Will straight grow Sanctity when here' (ll. 165–166); the ambiguity in 'grow' is very much like that in the lines on Daphne in 'The Garden'.

Marvell cannot quite persist in his characterization of the nun without paying attention to the notorious reliance of the Catholic Church on the senses, both in its customs and its ritual, to reinforce its abstract dogmas. The stanzas that Miss Wallerstein finds so objectionable (XXI–XXIII) do indeed contain their own commentary on the perversion of the natural delights of sense to illegitimate objects. And, lest we miss the point, Marvell couches the entire passage in terms that must recall the earlier arguments in favour of unadulterated naturalness as against the excesses of artifice.

> 'For such indeed are all our Arts;
> 'Still handling Natures finest Parts.
> 'Flow'rs dress the Altars; for the Clothes,
> 'The Sea-born Amber we compose;
> 'Balms for the griv'd we draw; and Pasts
> 'We mold, as Baits for curious tasts.
> 'What need is here of Man? unless
> 'These as sweet Sins we should confess.
>
> (ll. 177–184)

The sensuality is both subtle and arrogant, but Marvell pushes the effect further in the next stanza, where two nuns lying in bed are described

'As Pearls together billeted.
'All Night embracing Arm in Arm,
'Like Chrystal pure with Cotton warm.

(ll. 190–192)

As in the religious 'Dialogues', Marvell has presented the case of the sensual enemy so well and so attractively here that although we may not think that he is of the nun's party without knowing it, we must at least acknowledge that not the weakest aspect of the convent's threat is the genuine beauty and allure of the life it contains. The impulse to retreat into such a world of soft passivity will be dramatized again later in the poem, when the poet wanders in the wood. And there, too, his desire for contemplative and even mystical solitude will be subject to the same questions that obtain about the justness of Fairfax's decision. Although it is fairly clear that the nun's speech is meant to give a picture of luxurious indulgence that will be rightfully swept away by William Fairfax, and then by the English Reformation, the details of that picture have a powerful grip on Marvell's imagination. Icons, dainties, and silk stuffs do not attract him, but the caressing sweetness of nature does; the point is that the attitude of surrender to either set of temptations is much the same, and this gives to the nun's speech the imaginative integrity of a true and worthy enemy.

By contrast, William Fairfax's cry of 'Hypocrite Witches, hence avant' (l. 205) lacks in finesse what it displays in direct action. The man of action triumphs, of course, not only because historical fact would have it that way, but because Marvell must establish the pedigree of the Fairfaxes in a way that will lead naturally to the deeds of the Lord General. But the victory is not won without a moment of puzzled hesitation, as Fairfax ponders the necessity to take Isabella from the convent by force:

He would respect
Religion, but not Right neglect:
For first Religion taught him Right,
And dazled not but clear'd his sight.
Sometimes resolv'd his Sword he draws,
But reverenceth then the Laws.

(ll. 225–230)

The indecision is resolved, strangely enough, by the poet's reminder that William Fairfax is 'he whose Offspring fierce/Shall fight through all the *Universe*' (ll. 241–242). The actual siege of the convent is painted in burlesque terms; rosaries are compared to 'gingling Chain-shot' and Marvell says of the nuns that their 'sharpest Weapons were their Tongues' (l. 256). It is hard to tell whether the burlesque continues into the next stanza, but there is a touch of amused irony at the vigour with which, 'waving these aside like Flyes,/Young *Fairfax* through the Wall does rise' (ll. 257–258).[32]

At the touch of the man of action the haven of corrupt seclusion crumbles; Marvell compares it to the enchanted castle of legendary tales. And in an instant we are thrown forward from the marriage of Isabella Thwaites and her subsequent inheritance of Nunappleton after the dissolution of the religious houses to the prematurely truncated career of the Lord General himself. The third large movement of the poem begins with an account of the retired warrior's garden, which is as unlike 'wild' nature as it is unlike the stony fortresses it imitates. Fairfax is the hero

> Who, when retired here to Peace,
> His warlike Studies could not cease;
> But laid these Gardens out in sport
> In the just Figure of a Fort;
> And with five Bastions it did fence,
> As aiming one for ev'ry Sense.
>
> (ll. 283–288)

The contrast with the lines from 'An Horatian Ode' could not be more pointed: 'So restless *Cromwel* could not cease/In the inglorious Arts of Peace' (ll. 9–10); and both the rhymes and the thoughts behind them suggest that the problem of the choice between public affairs and passive retirement usurped Marvell's deepest concern during the years between the execution of Charles I and Marvell's departure from Nunappleton. Neither 'Upon Appleton House' nor 'An Horatian Ode' tells us very much, I believe, about Marvell's explicit political affiliations, for both poems are much more profoundly occupied with the question of the right course of action in a revolutionary time than they are with siding with one party or the other. Just as the praise of Cromwell in 'An Horatian Ode' is tempered by the realization of the violence behind his rise to power, so the figure of Fairfax relinquishing the great affairs of state for the pale imitation of martial prowess in his garden is subject to undeniable critical scrutiny.

But Marvell's humour, as always, is complicated. The five-pronged garden 'In the just Figure of a Fort' is seen not merely as a toy model of the real fortresses that had witnessed Fairfax's brilliant leadership not many years before. The image also calls up the connotations of the spiritual fortress that every man is enjoined to construct within himself against the temptations of the corrupt world. As in Spenser's allegory of the House of Alma (*FQ*, II, ix), the senses are regarded not only as the avenues of wisdom but also as gates vulnerable to the assaults of sin.[33] The tradition of picturing the body as a fortress of the spirit stems from medieval literature, but Marvell has justified his use of it by a topical reference to a kind of elaborate garden-decoration that was popular in this time.[34] The spiritual significance of the shape of the garden is ignored, however, in Marvell's eagerness to develop the potentialities for witty conceits inherent in the 'Figure of a Fort', In a style closely related to the ninth stanza of 'The Garden', he elaborates the initial military metaphor so that the garden becomes less a static, formal symbol of a military stronghold than a living model of the life and discipline Fairfax had supposedly left.

> When in the *East* the Morning Ray
> Hangs out the Colours of the Day,
> The Bee through these known Allies hums,
> Beating the *Dian* with its *Drumms*.
> Then Flow'rs their drowsie Eylids raise,
> Their Silken Ensigns each displayes,
> And dries its Pan yet dank with Dew,
> And fills its Flask with Odours new.
>
> (ll. 289–296)

The conceit is worked out with precision, from the bee's drumming of reveille to the flowers' recharging of their imaginary muskets. And whatever Marvell's serious intent in organizing the garden into a military encampment, the strongest impression left by the metaphors is one of gaiety and mental agility. He indulges in a typical metaphysical confusion of senses when he speaks of the 'fragrant Vollyes' shot off by the ranked flowers to salute Fairfax and his daughter as they go through their morning 'tour of inspection' of the garden.[35] And again, in

> Well shot ye Firemen! Oh how sweet,
> And round your equal Fires do meet;

> Whose shrill report no Ear can tell,
> But Ecchoes to the Eye and smell,
>
> (ll. 305–308)

the device of synesthesia is intended to convince us of the justice of the metaphor, as if the strangeness of such deliberate transmutations can itself fix the poet's idea in our minds. The lines that follow,

> See how the Flow'rs, as at *Parade*,
> Under their *Colours* stand displaid:
> Each *Regiment* in order grows,
> That of the Tulip Pinke and Rose,
>
> (ll. 309–312)

return to the purely visual comparison and a fairly orderly kind of wit. But stanza XL, with its echoes of Milton,[36] prepares us for the more weighty interpretation to be placed upon this garden shortly, even though it continues the witty mode of the preceding lines by comparing leaves to folded banners and the stinging bee to the sentry who demands the password on pain of running the intruder through. The preparation is insufficient, however, to allow for the abrupt transition to stanza XLI, which brings in a lament for the vanished peace and concord of England.

> Oh Thou, that dear and happy Isle
> The Garden of the World ere while,
> Thou *Paradise* of four Seas,
> Which *Heaven* planted us to please,
> But, to exclude the World, did guard
> With watry if not flaming Sword;
> What luckless Apple did we tast,
> To make us Mortal, and Thee Wast?[37]
>
> (ll. 321–328)

The order and serenity of the garden at Nunappleton has summoned, irresistibly, the memory of the 'Garden-state' of Britain before the Civil War, and the comparisons between that age and the mythic state of Paradise are not veiled in the least by conceited diction. The image of England as a type of the Garden of Eden was sanctioned by traditional legends and sagas, as well as by the common Elizabethan practice. But Marvell's appeal is given added force by the verisimilitude of the analogy he draws while describing Fairfax's well-disciplined realm. The loss of Paradise is the tragic event that goes almost unmentioned, but it is interesting to notice that Marvell, as well as Milton,[38] thinks of Eden not only as Heaven's most perfect earthly creation, but also as a symbol of perfection constantly threatened by 'the World'. The conditions of external reality have for the moment impinged on the playful contentment of Fairfax's floral regiment, and we are reminded not only of the events of the Civil War itself but also of the failure of the convent to protect itself ultimately from the brute force (albeit legal and justified) of Fairfax's ancestor. To see 'Upon Appleton House' as a fanciful retreat from political reality into a world of rural mindlessness is to misread a poem which at almost every moment is torn between the divergent demands of the world and the self.

Nor would Marvell elevate the condition of the English polity to an image of the fall of mankind if he were merely playing with the analogy. England had indeed become a 'Wast',[39] and men whose loyalties were attached to ancient institutions and the stable procedures of monarchical successions found the knowledge of mortality in the events of 1642–1649. What Marvell cannot say, and what the poem finally cannot tell us, is what was the 'luckless Apple' that brought this all about—was it worldly ambition, pride, or the nerveless taste for ease that banished Englishmen from the paradise Providence gave to them particularly?

When, in stanza XLII, the military metaphor is applied once more to gardens and flowers, it is with the purpose of recalling that imaginary Golden Age from which contemporary England has declined. Then 'Gardens only had their Towrs,/And all the Garrisons were Flowrs' (ll. 331–332); and the point is that this was once the reality, not the mock-reality of Fairfax's flowery militia, whose mimicking of the discipline of the Parliamentary army becomes somehow sinister when seen against the background of a true pastoral, where military discipline was a symbol only of innate natural order. The change is a bitter one for Marvell, as is evident in the tone of the transformations in stanza XLIII.

> The *Gardiner* had the *Souldiers* place,
> And his more gentle Forts did trace.
> The Nursery of all things green
> Was then the only *Magazeen*.
> The *Winter Quarters* were the Stoves,

> Where he the tender Plants removes.
> But War all this doth overgrow:
> We Ord'nance Plant and Powder sow.
>
> (ll. 337–344)

In other words, the gardener *was* once the figure of order and ability, and there was no need for the soldier to pretend to be a gardener. The opposition between images of natural growth and images of military activity owes nothing to the conventional use of military terms in the poetry of courtly love; Marvell has by now established a wide range of symbolic meanings for his natural imagery, and we can judge it by the nostalgic tenderness of line 339, and by the cold perception of man's destructive absurdity in line 344. The evils of the external world have impinged indeed on the carefully shaped miniature world of Nunappleton, and the measure of their effect is given in the unspoken questions of the next stanza.

> And yet their walks one on the Sod
> Who, had it pleased him and *God*,
> Might once have made our Gardens spring
> Fresh as his own and flourishing.
> But he preferr'd to the *Cinque Ports*
> These five imaginary Forts.
>
> (ll. 345–350)

It would be a mistake, I think, to read these lines as if Marvell had been barely able to control his own disapproval of Fairfax's course. He does not underestimate the importance of the will of God in matters of such moment; and further, the choice Fairfax has made and the reasons for it are obviously congenial to Marvell. The poet will follow a similar path in the later parts of the poem. All that can be attributed to the lines legitimately is the same note of regret that informs stanza XLI, especially since the justification of Fairfax that follows is in the same uncompromising terms that we observed in 'Upon the Hill and Grove at Bill-borow'.

> For he did, with his utmost Skill,
> *Ambition* weed, but *Conscience* till.
> *Conscience*, that Heaven-nursed Plant,
> Which most our Earthly Gardens want.
> A prickling leaf it bears, and such
> As that which shrinks at ev'ry touch;

> But Flowrs eternal, and divine,
> That in the Crowns of Saints do shine.
>
> (ll. 353–360)

Aside from the suggestions of mystical ecstasy in the passage describing the poet's sojourn in the woods in stanzas LXXI to LXXVII, this is the nearest approach Marvell makes in 'Upon Appleton House' to the full recognition of the religious beliefs that lie beneath his explicit social and philosophical attitudes. The passage has obvious relations to 'The Garden',[40] and it again emphasizes the virtuous aspect of Fairfax's rejection of the pride of position in favour of inner purity; but it also carries on the implication that virtue as such must always shrink from and be menaced by the outside world. Nowhere in the poem does Marvell weaken the cogency of his dialectic by pretending that the world's attractions are illusory and easily conquered; but at this point he does indicate rather openly that the reward of self-sacrificing integrity can come only in Heaven. Quite clearly, the point of view of this stanza is from 'here below', but Marvell carries his glance at the supernatural realm no further, returning immediately to the contemplation of the scene actually before him. And with the return to the natural setting we find a return to the conceits and ambiguous diction of the lines on the flower-garden.

> The sight does from these *Bastions* ply,
> Th' invisible *Artilery*;
> And at proud *Cawood Castle* seems
> To point the *Battery* of its Beams.
>
> (ll. 361–364)

Now the armament of the flowery fortress is alleged to be the sense of sight itself, and the eye's beam is compared to the shot from a cannon. The idea allows Marvell a joke at the expense of the Archbishop of York, but it also redirects our attention to the world surrounding Nunappleton, since the poet is about to descend into the meadows he has already mentioned, and thus begin the third major portion of the poem. He is moving (or 'escaping', as some critics will have it) from the world of ordered artifice to the realm of nature, the meadows; but he will find that the grass, as reflecting symbol of mortal life, is subject to the same vicissitudes that spoil the perfection of the garden and the greater world outside

—and there will follow the further retreat to the solitude of the woods. But first he must undergo the transformations of the strange meadows.

> And now to the Abbyss I pass
> Of that unfathomable Grass,
> Where Men like Grashoppers appear,
> But Grashoppers are Gyants there.

(ll. 369–372)

Whether Marvell is remembering Lovelace's poem 'The Grasse-hopper'[41] or intending a biblical allusion,[42] the dominant ideas of the passage are the inversion of human and natural characteristics, and the suggestion of the strange visions that arise when the human consciousness immerses itself in the instinctive processes of growing things. Not only is the meadow an abyss, but it is easily and cogently compared to a sea, and the analogy obviously attracts Marvell. He imagines the mowers diving into the depths of the green sea, and the wit with which he compares sailors taking a sounding to the men who 'bring up Flow'rs so to be seen,/And prove they've at the Bottom been' (ll. 383–384), is a lighter version of the extraordinary but similar image in 'Mourning'.

It must be remembered that these are not the meadows with which the Mower Damon was so intimately identified; the poet sees them as a scene of successive wondrous changes, even comparing them to the elaborate stage machinery of the court masques. Marvell uses imagery of the theatre rarely, but always with clear intent;[43] and here his purpose is to strengthen the impression of kaleidoscopic variety in nature, which in turn contributes to our sense of patterns and discipline gone awry. The ordinarily sympathetic pastoral scene now presents itself as a shifting vision of man's history and human folly, so that it becomes more exemplary than comforting. Not only do the visions change as Marvell watches, but we must also be aware of the gradual but unswerving succession of the seasons that moves through the poem as the poet moves through the grounds of Nunappleton. All of nature is in flux, constantly—and 'Upon Appleton House' is one major evidence that Marvell did not long conceive of the natural world as a static emblem of metaphysical truths. He shows himself unfailingly aware of the unceasing process of metamorphosis that dominates both nature and human society.

231

Once he has entered the meadows—and their greenness suggests, as does the appearance earlier of the flowers in Fairfax's garden, that his symbolic journey has begun in the spring—the summer's heat gives way to the season of harvest, and the mowers enter to the accompaniment of a series of images comparing them to the Israelites crossing the Red Sea.[44] The analogy has no meaning deeper than the visual similarity, however, as we can see in stanza L, where the central incident is either an echo or a foreshadowing of the climactic stanzas of 'Damon the Mower'.

> With whistling Sithe, and Elbow strong,
> These Massacre the Grass along:
> While one, unknowing, carves the *Rail*,
> Whose yet unfeather'd Quils her fail.
> The Edge all bloody from its Breast
> He draws, and does his stroke detest;
> Fearing the Flesh untimely mow'd
> To him a Fate as black forebode.

(ll. 393–400)

Death is present in these meadows too, but it is accidental as it was in the 'Mower' poems, and elicits thoughts about individual mortality and the apparent meaninglessness of the way in which death strikes down all creatures. In stanzas LIII and LIV the mowers themselves will be compared to a victorious army, but at this moment the 'Massacre' of birds and grass does not have the diverting embellishments of the panoply and order of armed combat. Fairfax's troopers had been able to believe that slaughter of their enemies was necessary to preserve religion and purify the state. But the murder of the rail occurs with no such sanction, and figures as the sign of gratuitous bloodshed. And Thestylis in stanza LI shows that not all rustics feel the innate sympathy for unspoiled nature that Marvell's pastoral characters usually do. She throws back at the poet his superficial analogy with the escaping Israelites and blasphemously makes use of his own kind of wit to strip the analogy of any religious significance: 'Rails rain for Quails, for Manna Dew' (l. 408). Marvell takes the bloody occasion for a brief homily on the precariousness even of humility in a society where all principles of hierarchy have been overthrown by force.

> Unhappy Birds! what does it boot
> To build below the Grasses Root;

232

When Lowness is unsafe as Hight,
And Chance o'retakes what scapeth spight?

(ll. 409–412)

Heroes fall before the cunning assaults of envious men, and the
lowly are trampled by the sheer force of the march of events; the
only advice the poet can offer contraverts the natural order that
governs the humble rails: 'Or sooner hatch or higher build' (l. 417).

Once again the mower appears as the surrogate of death, but
now his stance is complicated by the machinery of a kind of pseudo-
epic that Marvell constructs around him.

> The Mower now commands the Field;
> In whose new Traverse seemeth wrought
> A Camp of Battail newly fought:
> Where, as the Meads with Hay, the Plain
> Lyes quilted ore with Bodies slain:
> The Women that with forks it fling,
> Do represent the Pillaging.[45]

(ll. 418–424)

It is hard to believe that Marvell fastened on this conceit only
because he was taken with the visual similarities between a newly
mown field and a battlefield (although the image of death as a
reaper was certainly present in his mind); surely the harvest scene
must have impressed him with the ubiquity and the cold casualness
of death, and must have led him to question the elaborate pretences
man erects to justify his acts of organized, political massacre. In
any case, the insouciant figures of the mowers and the women are
dignified in the next stanza by epic and pastoral images.

> And now the careless Victors play,
> Dancing the Triumphs of the Hay;
> Where every Mowers wholesome Heat
> Smells like an *Alexanders sweat*.
> Their Females fragrant as the Mead
> Which they in *Fairy Circles* tread:
> When at their Dances End they kiss,
> Their new-made Hay not sweeter is.[46]

(ll. 425–432)

When Benlowes in Canto XIII of *Theophila* attempted to relate the realities of the pastoral life with the spiritual values they were supposed to symbolize, his ennobling description of the mower was:

> Then, view the mower, who with big-swoln veins,
> Wieldeth the crookèd scythe, and strains
> To barb the flow'ry tresses of the verdant plains.

(ll. 4–6)

The predictable adjectives combine to give an impression of strenuous effort, but they are not aimed at the comparison Marvell is seeking between the mower and the legendary hero. The allusion to Alexander raises the continuing military image to a higher level, while at the same time it underscores the humour of the entire figurative description of the battlefield of hay. But after one last reference to the haystacks as 'Roman Camps' that 'rise/In Hills for Soldiers Obsequies' (ll. 439–440) the stage machinery whirls again and presents the poet with a bare, flat surface (the harvest is over) and becomes, within sixteen lines, one of Lely's canvases, the bull-ring at Madrid, an image of the society the Levellers would create, a cattle-pasture, and a scene from Davenant's *Gondibert*, successively. The metamorphoses throng in upon the mind of the poet, and once he has thought of the meadow, shaven first by the scythe and then by the grazing cattle, as a reflecting glass, the image immediately leads to successive conceits based on the resemblances between the cattle and freckles on a face, insects under a microscope, and finally on stars within the slowly moving constellations. Apart from the contemporary interest in experimental optics, nothing justifies this spate of far-fetched analogies except Marvell's determination to create the power of the meadow to change and be changed as compellingly as possible. One of his methods is to accumulate many examples quickly, so that the swift transmutations in the poet's mind seem to transfer their speed and oddness to the natural setting.

These tumbling speculations are swept away by the rising of the River Wharfe, but Marvell holds fast to his perception of metamorphosis in all natural changes. The river, for example, 'makes the Meadow truly be/(What it but seem'd before) a Sea' (ll. 467–468); and Marvell finds an instance of his favourite phenomenon, the inclusion of a thing within itself, as 'The River in it self is drown'd' (l. 471). And with the overwhelming inundation,[47]

Marvell brings down the curtain on the changing stage of the meadows at the moment of supreme chaos, when denizens of sea and land have exchanged their habitats and every semblance of natural order has disappeared from the meadows that not long before were marked by at least the mock-discipline of the pillaging hay-gatherers. The sea may, when calm, be a true and reflecting surface, but in moments of disorder it threatens human communities—and the world of the fields—with monstrous disruption. It is from this confused terror that the poet retreats in stanza LXI.

> But I, retiring from the Flood,
> Take Sanctuary in the Wood;
> And, while it lasts, my self imbark
> In this yet green, yet growing Ark.

> (ll. 481–484)

There can be no doubt of the biblical allusions in these lines, and Marvell goes on to point out that Noah might well have chosen the wood for *his* Ark from this venerable forest. The mention of 'Sanctuary' shows that Marvell is aware of both the allusions to Noah's Ark and the Ark of the Covenant; and it is possible that the confidence with which he 'imbarks' himself (a pun on 'embark' and 'bark') is meant to be contrasted with the arrogance with which man, the 'Mote of Dust', 'imparked' himself in stanza III. But the word-play does not obscure the sense of safe and virtuous solitude that Marvell, once again, discovers amongst the trees.

The change in the poet's mood recalls the part in the poem that Fairfax and Nunappleton are meant to play; the trees are made the subject of an extended conceit intended as a compliment to the families of Fairfax and Vere, which includes a reference to the military fame of both houses.

> Of whom though many fell in War,
> Yet more to Heaven shooting are:
> And, as they Natures Cradle deckt,
> Will in green Age her Hearse expect.[48]

> (ll. 493–496)

Not only are the trees regarded as emblems of the bravery of their masters, but they are characterized as living pillars of continuity. To have 'deckt' 'Natures Cradle' is remarkable enough, but to live long enough to 'expect' 'her Hearse' is to accomplish a miracle of longevity that can be attributed only to the abstract essence of a political institution. Marvell adds to the wit of the concept by the paradoxical 'green Age', a quality that can be posited only of trees and other growing things.

The following stanzas display the accuracy of visual observation for which Marvell has often been praised.[49] But every detail of the description of the wood is made to serve the end of a metaphysical conceit. Seen from afar the trees seem to form a solid mass, so bulky and coherent that it suggests a *'Fifth Element'* (ll. 497–502); within the wood, the trees appear as columns supporting *'Corinthean Porticoes'*[50] and the wood itself a temple whose choristers are the singing birds. Once again the process of animating inanimate objects is reversed, and growing things are said to follow the designs of architecture. Marvell also distinguishes between the studious songs of the nightingale and the emblematic love-songs of the stock doves, which give him the opportunity for some plays on words in the style of his early hyperbolical, courtly verse. Stanzas LXVII and LXVIII are curiosities of ornithology; they tell us more about Marvell's interest in the human-seeming habits of certain birds than they do about the greater concerns of the poem. But he finds a sermon in the behaviour of the woodpecker (hewel), which reminds him both of the actual woodcutter and the allegorical effects of sin on the human soul.

> Who could have thought the *tallest Oak*
> Should fall by such a *feeble Strok'*!
>
> Nor would it, had the Tree not fed
> A *Traitor-worm*, within it bred.
> (As first our *Flesh* corrupt within
> Tempts impotent and bashful *Sin*.)
>
> (ll. 551–556)

The hewel, like sin, is only the instrument that brings about the fall that our innate fleshly corruption has already made inevitable.

The thought, which in another context might be expected to elicit weighty pronouncements, propels the poet into an easy and supremely witty transformation of his own.

> Thus I, *easie Philosopher*,
> Among the *Birds* and *Trees* confer:
> And little now to make me, wants

Or of the *Fowles*, or of the *Plants*.
Give me but Wings as they, and I
Streight floting on the Air shall fly:
Or turn me but, and you shall see
I was but an inverted Tree.

(ll. 561–568)

As in 'The Garden', the peculiar sympathy of the wooded setting makes every metamorphosis possible in the mind of the poet. The image of the winged soul should be so familiar by now that it should not be necessary to comment on the wit that has a man ask for wings so that he may fly, while knowing that in the light of Divine Revelation he *does* have wings. By the same token, reversing his normal upright state will make him look like a forked Y; and the visual pun is meant to justify his statement that he is at heart one with the birds and the trees.[51]

His imagined identification with the nature of the woods extends to an ability to speak 'In their most learned Original' (l. 570), and we are reminded of Adam's prelapsarian power to converse with and understand the rest of creation. This wood is like 'The Garden' in that it takes man's mind back to its primal condition of intelligent sympathy with his uncorrupted surroundings. Indeed, he pretends, with the natural philosophers of the Platonic tradition, to absorb wisdom and the faculty of prophecy from the inarticulate mentors he finds in the wood.

The falling leaves are compared to '*Sibyls* Leaves', and become the materials with which the poet 'weaves' his prophetic vision; again, they are the multicoloured feathers used in the composition of Aztec garments and 'paintings'.[52] But the 'curiosity' of these comparisons is brought to its peak by the sweeping statement: 'What *Rome, Greece, Palestine*, ere said/I in this light *Mosaick* read' (ll. 581–582). The worldly and divine wisdom of classical antiquity and the Old Testament dispensation is summed up in one line, and the poet claims that all their teachings can be understood from the speaking colours of the falling leaves. The play on '*Mosaick*' is not precisely a pun,[53] but it does draw an implicit analogy between the Old Law and the varicoloured world of nature and natural philosophy. Marvell is relying on a vast tradition of cosmological theory, especially in the couplet: 'Thrice happy he who, not mistook,/Hath read in *Natures mystick Book*' (ll. 583–584). The only unusual aspect of this notion, since for the most part it can be found in many versions in innumerable writers of the Renaissance,[54] is that thus far in the poem Marvell has simply observed and interpreted nature, and has not extracted any of the 'mystical' truths that the created world was supposed to express about the structure of the entire intelligible universe. Nature, in 'Upon Appleton House', will not remain static and emblematic long enough for Marvell to launch the conventional disquisition on its divinely symbolic essence. The leaves and ivy behave like the fruits in 'The Garden', reaching out and enveloping the poet in an *'antick Cope'* of verdure so that he looks 'Like some great *Prelate of the Grove'* (l. 592). But the disguise penetrates no deeper than the surface, since the poet's bishopric is populated only by trees. There is no place here for either the outward rituals or deeper religious meanings of the Church. Nor does the poet behave as a prelate when, 'languishing with ease' he rests on 'Pallets swoln of Velvet Moss' and enjoys the ministrations of the breezes which 'winnow from the Chaff [his] Head'. The unassertive and undemanding sympathy of nature clarifies his imagination and purges it of the disturbed images that had crowded in while he viewed the garden and the meadow. He discovers the final, impregnable retreat for the mind that can read *'Natures mystick Book'* but can discern only the mockery of true order and sanctity in the world that man has touched or despoiled.

> How safe, methinks, and strong, behind
> These Trees have I incamp'd my Mind;
> Where Beauty, aiming at the Heart,
> Bends in some Tree its useless Dart;
> And where the World no certain Shot
> Can make, or me it toucheth not.
> But I on it securely play,
> And gaul its Horsemen all the Day.
>
> (ll. 601–608)

This is another version of the metaphorical fortress, but it does not betray its pretence, as does Fairfax's garden, by assuming the same shapes and proportions of the evils it is meant to exclude. The use of 'incamp'd' suggests that Marvell wanted to recall the military imagery of the opening stanzas, and also to refine the distinction he had made already between 'impark'd' and 'embark'd'. The two enemies against which the wood defends him are 'Beauty' and 'the World'; 'The Garden' shows how nature can purify the passion of sexual love, and the forest at Nunappleton now shuts out the world of civil war, the world that was playfully but mistakenly symbolized by the mowers in the meadows. Secure in his retirement, and in amused defiance of the mortal dangers he has escaped, the poet gives himself for a moment to an image of vigorous activity: 'But I on it securely play,/And gaul its Horsemen all the Day' (ll. 607–608). The joke is that the poet has conquered the horrors of wartime savagery by triumphing over the cavalry that was the greatest weapon on both sides in the Civil War; he 'gauls' the riders as they have spurred their horses and as their image has driven the poet into his forest retreat.

But even this safety is precarious, and so he appeals to the plants to force their active sympathy still further and bind him permanently to the spot.[55] He is conscious, however, that the analogy between the human spirit and the natural forces that govern the plants is an abstraction whose source is in the imagination; and it is that mental faculty that divides the human and the natural ultimately and decrees that man will be both destroyer and gardener. In anticipation of his own inevitable defection, he pleads,

> But, lest your Fetters prove too weak,
> Ere I your Silken Bondage break,
> Do you, O *Brambles*, chain me too,
> And courteous *Briars* nail me through.
>
> (ll. 613–616)

The last lines are shocking, not simply because Marvell seems to be alluding to the Crucifixion, but because any such reference is beside the point here. Only by stretching the limits of tolerance can we see that Marvell is asking to be martyred by the trees so that he can extend his triumph over the world eternally. The analogy is false in so far as his faith is supported by nature, and since the hostile world of war and society has been defeated in the very passage that leads to this climax. And the poet abandons it rather swiftly in order to return to the vision of the meadows, from which the flooded river has receded.

After the ecstatic incident among the trees, the diction once again becomes ornate and conceited. Natural description resorts to terms of artifice, and the metaphysical play on identity appears in the final couplet of the stanza.

> For now the Waves are fal'n and dry'd,
> And now the Meadows fresher dy'd;
> Whose Grass, with moister colour dasht,
> Seems as green Silks but newly washt.
> No *Serpent* new nor *Crocodile*
> Remains behind our little *Nile*;
> Unless it self you will mistake,
> Among these Meads the only Snake.
>
> (ll. 625–632)

The scene reveals the same shaping attitude toward nature that Milton showed in *Arcades* (l. 84) and 'Lycidas' (l. 139); and while the last four lines are primarily a joking allusion to the theory that the Nile mud spawned crocodiles, they contribute a visual image of the Wharfe meandering through the meadows and also remind us in passing of the serpent present in every garden-paradise. This serpent, however, is harmless; the poem's atmosphere demands it, and it is in reality nothing more than the familiar river, whose appearance gives Marvell the opportunity for an oblique compliment to Fairfax.

> And its yet muddy back doth lick,
> Till as a *Chrystal Mirrour* slick;
> Where all things gaze themselves, and doubt
> If they be in it or without,
> And for his shade which therein shines,
> *Narcissus* like, the *Sun* too pines.
>
> (ll. 635–640)

The lines are a free reworking of stanza 12 of Fairfax's translation of Saint-Amant's 'La Solitude'.[56] But they show Marvell's typical delight in an image of confused identity, and hark back to the underwater transmutations in the passage on the meadows, stanza XLVIII. The delight extends into the next passage, whose humour is directed at the poet himself, and which ends with an obviously self-conscious pun.

> Oh what a Pleasure 'tis to hedge
> My Temples here with heavy sedge;[57]

Abandoning my lazy Side,
Stretcht as a Bank unto the Tide;
Or to suspend my sliding Foot
On the Osiers undermined Root,
And in its Branches tough to hang,
While at my Lines the Fishes twang!

(ll. 641–648)

The poet has reached the utmost state of passivity, abandoning his consciousness to the care of the trees and vines; but he cannot relinquish an attentive audience, even if it is made up of fish!

Yet even this moment of unthinking ease is transient; the appearance of Mary Fairfax in stanza LXXXII draws him back forcibly into the world of order and value that he left for the spiritual simplicity of the forest. In the final fifteen stanzas of 'Upon Appleton House' Mary will assume metaphorical proportions comparable to the Elizabeth Drury of Donne's 'Anniversaries'; she is now 'her *Ages Aw*' but more important she will become a figure of hopeful prophecy for the restoration of stable and ordered peace in England. In recognition of her imagined power, Marvell shamefacedly puts away his 'idle Utensils' lest Mary's 'judicious Eyes/Should with such Toyes a Man surprize' (ll. 653–654). He defers to the necessity of returning to the ostensible concerns of the earlier part of the poem, and in doing so must assume a stance that belittles the delights and the surcease he had found in the wood. The pursuits are now called immature that a short while ago were the source of ecstasy; the hurried shift in viewpoint is almost a précis of the poem's method.

The decorum of compliment necessitates, in this case, the conceited diction that had begun the poem; but each conceit is used to advance the general argument of the compliment. Thus, since Mary must represent the civilized alternative to the wild and permissive disorder of Nature, Marvell first points out 'how loose Nature, in respect/To her, it self doth recollect' (ll. 657–658); and the pun on 'recollect' ('remember' and 'pull together again') intensifies the correspondence between the embarrassment of Nature and the poet's own shame at his idleness. The sun's behaviour in lines 661–664 both justifies the introduction of a night scene and does indirect homage to the innocence and chastity of the heroine.[58] Then, for eight lines Marvell writes a kind of 'mood piece' that

241

was extremely unusual in seventeenth-century poetry as he explores the possibilities of describing the descent of darkness upon the river and meadows. The imagery is not evocative or vague, as it might tend to be in a Romanticist 'night-piece'—in fact it conjures up fish lying still in the water as if they were stuck in amber, and the sky taking its dark blue colour from the wings of the passing halcyon—but it does create a cumulative effect of strange and subdued transformations as the visible world changes once again under the changing light.

At the morning parade Mary had been compared to a flower, but now she is named as the true *genetrix* of the garden and the source of the essential being of all nature.

> 'Tis *She* that to these Gardens gave
> That wondrous Beauty which they have;
> *She* streightness on the Woods bestows;
> To *Her* the Meadow sweetness owes;
> Nothing could make the River be
> So Chrystal-pure but only *She*;
> *She* yet more Pure, Sweet, Streight, and Fair,
> Then Gardens, Woods, Meads, Rivers are.
>
> (ll. 689–696)

This is simply the reverse of the conceit in 'The Match' where all the beauty in Nature's 'store' was concentrated in Celia; it is also one of the most prevalent conceits in all of metaphysical love poetry.[59] And Marvell seems to drive the meaning home by the use of repeated monosyllables in line 695, as well as by the further inversions of stanza LXXXVIII:

> Therefore what first *She* on them spent,
> They gratefully again present.
> The Meadow Carpets where to tread;
> The Garden Flow'rs to Crown *Her* Head;
> And for a Glass the limpid Brook.
>
> (ll. 697–701)

The point is that the beauty of nature, which the metaphor attributes to the influence of Mary Fairfax, finds its true purpose in serving her in the form of artifacts, just as her father gave meaning to the garden by converting it into a symbol of one kind

of social organization. Mary's ultimate goals are more exalted
than Fairfax's, however, as Marvell declares:

> For *She*, to higher Beauties rais'd,
> Disdains to be for lesser prais'd.
> *She* counts her Beauty to converse
> In all the Languages as *hers*;
> Nor yet in those *her self* imployes
> But for the *Wisdome*, not the *Noyse*;
> Nor yet that *Wisdome* would affect,
> But as 'tis *Heavens Dialect*.
>
> (ll. 705–712)

The stanza, whose diction is moderately obscure, nevertheless
delineates a miniature ladder of perfection; Mary Fairfax discounts
her physical beauty in comparison to the beauty of the knowledge
of 'Languages', a notion that recalls the poet's ability to converse
with the birds and the trees in 'their most learned Original'. But
the girl does not enjoy the birds' song for its sensuous loveliness,
as the poet does; she speaks only for wisdom, and only, we learn,
for the wisdom that reveals itself in the accents of Divinity.

The world of armed strife intrudes into the speculative atmosphere in stanza LXXXX as the metaphors of battle appear again,
but this time they are consciously related to the conventional world
of the Petrarchan love-poem; tears are 'watry Shot' and sighs are
'Loves Cannon charg'd with Wind'. If Mary Fairfax is to be the
chaste inspiration of a new natural order, she must be shown to be
invulnerable to the temptations that beset a young woman. Thus
her skill in evading the types of the passionate suitor is credited to
the military discipline taught by her father's example. Her success
in carrying on the Fairfax virtues gives Marvell the occasion for a
brief diatribe against worldly women, the sex that studies not the
languages of wisdom but the arts of the 'Face', the sex that dare not
frown at vice because it might wrinkle the 'smooth Forehead'.

But Mary shares the natural innocence of the trees, and thus
justifies Marvell in calling her 'a *sprig of Misleto*' that 'On the
Fairfacian Oak does grow'. The importance of lineal descent, the
guarantee of legitimacy, is emphasized here as it had been in the
long episode of William Fairfax and Isabella Thwaites earlier. And
Marvell deals with the question of inheritance in lines that contrast
illuminatingly with the final stanzas of 'The Picture of little T.C.':

Whence, for some universal good,
The *Priest* shall cut the sacred Bud;
While her *glad Parents* most rejoice,
And make their *Destiny* their *Choice*.

(ll. 741–744)

The implication, of course, is that this bud will be cut not for adornment but for grafting to another distinguished stock, as the Veres and the Fairfaxes combined to produce this unparalleled sprig. Marriage opens up the vistas of the future for Marvell, now that he has traced the history of the family and the estate from its source to its latest glory. He exhorts the 'Fields, Springs, Bushes, Flow'rs' to profit from Mary's presence while she remains unmarried (her chaste state is equated with 'studious Hours' as if her pursuit of wisdom must cease with the end of her virginity), and to 'preferr' themselves so that they will exceed the rest of nature in the same degree that she surpasses all other women. To substantiate the compliment Marvell adduces a number of contemporary and legendary garden-seats of beauty—except that Idalia and the Elysian Fields are scorned as unworthy of being compared to the garden ruled by Mary Fairfax. But the light arrogance of the exaggerated flattery dissolves in the obviously sincere and hopeless sorrow of,

'Tis not, what once it was, the *World*;
But a rude heap together hurl'd;
All negligently overthrown,
Gulfes, Deserts, Precipices, Stone.
Your lesser *World* contains the same.
But in more decent Order tame;
You Heaven's Center, Nature's Lap.
And Paradice's only Map.

(ll. 761–768)

Despite the demands made by the genre, this is not simply the tone of courtly compliment. It is the pastoral lament for the lost Golden Age; it could be a verse paraphrase of the tenor of Godfrey Goodman's *The Fall of the World*, and it resonates to the same notes of despair and disgust that inform Donne's 'An Anatomy of the World'.[60] The bare, harsh stress on 'Stone' conveys exactly the desolation of this view of the corrupt world of chaotic self-seeking. And the integrity of Marvell's vision is assured in his recognition that the 'lesser *World*' (which is both Mary Fairfax and Nunappleton) is made up of the same intractably decadent materials as the great world, or macrocosm, that it has come to symbolize through the various movements of the poem. 'More decent Order tame' is the only bulwark, passive as it is, that can shore up man's ruins against the assaults of the rude world; it governs the military garden of Lord Fairfax, it directs the seasonal transformations of the river and the meadow, and it gives Mary Fairfax a pattern to impose upon unruly nature so that it may best fulfil its potentialities. And because there is still hope that Mary, or what she symbolizes, will restore the garden-state from which England has banished itself, she is called *'Heaven's Center, Nature's Lap'*—the pole-star of spiritual value and the nursery of all things green. The irony in the last line is neither sharp nor critical; if anything, it is a pathetic admission that beneath the high-flown flattery there is a disconcerting core of truth. Although 'only' commonly meant 'foremost',[61] it has its modern meaning as well in the last line—and Marvell's point is that all there can be of Paradise for man is contained in the 'decent Order' of Nunappleton, despite its stones and precipices. The imposition of a meaningful pattern on nature is man's peculiar ability; yet it can never eradicate the effects of man's evil propensities or the mindless chaos of unformed nature.

The final stanza of the poem has attracted the same charges of irrelevance and extraneousness that are usually laid to the end of 'The Garden'. It is true that after the profound and moving statement of stanza LXXXXVI this conceited imitation of Cleveland[62] is responsible for a disconcerting lapse of tone. But the poem is framed in passages of precise observation, as if to assure us that all the wide-ranging thoughts have started from a firm centre of physical reality. That reality has undergone uncounted transmutations within seven hundred-odd lines, and even at the end of the long season's vigil Marvell's mind is still alert to the analogical possibilities of the odd sight presented by the fishermen carrying their coracles. With 'their *Heads* in their *Canoos*' the fishermen provide yet another instance of the principle of inversion that has motivated so many of the metaphors and the incidents of 'Upon Appleton House'. And 'rational *Amphibii*' is indeed a pertinent phrase for the human figure, which in this poem has been thrust below the seas, has lived through harvest and massacre, and finally immersed itself in nature and felt its soul released from the galling bonds of the world. The poet's life, if not his consciousness, has shown itself to be 'amphibious', and the deliberate confusion among the elements and the senses has in some ways sustained the metaphorical modes of the entire work.

Thus there is no strain in the comparison with which 'Upon Appleton House' ends; the night sky begins to look like the dark shell that covers the men's heads, the hemisphere has become dark, and the time has come for the poet to go back through the woods and meadows he has known and described, and finally through the emblematic door that opens the poem. We have been given an exhaustive and varied picture of the dangerously disordered state of England and the world; and we have learned something of the 'green' virtues that may redeem them. The poet has presented the opposed and complementary claims of the life of public action and of private retirement; and to call his attitude 'complex' is to do a disservice to the way in which his reactions to the two ways of life interact with and modify each other. The safety and solitude of the woods attract Marvell almost irresistibly, yet his feelings for the profundity and worth of the roots of human society will not permit him to dismiss responsibilities outside the garden and the forests. The fluctuation of the poem between poles of realism and symbolic extravagance reflects the constant oscillation between these two poles of moral action. If there is any resolution it is in the metaphors themselves that form the substance of 'Upon Appleton House'.

Notes

1 See Legouis, *Andrew Marvell*, pp. 17–20.

2 Legouis, p. 19.

3 See C. R. Markham, *A Life of the Great Lord Fairfax* (London, 1870), pp. 365–366.

4 See *The Poems of Thomas, Third Lord Fairfax, passim*.

5 G. R. Hibbard, 'The Country House Poem of the Seventeenth Century', *Journal of the Warburg and Courtauld Institutes*, XIX, 1–2 (January–June 1956), pp. 159–174.

6 Margoliouth, I, pp. 56–58.

7 *A Life of the Great Lord Fairfax*, p. 58.

8 See Margoliouth (I, p. 229) for the reliability of lines 29–32. The hill is neither so commanding nor so perfectly shaped as Marvell would have us believe.

9 See *Elizabethan and Metaphysical Imagery*, pp. 94–95.

10 Cf. *FQ*, VI, x, 23.

11 See Margoliouth, I, 229.

12 See above, p. 151.

13 Cf. Sophocles, *Oedipus at Colonus*, ll. 261–678.

14 We do not know whether 'Upon the Hill and Grove at Bill-borow' or 'The Garden' was written earlier, but they are connected by Marvell's interest in the metaphorical use of the practice of carving the beloved's name in the bark of a tree.

15 For a typical example, see *Macbeth*, I, iv, ll. 29–30.

16 See Markham, p. 338. For a poem written by Fairfax to express his revulsion at the trial and sentencing of Charles, see Markham, p. 352.

17 Margoliouth (I, p. 229) points out that the phrase appears in Waller's 'The Battle of the Summer Islands' and that it was a commonplace in contemporary French poetry. It is used primarily to create an epic tone, and this fact deepens the contrast between the warlike forests of weapons and the oak groves of Bilborough. The irony of the symbolism is present, too, in the fact that the oak was the emblematic reward for military bravery.

18 See Margoliouth, I, p. 229.

19 Jonson, 'To Penshurst', l. 51, *The Complete Poetry of Ben Jonson*, ed. W. B. Hunter, Jr. (New York, 1963), pp. 77–81.

20 Jonson, 'To Penshurst', ll. 67–68.

21 Cf. Carew, 'To my friend G. N. from Wrest', ll. 20–24, *Poems*, pp. 86–89.

22 See Margoliouth, I, p. 231, for Fairfax's poem, from Bodleian MS Fairfax 40.

23 *The Happy Man*, p. 90. Miss Røstvig actually cites Martial, *Epigrams*, X, 47, but this seems to me less useful as an illustrative source than the description of Baian villa. See also her article, 'Benlowes, Marvell, and the Divine Casimire', *Huntington Library Quarterly*, XVIII, 1 (November 1954), pp. 13–35.

24 Some recent critiques of the poem, while acknowledging its apparent lack of coherence, attempt to provide a rationale for its structure; see M. S. Røstvig, ' "Upon Appleton House" and the Universal History of Man', *English Studies* XLII (1961), pp. 337–351; D. C. Allen, 'Upon Appleton House', in *Image and Meaning*, pp. 115–153; Tayler, *Nature and Art in Renaissance Literature*, pp. 150–154; Toliver, *Marvell's Ironic Vision*, pp. 113–129; Kitty Scoular, *Natural Magic* (Oxford University Press, 1965), pp. 120–190; M. J. K. O'Loughlin, 'This Sober Frame: A Reading of "Upon Appleton House" ', *Andrew Marvell. A Collection of Critical Essays*, ed. G. deF. Lord (Prentice-Hall, 1968), pp. 120–142.

25 Margoliouth (I, p. 231) gives reasons for rejecting the Folio reading

'Mose' and Cooke's emendation 'Mole'. The biblical echoes of 'Mote of Dust' are germane to Marvell's intent in this passage.

26 Marvell's details correspond to the sketch of Nunappleton given in Markham, p. 363, and in Grosart, I, facing p. 1.

27 Matthew 7:14.

28 Moral Essays: 'Epistle IV: To Richard Boyle, Earl of Burlington', l. 179; *The Poems of Alexander Pope*, ed. J. Butt (Methuen, 1963), pp. 586–595.

29 'To Penshurst', ll. 13–14. Of course, Sir Philip Sidney is meant.

30 Miss Wallerstein (*Studies in Seventeenth-Century Poetic*, pp. 297–298) believes that Marvell's anti-Catholicism is typical of his time and cultural position—and quite uncompromisingly. In particular she finds that in the sensuously seductive stanzas, XXI-XXIII, 'there is an attack upon that use of the senses or sensual sublimation as a key to ecstasy or in ritualistic symbolism which was an important element in the devotion of the Counter-Reformation'. L. Hyman, in 'Politics and Poetry in Andrew Marvell', *PMLA*, LXXIII, 5: 1 (December 1958), pp. 475–479, interprets the nunnery passage as an example of 'Marvell's impatience with Fairfax's retirement from the world. For Marvell is not only satirizing convents, which is hardly remarkable in this period, but he is attacking the whole idea of withdrawal from action'. I think this circumscribes Marvell's feelings, ideas, and modes of thinking much too sharply. It is impossible to read 'Upon Appleton House' as a criticism of Fairfax and an exhortation to return to public affairs unless we are willing to say that Marvell is disguising very deep feelings (and apparently not very successfully) in a poem that at the same time draws upon most of his characteristic interests and beliefs. Christopher Hill, too, exhibits this tendency to reduce Marvell's thinking to formulae that are much more meaningful to a twentieth-century mind than they would have been to Marvell, *viz*: 'the retirement, the cultured and indeed opulent ease of the nunnery is frankly opposed to the claims of a Protestant and commercial civilization' (*Puritanism and Revolution*, p. 353.)

31 Why, for example, does he choose to elaborate on this story when Fairfax's family history was full of illustrious actions?

32 There is also a faint echo of 'An Horatian Ode', ll. 15–16.

33 Cf. 'A Dialogue Between The Resolved Soul, and Created Pleasure'.

34 Miss Røstvig (*The Happy Man*, p. 244) suggests that stanza XXXVI is based on Benlowes' *Theophila*, XII, 41: 'For fields of combat, fields of corn are here,/For trooping ranks, tree-ranks appear'. However, this ignores the fact that such gardens were common in seventeenth-century England, and that there is, presumably a factual basis for Marvell's

description. My remark is qualified because although most editors refer to Markham's description of Fairfax's garden, where 'the flowers were planted in masses—tulips, pinks, and roses each in separate beds, which were cut into the shape of forts with five bastions' (p. 366), none seems to have remarked that Markham cites as his authority Marvell's poem! I have been unable to find, in works on Fairfax or in Yorkshire county records, any independent corroboration of Marvell's description. Nevertheless, it seems very probable that the garden at Nunappleton was as he pictures it.

35 The poem's concluding compliment to Mary Fairfax is heralded in stanza XXXVIII by 'She/Seems with the Flow'rs a Flow'r to be' (ll. 301–302), although we shall find later that she is really their governing spirit.

36 Cf. ll. 313–314 and 'On the Morning of Christ's Nativity', l. 21; *Complete Poems*, p. 43.

37 Margoliouth gives 'The', but Aitken's emendation (1829) seems preferable, as an indication of the desired stress.

38 See the long passage in *PL*, IV, ll. 268–285, where Eden is compared to numerous gardens where treasures were hidden and protected from external dangers.

39 Contrast this with the 'sweetly wast' park of Nunappleton in l. 78.

40 Cf. the 'sacred Plants' in stanza II, and the underlying suggestion that the imagined garden is something more than natural.

41 *Poems*, pp. 38–40. Lovelace's poem is a humorous address to the grasshopper on the dangers of life amidst nature.

42 Miss Joan Grundy, in 'Marvell's Grasshoppers', *NQ*, N.S. IV, 4 (April 1957), p. 142, cites Numbers 13:32–33. Legouis later rejected more extensive suggestions of Old Testament parallels by Miss Grundy in 'Upon Appleton House'.

43 Cf. 'An Horatian Ode', ll. 53–58; 'A Poem upon the Death of O.C.', ll. 7–12.

44 This is another of the images cited by Miss Grundy (see above, note 42) to show that Marvell was working out an elaborate structure of biblical reference in this poem. However, it seems to me that he was simply fascinated by the actual pattern formed in the grass as the mowers cut their way with their scythes.

45 Cf. Saint-Amant, 'Sur la Moisson d'un Lieu Proche de Paris': 'L'or tombe sous le fer; desjà les moissonneurs,/Despouillant les sillons de leurs jaunes honneurs,/La desolation rendent et gaye et belle' (ll. 9–11).

As Davison points out (p. 228), it was much more common to describe a field of battle as if it were a harvest scene.

46 For lines 427–428 Margoliouth (I, p. 233) cites North's translation of Plutarch's *Life of Alexander* wherein Alexander's body is reported to have given off a peculiarly sweet odour.

47 Cf. Horace, *Odes*, I, ii; Ovid, *Metamorphoses*, I.

48 Both Margoliouth (I, p. 234) and Macdonald (p. 183) remark that the lines probably refer to the felling of trees during wartime. The conceit applies equally well to the trees and to the scions of Fairfax and of Vere.

49 The lines on the hewel (woodpecker) and 'hatching thrastles shining eye' (ll. 537–544, 532) are most often quoted in this regard. Marvell's technique of passing from one observation quickly to another is illuminated by a remark of Miss Mourgues' (*Metaphysical Baroque and Précieux Poetry*, pp. 93–94) on similar devices in the poetry of Théophile, Saint-Amant, and Tristan. She says they 'consider nature as a succession of landscapes to be enjoyed for their own sake and depicted with some precision; and precision for them consists in putting the stress on concrete details in landscape. . . . The second noticeable aspect of their technique in landscape painting is to pass from one object to another without supplying the connexion . . . .'

50 The choice of the Corinthian order is exact, since its capitals are decorated heavily with leaves. Marvell even uses the technical architectural term 'order' in line 507.

51 See A. B. Chambers, ' "I Was But an Inverted Tree" ': Notes toward the History of an Idea', *Studies in the Renaissance*, VIII (1961), pp. 291–299.

52 See Margoliouth (I, p. 234) for contemporary notes on the practice.

53 Cf. 'Musicks Empire', l. 17: 'Mosaique of the Air';Margoliouth, I, p. 47.

54 The idea of Nature as the Book of God occurs at almost every stage in intellectual history. From St Augustine it developed into a major doctrine of the medieval realists. In Marvell's period there are countless examples. Sir Thomas Browne in *Religio Medici* says 'there are two Books from whence I collect my Divinity; besides that written one of GOD, another of His servant Nature, that universal and publick Manuscript, that lies expans'd unto the Eyes of all'; Rowland Watkyns, *Flamma Sine Fumo* (1662): 'High meditations doe my soul possesse,/ Like *John* the Baptist's, in a wildernesse,/When secret fields I tread, I do refuse/The books of men, and Nature's book peruse'; Mildmay Fane, in 'To Retiredness', uses a diction resembling Marvell's own: 'I am taught Thankfulness from trees./Then turning over Natures leaf,/I mark the Glory of the Sheaf,/For every Field's a severall |page,/Dis-

ciphering the Golden Age'; William Drummond of Hawthornden, in a sonnet written in 1623: 'Of this faire Volumne which wee World doe name,/If wee the sheetes and leaves could turne with care,/Of Him who it correctes, and did it frame,/Wee cleare might read the Art and Wisdome rare?'; William Habington, in 'Nox Nocti Indicate Scientiam' (1640), transfers the metaphor to the skies: 'My soule her wings doth spread/And heaven-ward flies,/The Almighty's Mysteries to read/In the large volumes of the skies'; J. A. Mazzeo, in 'Metaphysical Poetry and the Poetic of Correspondence', *JHI*, XIV, 2 (April, 1953), pp. 221–234, remarks that Renaissance poets thought of the world not only as 'God's poem' but also as a 'metaphysical poem full of witty conceits'. Miss Røstvig (*The Happy Man*, pp. 35–36) says that 'the interpretation of nature as a divine hieroglyph, or a mystic book shadowing forth deeper truths, is an important part of the background of the philosophy of retirement. This philosophy received its most distinctive form on English soil at the time when the interest in nature was cross-fertilized by the new confidence in the ability of the individual to find truth for himself in the light of the "candle of the Lord" '. Sermons and religious treatises of the seventeenth century offer so many instances of the metaphor that quotation is unncessary.

55 As Margoliouth notes (I, p. 235), 'gadding vines' seems to echo 'Lycidas', l. 40.

56 Cf. Fairfax: 'Sometimes soe Cleare & soe serene/Itt seemes ast were a looking glass/And to our Vewes presenting seemes/As heavens beneath the waters was'. This translates Saint-Amant's 'Tantost, la plus claire du monde,/Elle semble un miroir flottant,/Et nous represente à l' instant/Encores d'autres cieux sous l'onde./Le soliel s'y fait si bien voir,/Y contemplant son beau visage,/Qu'on est quelque temps à scavoir/Si c'est luy-mesme, ou son image,/Et d'abord il semble à nos yeux,/Qu'il s'est laissé tomber des cieux'.

57 'Clorinda and Damon', l. 6.

58 Cf. Milton's early, Italianate, and notorious conceit in 'On the Morning of Christ's Nativity', ll. 229–231; *Complete Poems*, p. 49.

59 Among many possible examples, see Nicholas Hookes, 'To Amanda walking in the Garden', in *Amanda* (1653); Cleveland, 'Upon Phillis walking in a morning before Sun-rising'; *Poems of John Cleveland*, eds. B. Morris and E. Withington (Oxford University Press, 1967), pp. 14–15; Cowley, 'The Spring', ll. 24–32, *Poems*, pp. 70–72; William Hammond, 'The Walk': 'Roses and lilies, and what beauteous stains/Nature adorns the Spring with, are but all/Faint copies of this fair Original./ She is a moving Paradise, doth view/Your greens, not to refresh herself, but you./This path's th'Ecliptic, heat prolific hence/Is shed

on you by her kind influence', Saintsbury, II, pp. 489–490; Waller, 'At Penshurst' (1645): 'Her presence has such more than human grace,/ That it can civilize the rudest place;/And beauty, too, and order, can impart,/Where nature ne'er intended it, nor art'; *Poems*, pp. 46–47.

60 There are verbal similarities in Henry More's 'Ad Paronem': 'A rude confused heap of ashes dead', *Philosophical Poems*, p. 136; and in a poem by John Joynes in *Lachrymae Musarum*, 'On the Incomparable Lord Hastings': 'and now this carcase, World,/Is into her first, rude, dark Chaos, hurl'd. This image derives ultimately from Ovid, *Metamorphoses*, I, 7.

61 Cf. *Hamlet*, III, ii, l. 132.

62 Cf. Cleveland, 'Square-Cap', *Poems*, pp. 43–45, l. 19.

6

The Great Work of Time

I

To consider 'Upon Appleton House' before discussing Marvell's three great poems on Cromwell, I have had to distort history slightly. Despite the manifold obscurities of the chronology of Marvell's poems, the circumstances in which these few poems must have been written allow us to date them with relative assurance. 'Upon Appleton House' and 'Upon the Hill and Grove at Billborow' could not have been written before Marvell took up his post as Mary Fairfax's tutor at Nunappleton late in 1650 or early in 1651. 'An Horatian Ode upon Cromwel's Return from Ireland'[1] marks the events of May–June, 1650; Cromwell returned from his successful campaign in Ireland to assume a position under Fairfax's command in the projected campaign against the Scots. However, Fairfax resigned his commission in protest over the Scots war, and Cromwell replaced him as commander-in-chief, leaving for Scotland at the end of June.[2] Thus at one moment in Marvell's career the two men who figured for him the highest representations of the opposed moral courses of action and contemplation came together in an incident that determined the coming fortunes of the Civil War, and provided Marvell with living images of the problems that were to fill his mind for at least a decade. The praise of Fairfax's decision in the Nunappleton poems sorts badly with Marvell's obvious awe at the relentless progress of Cromwell's military and political career; but the two points of view are contradictory only if we deny to Marvell's own thinking the balanced complexities that his verse reveals.

'An Horatian Ode' has been taken as the prime example of the 'intellectual poise'[3] of the metaphysical poetry of the late Renaissance, as an illustration of Marvell's ability to blend the symbols and concerns of public and private ethics,[4] and as the finest known instance of the recreation of classical Roman attitudes and tropes in English.[5] The puzzle implicit in the poem—that Marvell, whose Royalist sympathies had been revealed by 'To ... Lovelace' and 'Upon ... Lord Hastings', within a year had changed his political opinions radically enough to write a poem of apparently unstinting praise to Cromwell—precipitated a critical debate[6] in which Cleanth Brooks found that the terms applied to Cromwell's emergence as the supreme force in revolutionary England were tempered with a pervasive irony, and that the martyred King stood forth as the true hero of the poem. Douglas Bush replied that such a view did violence to the realities of seventeenth-century political ideas, and to Marvell's pre-eminent ability to perceive and dramatize the conflicting meanings implicit in events and personalities of such magnitude as the execution of Charles I and the rise of Cromwell. I hope to show that the poem is what it most pretends to be—a celebration of Cromwell's accession to power, and a profoundly serious justification of that power. Simply because Marvell's own career, from 1650 until the Restoration, is bound up with the fortunes of the Parliamentary party, is no convincing reason to assume that his poems in support or praise of Cromwell are mere time-serving. In all that has been written on 'An Horatian Ode' it is above all surprising that little attention has been paid to the elements in it that are truly 'Horatian'. It is not enough to point to the correspondences between his stanza (roughly, a tetrameter couplet followed by a trimeter couplet) and Horace's metres, for these are merely the bare bones of the inspiration Marvell found in the *Odes*.[7] It might be more useful to say that, in evaluating his own reactions to the phenomenon of Cromwell's meteoric career, Marvell would have found Horace's attitudes toward Augustus revealing and instructive. Indeed, here was the very type of the poet illuminating the path of the man of action while maintaining scrupulously his independence of thought and judgment. To face an absolute ruler with confidence in one's own ability to perceive the meanings of his acts against the background of history and national destiny is Horace's customary stance; it is also Marvell's.

The first eight lines state one part of the comparison that will be drawn at the first mention of Cromwell in line 9. It is commonly assumed that the 'forward Youth' of line 1 is a reference to Cromwell himself;[8] but it seems equally likely that the youth is the poet himself, and that the comparison thus made between himself and

Cromwell is meant to contribute to the general portrait of the age that is the main concern of the opening strophe of the poem. If I am correct, 'An Horatian Ode', at least in its initial phases, bears strong resemblances to 'Lycidas' in that it marks a crucial moment in the poet's career, and marks it with an intense consciousness of the many ways in which his talent and indeed his destiny are inter-twined with the conditions and prospects of the nation at large. Both poems begin with a forced and partially grudging acknowledg-ment that the 'times' must draw the poet from his study and from the orderly and congenial pursuit of his own imaginative goals. Milton abandons his regimen of preparation in order to deplore the waste of King's talent; and Marvell gives up the 'Numbers languishing' of his early love-poetry because the spirit of the age, embodied in Cromwell, has made it apparent that great things are to be fought for now, and that the battle calls for all men who would have a legitimate stake in England's rejuvenation, or who can grasp the intentions of Providence as revealed in moments of human history.

To suggest that the first lines refer to Cromwell is also to make nonsense of his activities and achievements in the years im-mediately preceding the Scottish campaign. In 1650 he was fifty-one years old, hardly a 'youth', and the veteran of Marston Moor and Naseby would not have had to 'oyl th' unused Armours rust' (l. 6). But the more important point is that these opening lines are meant to characterize the age itself, a time when England was approaching the climactic moment of the most significant political change in its modern history. Not only is the poet forced to leave his study and abandon the easy graces of court poetry and pastoral idylls, but England is moving finally away from the bright, and now naïve, visions of its Elizabethan period. The 'Garden of the World' is no longer shielded in its agrarian simplicity from the dissension and bloody strife that tears less fortunate isles; as the later Cromwell poems will show, the agony that England underwent in the 1640s brought it out not only on a new plateau of social and political organization but on to the stage of world affairs. The issues at stake in every battle and Parliamentary debate of the Civil War are of increasingly greater moment, and the summons that draws the 'forward Youth' from his books and 'Numbers' is as unavoidable as the painful onset of maturity. The confining 'Corslet' of action and political decision is uncomfortable, it has the harsh and stern lines of masculine responsibility; but it is also the only garment that will preserve the body politic through the great martial and moral battles to come. There may be nostalgia for what is being left behind, but I do not think that it can be said that the beginning of 'An Horatian Ode' is ambiguous or undecided in its attitude toward the necessity of taking action when history and Fate have joined to render retirement and the pursuit of individual pleasure not only irrelevant but somehow ignoble. It is in this sense, then, that the second part of the comparison, which deals with Cromwell, is prepared for.

The next lines raise a question of some importance for the entire poem: is the Providence that rules Cromwell's career a Christian power or Marvell's equivalent for the classical concept of Fate? The decorum of the poem would seem to rule out the possibility of a continuing reference to a Christian God, since Marvell is careful to have the details fit the imagined Horatian mould. But there are so many obvious similarities between the pagan idea and the profound sense of Divine Providence that permeated Christian (especially Puritan) thought that there was an equally small possibility that Marvell's audience would fail to read the Horatian poem as a sermon on the divine mission of Cromwell. Marvell's innate tact kept him from drawing the obvious parallels in the poem, and the effect is to make those parallels even more apparent to any reader acquainted with Protestant sentiments about individual election and the providential destiny of the English Puritans. Thus the Roman symbols maintain the Horatian atmosphere of the 'Ode' at the same time that they refer clearly to a body of religious doctrine that lay behind the Puritan Rebellion itself. It is this concept of the intervention of the supernatural in the affairs of men that informs these lines:

> So restless *Cromwel* could not cease
> In the inglorious Arts of Peace,
>   But through adventrous War
>   Urged his active Star.
> And, like the three-fork'd Lightning, first
> Breaking the Clouds where it was nurst,
>   Did thorough his own Side
>   His fiery way divide.

(ll. 9–16)

The 'Arts of Peace', it should be noted, are 'inglorious' only because the times have made them so; the reading that would take this phrase as Marvell's rejection of poetry and study commits the same error that it does in demanding that either Cromwell or Charles be painted uncompromisingly as a villain. More than any of Marvell's poems, 'An Horatian Ode' is filled with the sense that human values are mutable, subject to larger forces of history or universal destiny. Abstract values may indeed be absolute, but as they appear to men they are only momentary shadows of their greater meanings. But Providence also sees to it that great men appear at moments of change to interpret the will of history or God to those who are bewildered by the varicoloured surface of sublunary events. Nor are these men simply the passive instruments of a transcendent Will; although Cromwell is supported and guided by his 'active Star',[9] he 'urges' it along its destined course as well. In combining his personal genius and force with the influence of his heavenly guardian, Cromwell best exhibits the behaviour of the man 'That does both act and know' (l. 76), a type that integrates the faculties of action and of contemplation that have formed the poles of human possibility for Marvell. In the political sphere, Cromwell proves his 'election' by acting in a way that identifies him as the choice of Providence; his relation to the irresistible forces of history is most clearly paralleled by that of one of the Puritan 'elect' to the powers of Grace that have chosen him to be saved. The paradox is one that cannot be resolved, since it is inherent in the very idea that certain individuals can represent the inner processes of universal destiny on earth. Perhaps frustration at this deliberate and intractable paradox was part of Professor Brooks's motive for insisting that Marvell could not have admired Cromwell for abetting his own career—for behaving, in short, in the way he must to justify his election and his mission to a contemporary audience. Precisely Cromwell's ability to 'urge' his star was the best guarantee of his providential role, and we must understand in this sense the violent images of lightning and fire that follow.

Margoliouth (I, p. 238) tells us that the image of lightning breaking through a cloud may refer to Cromwell's forceful emergence from the Parliamentary 'side' in 1644; but aside from the pun the lines carry other meanings perhaps more important. There is violence not only in the physical act of slashing through the cloud but in the callous indifference to the cloud itself 'where it was nurst', as if this elemental force can take no cognizance of normal human ties and affections. But there is also a suggestion that the lightning and the cloud are one thing, self-generated, so that Cromwell has, while resting in the 'inglorious Arts of Peace', been nurturing his own abilities until the time when the need for them will overmaster any reasons for consideration or delay.[10] Finally, the lines are an indirect description of a Caesarean birth, an event that the Romans believed to be a fortunate augury. Taken with the internal echoes of May's translation of Lucan, this allusion is an indication that Cromwell is being presented as a type of the victorious, irresistibly powerful Caesar. This presents a difficulty when, in lines 23–24, there is a clear reference to Charles I as a type of Caesar. But there is neither confusion nor negligence in Marvell's method. 'Caesar', after all, became a generic title after Julius' reign, and there is no problem in portraying different embodiments of the spirit of absolute government. In one sense 'An Horatian Ode' envisages the transition from a monarchical state ruled by a Caesar whose power is based on his concept of Divine Right to a republican state ruled by a true Caesar who represents the will and best interests of the governed. Certainly the entire poem is informed with the hope that a tyrannous and ultimately weak monarchy will be replaced by the rule of a man whose wisdom is the sanction for his power, and whose destruction of tyranny is ordained by 'angry Heaven'. Both Charles and Cromwell are 'Caesars' then, but Heaven has proved the right of the latest Caesar to abrogate the divine right of the fallen Caesar; since Heaven is the justification claimed by both, Marvell has made it perfectly clear that the victory must go to Cromwell. There is no debate about 'right' or 'wrong' here; the course of events defines the power and the worth of the values that prevail.

To vary and deepen the portrait of Cromwell, Marvell also makes use of images drawn from natural science, and these contribute to the impression of Cromwell as an elemental force, driven not by calculation or rational choice but by the sheer physical necessity of its essence. Thus, in characterizing Cromwell's ascendancy over the Parliamentary 'side', Marvell remarks,

> 'tis all one to Courage high
> The Emulous or Enemy;

> And with such to inclose
> Is more then to oppose.   (ll. 17–20)

The force of Cromwell's destined purpose is so incommensurable
with ordinary political ambitions that he does not discriminate
between active hostility and the restriction that weaker men,
albeit his associates, would put upon his actions. In line 42 Marvell
will speak of the contemporary theory that two bodies cannot
occupy the same space at the same time; here the terminology of
physical science is used to explain why Cromwell was destined as
inevitably to rise above considerations of party as he was to conquer
his more obvious enemies on the battlefield. The analogy between
the military leader and the force of nature is carried on in the lines
that follow:

> Then burning through the Air he went,
> And Pallaces and Temples rent:
>   And *Caesars* head at last
>   Did through his Laurels blast.
> 'Tis Madness to resist or blame
> The force of angry Heavens flame.
>
>   (ll. 21–26)

The 'Pallaces and Temples' can be, with equal validity, features of a
Roman landscape or symbols of the overthrow of Charles and the
prelatical tyranny against which the Puritan Rebellion was aimed.
Nothing is proof against 'angry Heavens flame', not even the
laurel wreath that traditionally protected its wearer against
lightning.[11] In mentioning this superstition Marvell adds a touch
to the pagan details of the 'Ode', reinforces the metaphor of Cromwell as a lightning-bolt, and also drives home the realization that
such legendary beliefs no longer apply to the vindictive power that
has chosen Cromwell as its scourge. Perhaps there is a note of
ambivalence in 'Madness'; but Marvell is not considering alternate
ways to judge Cromwell's actions, he is stating rather baldly the
absurdity of protesting against the direction taken by the running
tide of history. This is especially true if history is understood
providentially, since to protest, then, is to complain against the
will of God, an act that combines futility with blasphemy.

Nevertheless, Marvell is aware that a portrait drawn only in such
figures must inevitably destroy Cromwell's claim to individual

distinction. He had mentioned Cromwell's 'urging' of his 'Star'; now he focuses the verse squarely on the emerging hero and fore-stalls criticism by pointing to his personal achievements.

> And, if we would speak true,
> Much to the Man is due.
> Who, from his private Gardens, where
> He liv'd reserved and austere,
> As if his highest plot
> To plant the Bergamot,
> Could by industrious Valour climbe
> To ruine the great Work of Time,
> And cast the Kingdome old
> Into another Mold.
>
> (ll. 27–36)

Again, the classical motifs are kept in play by the allusion to Cincinnatus, whose story epitomizes not only the choice between rural retirement and public affairs, but also the justified seizure of supreme political power by a man whose only interest is the welfare of his country. Beyond that, we have seen how deep and varied are the meanings, for Marvell, of those 'private Gardens' from which Cromwell has willingly absented himself. They are the crown of earthly felicity and the seed-bed of the transcendent virtues of contemplation.[12] However, Marvell senses the dis-crepancy between his idea of the 'garden-State' and the figure that Cromwell actually cuts in the world at large; Cromwell was no lover of rural simplicity, no philosopher of the meadow or the quincunx. Thus the phrase 'As if' qualifies the picture we are given, and allows us to see with Marvell that Cromwell's earlier days of obscurity gave only the appearance of being devoted to the humble pursuits of the country landowner. Lines 31–32 offer an opportunity for the view of Professor Brooks to muster some support. Marvell seems to be saying, ironically, that Cromwell conducted himself in the years before his rise to prominence as if all that interested him were horticultural matters. Yet the mention of 'plot' appears to look forward to the 'wiser Art' with which Marvell claims he lured Charles to Carisbrooke and eventual capture. Furthermore, the bergamot is not simply a 'kind of pear' as Margoliouth tells us (I, p. 238) but was known as the 'King's Pear'.[16] In other words, what the lines might appear to say is that

Cromwell, all the while he cultivated his powers against the day when they could be exercised, was planning always to supplant Charles and establish himself as monarch.

But the underlying argument is that in comparison to the true significance of Cromwell's achievements his 'plot' to overthrow Charles would have been inconsiderable in any case. Marvell does not hesitate to admire the political skill and cunning with which Cromwell realized his potential genius; they are essential aspects of the man who can both act and know, they effect the political events that angry Heaven decrees. In the end, although Marvell does appear to have believed that Cromwell tricked Charles into escaping from Hampton Court,[14] I do not think that the troublesome lines 31–32 mean to imply that his austere privacy concealed a scheming and treacherous mind. The plot to plant the bergamot would have been the work of a lesser man; Cromwell's true ambition, guided by Heaven and Destiny, was to 'ruine the great Work of Time'. If we are seeking meaningful ambiguities, this is the place to find them.

Notice that Cromwell's 'Valour' is referred to twice in the poem, once in line 33 as 'industrious' and again in line 107 as 'sad', or 'grave', 'sober'. The linking of industry and bravery repeats the idea that Cromwell's success is due equally to divine sanction and to his own energies and abilities. Courage alone could not aspire to an act of such magnitude, since intelligence and determination are necessary as well even to conceive the idea of casting 'the Kingdome old/Into another Mold'. In effect, this is to try to accomplish by the skills and spiritual dedication of a single man the work of men and institutions labouring through the history of centuries of civilization. It also grants to Cromwell the creative and shaping power of Fate, since he moulds a new England just as history had moulded the society that is being destroyed.

The point at issue, of course, is how Marvell feels about the ruination of 'the great Work of Time'. Beyond doubt his earlier (and later) poems show him to be acutely sensitive to the values of a stable and traditional society. His revulsion at any sort of interference with natural and long-sanctioned processes is evident in all his work. However, there is, finally, nothing in this passage of 'An Horatian Ode' to indicate that the massive creation of Time and Man, the English state, has any more compelling claim against the judgment of Heaven than that of age. Whatever the values or even

the beauties of that great work (and we shall see them dramatized
in the passage on the King's execution) they have not been sufficient
to maintain it in existence; this is Marvell's rigorously realistic
observation, and his sympathies with the England that is about
to disappear are not allowed to interfere with his objective judgment.
Some may detect a note of powerless grief in the lines that follow,
but I see no reason why they should not be read as they ask to be
read, as a statement of the supercession of venerable but weak
ideas of right and justice by newly created forces responsive to
the demands of a new civilization.

> Though Justice against Fate complain,
> And plead the antient Rights in vain:
> But those do hold or break
> As Men are strong or weak.

(ll. 37–40)

This is a hard saying, but it is also a just estimate of the relative
powers of human and providential wills. No one, in fact, pleaded
the cause of justice and ancient right more eloquently than did
King Charles at his trial, when he refused, and rightly, to recognize
the Parliamentary tribunal as able to try or judge him. Marvell does
not deny to Charles any of the honour or admiration he deserves
for his courageous and hopeless stand; his praise of Cromwell
does not require such petty manoeuvres. The point is made simply
by saying that justice is a concept subject to revisions by the society
that enforces it, and that ancient rights have no power over a people
when they have failed to secure for that people the peace and
stability they were meant to guarantee. The most noble ideals of an
England much more glorious than that of the Civil War may be
enshrined in 'the great Work of Time', but shrines as well as palaces
fall before the decree of Providence, and their beauty is no argument against strict historical necessity. The process may be tragic,
but it is, above all, inevitable, as Marvell indicates:

> Nature that hateth emptiness,
> Allows of penetration less:
> And therefore must make room
> When greater Spirits come.

(ll. 41–44)

The failure of the 'antient Rights' and the collapse of 'the great
Work of Time', then, have left Nature no defence against its own

physical laws that decree that a superior force must replace an inferior one. Notice that the monarchic state is seen as the creation of 'Time', and that Marvell is careful to attribute Heaven's sanction only to Cromwell's act of creative destruction. For it will be part of his argument that the construction of a new English polity not only follows the crumbling of the monarchy but that it is founded upon its ruins. In any case, he does not temporize about the fact that Cromwell is a 'greater Spirit'. The proof is in his ability to match 'The force of angry Heavens flame' with 'wiser Art'; the same combination of innate force and active skill is suggested in the ambiguous lines: 'What Field of all the Civil Wars,/Where his were not the deepest Scars?' (ll. 45–46). The scars are either those inflicted or those suffered, or both; all the possible statements would be true of Cromwell, and this is what Marvell wants to show. By the same token, the plays on words in the following, much-debated passage imply the complex intertwining of moral and prudential considerations in all of Cromwell's actions:

> And *Hampton* shows what part
> He had of wiser Art.
> Where, twining subtile fears with hope,
> He wove a Net of such a scope,
> That *Charles* himself might chase
> To *Caresbrooks* narrow case.

> (ll. 47–52)

The syntax keeps us from deciding whether it is the net that hunts Charles down to Carisbrooke or whether the super-subtle King is said to 'chase' himself into what proved to be a fatal net. And it seems to me that '*Caresbrooks* narrow case' is a deliberate pun on the strait confinement in which Charles found himself at Carisbrooke and on the casement-window through which he failed to make his escape.[15] But from the approval of Cromwell's diplomatic skills Marvell moves quickly, at the suggestion of Carisbrooke's consequences, to the climactic and deservedly famous passage on the beheading of Charles. Marvell has often been praised for the brilliance of his use of stage imagery in describing the moving and momentous scene.[16] But it has not, apparently, occurred to his critics to ask whether there was any specific intent in his choice of images, other than the familiar Stoic comparison between life and the drama. The question gains a certain urgency when we realize that 'A Poem upon the Death of O.C.' begins by describing the people waiting as at a play for the properly impressive demise of their great leader, only to be disappointed when Fate can find none brave or hostile enough to dispatch Cromwell in a manner violent enough to suit his career and his ultimate position. Cromwell, in short, never comes to the stage, while Charles is seen as perfectly suited to his role. I think the underlying suggestion is that, whereas Cromwell's actions blend the deed, the thought, and the power to effect both, Charles can only act out the gestures befitting a king, since he has forfeited the true foundations of his sovereign power. Cromwell acts, but Charles is the actor, because there is no substance in his actions any longer. Nevertheless, Marvell does not minimize the grace, the heroism, and the pathetic subservience to the powers of Fate that mark Charles's last hour.

> That thence the *Royal Actor* born
> The *Tragick Scaffold* might adorn:
> While round the armed Bands
> Did clap their bloody hands.
> *He* nothing common did or mean
> Upon that memorable Scene:
>
> (ll. 53–58)

'Scaffold', of course, was the term applied both to the platform on which the execution took place and to the trestle stage used for dramatic performances in the earliest days of English church and secular drama. The pun drives home the gravity of the occasion by making clear the several different kinds of events that are subsumed in the execution. For Charles it is the ultimate personal tragedy, and his manner of meeting it is in the finest traditions of doomed heroes. In his 'role' as King, Charles represents the England that is dying with him, and none of the significance of its being a violent death is lost. In the yielding dignity of his carriage he symbolizes the helplessness of 'antient Rights' before the forces of history that he himself has helped to call into existence. There is a tragic irony in our realization that the very qualities of the monarchic system that make it an object of reverence and pity have contributed to its fate and to its passive subjection to Cromwell's vigour. The King who mounts the scaffold is not the same King who ensnared himself in nets of intrigue that far surpassed Cromwell's modest 'plots'. The tragic moment has stripped him of most of the

attributes of the wily and foolish political schemer, and left him in
the purified and symbolic garments of the sacrificial hero. In this
role he assumes the wisdom and humility that should have marked
his behaviour as a divinely ordained king, but which he forfeited
in his fated desire to maintain a power that Providence had transferred to another instrument.

> But with his keener Eye
> The Axes edge did try:
> Nor call'd the *Gods* with vulgar spight:
> To vindicate his helpless Right,
> But bow'd his comely Head,
> Down as upon a Bed.
>
> (ll. 59–64)

Margoliouth (I, p. 239) suggests the possibility of a pun on *acies*,
which means both 'eyesight' and 'blade', and Miss Wallerstein
adds to the richness of the word-play by pointing out that 'it may
be remembered further that in neo-Platonic psychology, *acies*
denotes not only the gaze of the eye, but the intention of the mind
upon the image presented to it by the imagination'.[17] In short,
Charles is shown at the last moment to be aware of the personal,
the political, and even the symbolic meanings of the fate he is about
to meet. Whether it is through assumed dignity or final resignation,
he does not plead against the destiny that has already rendered his
justification impossible. In the phrase 'his helpless Right', Marvell's
point is that in the great world of politics and national destinies
'helpless' is ultimately as important a word as 'right'. According
to the laws of providential history, Cromwell's 'vindication' is
simply in his ability to bring Charles to the block and with a blow
to sever the ancient ties that have bound king to people through the
mediation of Divine Right. Marvell's argument is that the blow
could not have been struck without the intervention of Heaven's
influence, and that it would not have been struck without
Cromwell's ordained appearance. The acceptance of this view is
reflected in the swiftly falling accents of lines 63–64, where the
homely image grimly underlines the simple grace of an act that is in
its implications bloody, revolutionary, and shatteringly important
as only great acts of state can be.

But Marvell is not distracted by the tragic drama so long that he
can forget its meaning for the visionary future of the common-

wealth: 'This was that memorable Hour/Which first assur'd the forced Pow'r' (ll. 65–66). He does not evade the fact that until Cromwell had drawn sacred blood it could not be believed that the King's right to rule was not sanctioned by Heaven; until that moment the Rebellion was an unstable and treasonous eruption in the body politic. But with the demonstration of its power it also assures it continuance. The power is 'forced' both in that it has created itself by force and in that it has been forced into dominance by the pressure of events and destiny. But the nature of political power converts the unprecedented horror of a monarch's execution into the most solid possible foundation for the new state. To illustrate the paradox Marvell once again reaches into Roman history, and again into Pliny:

> So when they did design
> The *Capitols* first Line,
> A bleeding Head where they begun,
> Did fright the Architects to run;
> And yet in that the *State*
> Foresaw it's happy Fate.
>
> (ll. 67–72)

Marvell must have enjoyed the suggestive linking of 'Capitol' with 'bleeding Head', and yet the instance is fortuitous for his poem. The 'Architects' of the Puritan Republic did indeed begin with a bleeding head, and Marvell, of all poets, is conscious of the many implications of the work of architects.[18] They must cut and shape, often destroy and distort, in order to build a structure that will last and that will conform to the abstract notion that determined it and was produced by human imagination. The architects of Parliament may well have been frightened by this first step in the construction of their Capitol, but Marvell draws further on Pliny's legend and perceives that 'King Charles's Head' is not only a good augury but the only possible foundation upon which a republic can be built. That difficult and complex perception, in effect, sums up the purpose of the poem; it also provides an answer to those critics who still would have Marvell of the King's party without admitting it. There is neither personality nor tradition in the workings of historical necessity; the appeals of the King and of the 'Kingdome old' must be ineffectual, since they are couched in terms made obsolete by the course of events.

As an instance of the 'happy Fate' promised to England by Cromwell's impersonal execution of the will of Heaven, Marvell brings in the Irish campaign, in lines that always cause some embarrassment to defenders of Marvell's sincerity and objectivity in 'An Horatian Ode':

> And now the *Irish* are asham'd
> To see themselves in one Year tam'd:
>   So much one Man can do,
>   That does both act and know.
> They can affirm his Praises best,
> And have, though overcome, confest
>   How good he is, how just,
>   And fit for highest Trust.
>
> (ll. 73–80)

With the story of Drogheda in his mind, Marvell could not have meant this as a statement of fact. His point is that if the Irish could understand the true significance of Cromwell's relentless pursuit of political and ecclesiastical stability they would, as would the divided English, acknowledge the wisdom and the power of the man who had subdued their rebelliousness. To gauge the desperation with which Marvell and other moderates looked to Cromwell to save what the Civil War had already achieved, we may read these lines in the light of G.M. Trevelyan's assessment of the state of England immediately before Cromwell's Irish campaign:

> Scotland and Ireland, and half the Colonies across the Atlantic, had proclaimed another Government. The mastery of sea was challenged: a fourth part of the war ships had revolted to the new King; and privateers harbouring in the Royalist Scilly and Channel Islands, and in the Isle of Man, preyed upon English commerce almost at the mouth of our ports. . . . The sovereigns of Europe refused to recognize a Government whose principles they abhorred and whose power they as yet despised.[19]

Cromwell's tactics in Ireland gave the *coup de grâce* to the Cavalier vision of chivalric warfare, and announced the new dispensation of the Puritan Army whose swords were implements of God's will. The rigour of Puritan belief and behaviour was applied to the suppression of rebellion and heresy, and Cromwell's policy demonstrated that the preservation of the state and Protestantism was the prime concern of the military leader. Mercy to rebels was no mercy; the massacre at Drogheda was carried out under the inspiration of the fierceness of the Lord of Vengeance.

Lest Cromwell seem to be only a natural force, unattached to and uncontrolled by political considerations, Marvell turns his attention to the picture of Cromwell as the servant of the Republic he is creating by his unparalleled martial successes. And once again the description blends allusions to the career of Julius Caesar and precepts from the core of Puritan moral doctrine:

> Nor yet grown stiffer with Command,
> But still in the *Republick's* hand:
>   How fit he is to sway
>   That can so well obey.
> He to the *Commons Feet* presents
> A *Kingdome*, for his first years rents:
>   And, what he may, forbears
>   His Fame to make it theirs:
> And has his Sword and Spoyls ungirt,
> To lay them at the *Publick's* skirt.
>
> (ll. 81–90)

In later years Cromwell will refuse the offer of kingship from the Parliament, but even here he is seen as the dutiful servant who is as obedient to the will of his party as he is subject to the commands of 'angry Heaven'. Marvell's intent is to suggest an identification between divine and human will at this point, and both meanings hinge on 'obey', since Cromwell is the prime instance of perfect obedience to both masters. The image Marvell chooses to enforce his argument combines concisely the two aspects of Cromwell he wants to illumine: his submissive obedience and his terrible latent power of execution.

> So when the Falcon high
> Falls heavy from the Sky,
> She, having kill'd, no more does search,
> But on the next green Bow to pearch;
>   Where, when he first does lure,
>   The Falckner has her sure.
>
> (ll. 91–96)

As we might expect, the terminology of falconry is used with accuracy,[20] but the overriding impression is one of lethal force that exercises itself only upon the orders of the 'Falckner'. The argument that merciless slaughter is brutal and inhuman is as irrelevant to Cromwell's acts as it is to the killing stoop of the trained bird of prey. Neither kills for self-aggrandizement or even for survival, but solely in obedience to its master's commands. The simile both excuses and justifies unyielding sternness in Ireland, and shows that his victories in the Civil War have all been in the service of the Republic and not in the chivalric tradition of individual glory.

With the ideas of Cromwell's invincible, Heaven-guided force, and his subservience to the will of the Parliament secure, Marvell goes on to form a vision of the future of England under the surveillance of this supernaturally gifted bird of prey. To give the scale of his predestined achievements the poet reaches again for classical comparisons which also point forward to the problem of foreign hostility that the new English state was beginning to face. Naturally enough, its most obvious enemies were the Catholic powers of the Continent, and the danger from without was as much to the Protestant religion as to the polity itself. Thus,

> A *Caesar* he ere long to *Gaul*,
> To *Italy* an *Hannibal*,
>   And to all States not free
>   Shall *Clymacterick* be.
>
> (ll. 101–104)

Not only will he resume the careers of the great conquerors of antiquity, but he will achieve the millennial freedom of all oppressed nations. Cromwell thus becomes the figure not only of supreme military might but also of the inevitable downfall of all tyrannical monarchies, of which his success in the Civil War is the unmistakable sign.

This larger vision resolves itself into a prophecy of victory in the Scottish campaign about to open. The 'party-colour'd Mind' of the Pict[21] will find no defence against Cromwell's 'Valour sad', since in its very sobriety it reveals its impersonal determination, against which passionate plotting cannot stand. The 'sadness' of Cromwell's courage is the indispensable temper for its 'industriousness'; together they make up the driving force of the figure who draws strength both from his inner springs of accomplishment and from his inherent submission to the will of Providence.

But the poem ends, not only on this note of admiring and relieved prediction, but with an exhortation to Cromwell:

> But thou the Wars and Fortunes Son
> March indefatigably on;
>   And for the last effect
>   Still keep thy Sword erect:
> Besides the force it has to fright
> The Spirits of the shady Night,
>   The same *Arts* that did *gain*
>   A *Pow'r* must it *maintain*.

(ll. 113–120)

The basis of this appeal is Marvell's realization that Charles had failed egregiously to maintain the foundations of his power. If kingly rule had been sanctioned by God, then the wrath of Heaven that brought Cromwell down upon the helpless Charles was a sign that the King had offended the Providence that had granted him his crown. Marvell knows that Cromwell's enterprise is unprecedented; he has created and must sustain a state full-sprung from the forces of nature, with neither tradition nor *mystique* to 'hedge' it with divinity. Not only is the Republic thus precariously balanced upon its own sources of power, but it is threatened by enemies abroad. The destructive power inherent in Cromwell's figure is a neutral force, responsive to the pressures of history, but, saving the wisdom and humility of the man himself, easily turned aside into paths that will lead again to chaos and sterility. The arts that must maintain it in the victorious and fruitful course it has followed thus far are those same skills that Cromwell has demonstrated in war, diplomacy, and the instinctive understanding of the decrees of Providence and historical necessity. Since Cromwell has shown that a state may be created without the sanctions and supports that men have always thought indispensable, he must expect no aid from traditions or concepts he has rendered obsolescent in his own career.

Marvell does not underestimate the difficulty of the task, nor the unsleeping self-control and effort that it demands. The only relief Cromwell can look to is the signs of his 'election' by Providence to begin and continue the task of creative destruction. The last lines are carefully poised in their attribution of responsibility for

Cromwell's success, so poised, in fact, that Professor Brooks discovers in them a major ambivalence.

> Cromwell is the son of the wars in that he is the master of battle, and he seems fortune's own son in the success that has constantly waited upon him. But we do not wrench the lines if we take them to say also that Cromwell is the creature of the wars and the product of fortune.[22]

We do wrench the lines, however, if we insist that these two viewpoints are contradictory or mutually exclusive. Marvell's point is precisely that events have created Cromwell's triumphant role, but that his ability to capitalize on fortune and to express the intent of history is the sign of his being chosen for greatness. The attitude taken by Brooks, the belief that fortune is a harlot and her creatures only time-serving panders, is a good deal less subtle than Marvell's political realism, and does not correspond at all with either the pagan or Christian philosophies of history that recognized the arbitrariness of Fortune's graces as well as their providential significances. Brooks is unwilling to see that a hero may truly 'embody' the purposes of history while his actions, interpreted on the cynic level of political expediency, seem no different from those of a tyrant or an intriguer. His argument denies Marvell the right to look without illusion at the reality of Cromwell's rise to power and to perceive within its curve the marks of foredestined retribution for the sins of the monarchy and the promise of a greater 'Work' to be built upon its symbolic ruins.

Cromwell is exhorted to keep his sword in the attitude of alert defence, always ready to attack the state's enemies. As Margoliouth (I, p. 239) remarks, lines 117–118 suggest the power of the crossed sword-hilt to stay evil spirits,[26] so that the sword is said to represent both military and spiritual might. It may seem a quibble, but it is hard to see how an 'erect' sword, one held with the blade up, can present the shape of the cross to the 'Spirits of the shady Night'. I think Marvell is suggesting that the naked blade itself, since its use has been sanctified by 'angry Heaven', is enough to drive back the threatening evil that surrounds the newly founded state. Furthermore, it would break the carefully maintained classical decorum of the poem to introduce a specifically Christian symbol at this point. Throughout the poem Marvell has relied on the unspoken parallelism between Fate and Christian Providence to strengthen his portrait of Cromwell's mission, but it would be quite a different thing to shatter this delicate fabric of reference by mentioning the cross, and I do not think that Marvell would be so careless.[24]

For if 'An Horatian Ode' is entitled to be described as 'notable for its combination of Horatian structure, metre and diction and . . . of Horatian attitude',[25] then Marvell must accomplish this difficult task without making use of the Christian or specifically Puritan allusions that would naturally be expected to support such an argument in favour of Cromwell. And when we say that the 'Ode' does indeed catch the flavour of Horace's addresses to Augustus, I think we mean primarily that it shares Horace's faculty for weighing out with tact and integrity the measures of praise and correction that are due the military leader from the poet who observes and estimates his achievement. Within the four books of the *Odes*, Horace's attitude toward Augustus changes from careful reserve (I, ii) to open-handed admiration that always maintains the right to remind the Emperor that a reign propped up by military force can earn such admiration only by fostering the arts that are the beneficiaries of the sword, not its dependents (IV, v). In the earlier Odes, Horace's ironic view of his role as representative of poetry and the rustic virtues of simplicity and contemplation emerges in his recurrent claim that he is unfit to sing the praises of the powerful and magnificent Empire (I, vi); but he is never reluctant to offer the kind of farsighted advice that Marvell advances in the closing lines of 'An Horatian Ode'.[26] And of course the Roman poet is profoundly aware of the ironies implicit in the shifting decrees of Fortune (I, xxxiv, xxxv); even his prayers for the success of Augustus' military exploits are coloured by his recognition of the enormous importance of fate in a career that seems by human standards to be touched with supernatural favour. Nor is Horace blind to the inevitable concomitants of military power; in his Ode to Fortune (I, xxxv), in the midst of lines presaging Augustus' victory in a campaign against Britain, he recalls himself to a vision of the mortal cost of any military conquest: *eheu, cicatricum et sceleris pudet/fratrumque*.[27] Marvell's sense of the dual responsibility of Cromwell to the nation and to Providence is paralleled, in the famous first Ode of Horace's third Book, by the passage that points to the perilous balance of imperial power:

regum timendorum in proprios greges,
reges in ipsos imperium est Iovis,
  clari Giganteo triumpho,
    cuncta supercilio moventis.[28]

The lines are set off from the rest of the Ode, which is written in praise of the simple and contented life of retirement, an idea that Marvell touches and puts away in the first eight lines of his 'Ode', but which we know to have been of paramount importance to him. Because the world of the garden had more complex and more strictly symbolic significance for Marvell than it did for the Stoic philosophy of Horace, it could never become for the English poet a true and ultimate retreat from the affairs of the world. Thus Horace maintains throughout his career a view of the course of empire that is always pure, serene, and objective, while Marvell, in the poems on Cromwell, makes a deliberate decision to abandon the imaginative life of contemplation while using its values as criteria to judge and express the life of public action.

But 'An Horatian Ode' is more intrinsically related to the poetry of Horace, not in its subjects, nor even in its inventive imitation of Horace's metres, but in the subtlety of its range of attitudes and in its ability to suggest several meaningful interpretations of an event without emphasizing any one at the expense of the others. The technique (if it can be called a technique, rather than a quality of intellect) is perhaps most apparent in the 'Cleopatra' Ode (I, xxxvii) and the 'Regulus' Ode (III, v). The poem in celebration of the defeat of Cleopatra corresponds to the movement of Marvell's poem through the scene of Charles's execution. It begins with an unrestrained paean to Augustus' victory, a victory song that includes the expected execration of the Egyptian enemy—she is called *regina . . . impotens* and her cohorts *contaminato cum grege turpium/morbo virorum.* Augustus is imaged, as was Cromwell, as a hawk or a hunter, remorseless in his pursuit of whatever endangers the safety of the state.[29] But Cleopatra's demeanour when she commits suicide rather than be exhibited in chains in Rome earns Horace's full admiration: *quae generosius/perire quaerens nec muliebriter expavit.* In death she acts out the part of the tragic hero with the same regal command of gesture that distinguished Charles's last moments. The poem ends with the recognition that Cleopatra's triumph over the fear of death and over the ignoble plans of her

Roman enemies—*non humilis mulier*—is as complete as Augustus' military victory. The worth of inner integrity and self-command is set against the worldly success of Augustus, and both are judged in the light of their incommensurability. In Marvell's poem his great effort is to make Cromwell, by the powers of metaphor and imaginative sympathy, a figure of the union of the two kinds of success and the two kinds of integrity of purpose. If 'Upon Appleton House' suffers from a lack of internal coherence it is because Marvell was not so successful there at joining the moral significances of Fairfax's idea of self and his role as a public figure. The attempt was made through the consistency of the metaphors and images, but 'Upon Appleton House' is often distracted from this particular purpose by Marvell's equally demanding questions about his own relation to the world of innocent nature and the surrounding world of political upheaval and social change.

If Fairfax's retirement had offered one answer to the debate between the advocates of action and of contemplation, Cromwell's rejection of the 'inglorious Arts of Peace' proposed another. And Cromwell's importance for Marvell, as one critic has put it, was as 'the principle of order in the midst of chaos'.[30] Whatever Marvell's nostalgia for the settled and traditional ways of pre-Revolutionary England, he could not but recognize that Charles's reign had led inescapably to an age of destructive turbulence. The institutions and ideals that had preserved England as the 'Garden of the World' had lost their validity because they had lost their substance. Marvell saw in Cromwell's principled actions, as opposed to the more radical ideas of, say, Lilburne, the hope that the destruction of the monarchy would not be carried out in a spirit of unleavened vengeance. Cromwell's consciousness of a divine mission entrusted to him by God and by the course of fate was the only thing that could promise an orderly reconstruction of the English polity. And if that order was based on a bloody revolution, Marvell was humane enough to understand that in the fallen world good, very often, could emerge only from evil, and that the evil was frequently a purgative that cleansed the world and allowed the good to establish itself. Above all such considerations was the hope that Cromwell could restore a fruitful and intelligible order to the convulsed surface of English life; his vision was the one Horace described in *Odes*, IV, xv:

custode rerum Caesare non furor
civilis aut vis exiget otium,
non ira, quae procudit enses
et miseras inimicat urbes.

'The First Anniversary of the Government under O.C.'[31] and 'A Poem upon the Death of O.C.'[32] trace the history and the ultimate character of the period *custode rerum Caesare.*

II

'The First Anniversary' must have been written during or after December 1654, but was not published (in quarto) until 1655; Cromwell died in 1658, and Marvell's poem was not published until the Folio of 1681, although it was subsequently cancelled in all copies save the unique specimen in the British Museum. When Marvell left Nunappleton in 1653 he seems also to have left behind the impulse that helped to create his best-known lyric verse; the poems written after that date revert to the heroic couplets he had used before only in the verses to Lovelace and Hastings, and in the satirical 'Fleckno'.[33] 'The Character of Holland', written most probably early in 1653, also indicates the changes or developments in Marvell's interests and poetic techniques in the first years he spent in the capital after the pastoral seclusion of Fairfax's estate. These poems point the way to his later works, such as 'The last Instructions to a Painter', 'The Loyall Scot', 'Further Advice to a Painter'—all the poems in rhymed pentameter couplets that established his long-lived reputation as a master of political satire under Charles II.

Nevertheless, the Cromwell poems still exhibit some of the typical lyrical concerns this essay has been trying to disengage from Marvell's earlier poetry. Although 'The First Anniversary of the Government under O.C.' owes more to the 'correct diction' of Denham and Waller than it does to the metaphysical style of Cowley and Donne, many of the symbols and metaphors that Marvell uses to elevate his mythic interpretation of Cromwell's reign are drawn from the same sources that had enriched his earlier verse. The first six lines are based on the paradoxical relationships between the microcosmic scale of human life and the greater scope of the evolutions of the universe.

Like the vain Curlings of the Watry maze,
Which in smooth streams a sinking Weight does raise;
So Man, declining alwayes, disappears
In the weak Circles of increasing Years;
And his short Tumults of themselves Compose,
While flowing Time above his Head does close.

(ll. 1–6)

Man grows 'weak' as his years 'increase', and the point of the metaphor is that Cromwell alone imitates the planets and the cycles of history by growing stronger and more brilliant with each return. Where, in 'The Garden' and in 'To his Coy Mistress', Marvell had once imagined the human mind or passions achieving victory over Time by concentrating all experience into one point of transcendent meaning, now "Tis he the force of scatter'd Time contracts,/And in one Year the work of Ages acts' (ll. 13–14). On the surface, this refers to the completion of Cromwell's first year of successful government, but 'the work of Ages' recalls 'the great Work of Time' that he had been forced to 'ruine' in 'An Horatian Ode'. Now Marvell is assessing the structure Cromwell has raised upon those ruins, and he finds it more stable and more perfect than any of the famous works of 'heavy Monarchs'. The year during which all this has been done is an image of the Platonic Great Year (which is mentioned in line 17), the time-span in which the heavenly bodies were thought to complete one journey around their orbits, and which represented a kind of millennial vision for the classical world and for many poets of the Renaissance.

By contrast, the kings whom Cromwell has replaced are vilified for their petty deeds in a diction that clearly heralds the antithetical analyses of Pope:

Another triumphs at the publick Cost,
And will have Wonn, if he no more have Lost;
They fight by Others, but in Person wrong,
And only are against their Subjects strong.

(ll. 25–28)

The strongest protest raised against these arrogant and futile monarchs is that 'They neither build the Temple in their dayes,/Nor Matter for succeeding Founders raise' (ll. 33–34), and in both 'An Horatian Ode' and in this poem Cromwell is credited with the

combination of piety and constructive energy that can accomplish
both these tasks. The kings are compared to the hollow figures that
strike a meaningless music on an ornate clock; they are 'wooden
Heads unto the Viols strings' (l. 44), in an image that adds blunt
satirical humour to a conceit that will now be applied to Cromwell
and expanded to accommodate a mythological dimension.

> While indefatigable *Cromwell* hyes,
> And cuts his way still nearer to the Skyes,
> Learning a Musique in the Region clear,
> To tune this lower to that higher Sphere.   (ll. 45–48)

The symbolic value of the 'music of the Spheres' needs no comment,
except to say that it was as often used as an image of political
concord as it was to figure universal metaphysical harmony.
Cromwell's peculiar ability is to 'tune' the elements of the polity
to the harmony announced by Heaven; he does this by the 'wiser
Art' of political skill that distinguishes him from the greedy and
ineffectual kings Marvell has just dismissed. The musical metaphor
summons up almost inevitably the comparison with Amphion,
the legendary hero who built Thebes by charming stones and
bricks to fall into place by the beauty of his music. Marvell's
version of the Amphion myth, as applied to Cromwell, shows his
habitual technique of introducing witty topical references into an
epic simile that would ordinarily be used only to heighten the
tone of a political panegyric.

> So when *Amphion* did the Lute command,
> Which the God gave him, with his gentle hand,
> The rougher Stones, unto his Measures hew'd,
> Dans'd up in order from the Quarreys rude;
> This took a Lower, that an Higher place,
> As he the Treble alter'd, or the Base:
> No Note he struck, but a new Story lay'd,
> And the great Work ascended while he play'd.
>
> (ll. 49–56)

In effect, this is a general description of Cromwell's procedures
after his becoming Protector at the dissolution of the Barebones
Parliament in December 1653 and during the first months of the
first Protectorate Parliament. His major political problem was to
reconcile the dissenting parties within Parliament and to preserve

the military power in his own hands lest disagreement bring on again political chaos. The musical terms—'Measures', 'order', 'Treble', 'Base'—are apt images for Cromwell's attempts to shape the governing body to his purposes, and for his attempt to manage the differing classes of representatives in some degree of concord. This architect 'hews' with a 'gentle hand', but in the light of 'Upon Appleton House', l. 3, and 'A Dialogue between the Soul and Body', ll. 43–44, it is clear that Marvell, although writing a poem of unabashed praise, is never forgetful of the necessary costs, waste, and even cruelty that attend any act of political creation. Nevertheless, he gives his approval to Cromwell's attempts and to his accomplishments, and the phrase 'the great Work' appears again as if in earnest of his faith in Cromwell's sincerity. The entire passage is tied off in the famous pun in lines 67–68: 'Such was that wondrous Order and Consent,/When *Cromwell* tun'd the ruling Instrument'; where, while the musical metaphor is maintained and brought to a climax, Marvell also puns on the 'Instrument of Government', the constitutional act of Parliament that granted Cromwell his powers as Protector in 1653. The punning lines precede a long expository digression on the composition of the state, wherein the rebellious and intractable elements are variously compared to the components of a building. The scope of Cromwell's heroic task is indicated by the cynically severe question, 'All other Matter yields, and may be rul'd;/But who the Minds of stubborn Men can build?' (ll. 77–78). The answer is, of course, that Cromwell has surpassed even Amphion in discovering the 'art' that will charm men into composing their differences within an orderly political structure.

Although Amphion was often taken as the image of the founder of civilized institutions, it is instructive to look at Waller's version of the myth in 'Upon His Majesty's Repairing of Paul's', written to commemorate the project begun by Charles I to restore the Cathedral. (Ironically enough, the work was never completed because of the eruption of the first Civil War.) Waller makes the accepted comparison in these terms:

> He, like Amphion, makes those quarries leap
> Into fair figures from a confused heap;
> For in his art of regiment is found
> A power like that of harmony in sound. (ll. 11–14)

The metaphor is the same as Marvell's, and musical skill is equated with the art of governing recalcitrant materials. But in comparison to Marvell's extended play upon the idea of harmony as an ordering principle for the state, Waller's 'A power like that of harmony in sound' is disappointingly flat; it neither varies nor ramifies the conceit, nor does it find any more comprehensive significance in the analogy. Clearly, Charles I is described as another Amphion only to lend the aura of legendary deeds to a poem of court flattery.

This is not to deny that 'The First Anniversary' is flattery too; but the Horatian cast of Marvell's mind would not permit him to control his powers of invention in submission to what was rarely a fertile convention. From the image of Cromwell as supreme architect he passes to the suggestive image of a ruling planet, in a way that recalls the elemental force of the military scourge in 'An Horatian Ode':

> And in his sev'ral Aspects, like a Star,
> Here shines in Peace, and thither shoots a War.
> While by his Beams observing Princes steer,
> And wisely court the Influence they fear.
>
> (ll. 101–104)

The initial metaphor of the poem, the reference to the circling powers of the heavens, is maintained throughout most of its 402 lines; Cromwell will be characterized, naturally enough, as the sun, and will always stand for the serene and constant 'influence' that governs human destinies. But in this passage the analogy is meant to show that the perfection of Cromwell's character is revealed in his faculty for subsuming many opposed qualities in a transcendent sphere of power. Just as a musical harmony unites the treble and the bass, so Cromwell rationalizes the joint powers of peace and war, and reconciles the low and high estates in Parliament. Petty princes (and we are given a catalogue of them and their sins in lines 105–116) dissipate their forces in incoherent folly; and in a passage unique in his poetry, Marvell promises to chasten and instruct them 'once with graver Accents' (l. 121), 'Like the shrill Huntsman that prevents the East,/Winding his Horn to Kings that chase the Beast' (ll. 123–124). Marvell never did compose the 'graver Accents', but long after Cromwell's death deprived him of the inspiration for his self-imposed mission, his verse satires and his vigorous Parliamentary activities continued to be devoted to the exposure and the correction of the abuses of Charles II's reign. His simile is a precise and complicated characterization of his role as the poet of Cromwell's glory. His clarion warnings sound before the approach of Cromwell, the Sun; and Cromwell is now the true King that hunts the Beast of dissension and religious intolerance,[34] rather than the wily Charles I who 'chased' himself into '*Caresbrooks* narrow case' in his double role of huntsman and hunted. The 'Beast' is primarily a reference to the Catholic Church, although the subject of lines 105–108 is the vision of the Fifth Monarchy as adumbrated in the Book of Daniel and Revelation. The fall of the 'Beast' will usher in the rule of the Saints, a concept peculiarly appropriate to the early Parliaments of the Protectorate.

But the apocalyptic vision is only the metaphoric basis of this part of the poem; the surface diction still follows the prophecy of a time when 'High Grace should meet in one with highest Pow'r' (l. 132), terms that were used to describe Cromwell in 'An Horatian Ode'. Such an event would 'precipitate the latest Day' (l. 140) and fulfil in England all the promises of retribution and salvation at the Day of Judgment. Until this is proved by the direct intervention of Heaven, men can only guess at the commandments of Providence; and, as Marvell has shown in 'An Horatian Ode', the man best equipped to precipitate the Apocalypse is he

> Who in his Age has always forward prest:
> And knowing not where Heavens choice may light,
> Girds yet his Sword, and ready stands to fight.
>
> (ll. 146–148)

Cromwell is once again characterized as the 'world-historical' figure who is most able to interpret the course of history because he is ready to respond to its demands and wise enough to understand them. Most men stand 'unconcern'd, or unprepar'd' for the climactic moment of human history; and in describing the suspended condition of the fallen world, Marvell echoes Milton's 'Nativity Ode'.[35]

Cromwell alone has preserved himself from the state of sinful ignorance, and after some lines in praise of Cromwell's 'Saint-like' mother, Marvell embarks on a passage of fifty lines or so that elevates the incident of Cromwell's overturning his coach in Hyde Park in September 1654 into an occurrence of universal significance.

'Our Sins' are held responsible for the accident in lines that allude to the biblical Fall and to the Platonic myth of the unruly passions yoked and driven by the charioteer, Reason.

> How near they fail'd, and in thy sudden Fall
> At once assay'd to overturn us all.
> Our brutish fury strugling to be Free,
> Hurry'd thy Horses while they hurry'd thee.
>
> (ll. 175–178)

Miss Bradbrook suggests that the entire passage is tempered with an ironic awareness of its own exaggerations,[36] but this, if true, does not lessen the gravity that Marvell attaches to the possibility of Cromwell's violent death while his great work is still unfinished. He measures this gravity by reverting to the diction of his pastoral and philosophical poetry; and it is also interesting to see how within eight lines Marvell passes from symbolic statements that echo Milton to balanced observations that have both the precision and the conscious humour of Pope.

> Thou *Cromwell* falling, not a stupid Tree,
> Or Rock so savage, but it mourn'd for thee:
> And all about was heard a Panique groan,
> As if that Natures self were overthrown.
> It seem'd the Earth did from the Center tear;
> It seem'd the Sun was faln out of the Sphere:
> Justice obstructed lay, and Reason fool'd;
> Courage disheartned, and Religion cool'd.
>
> (ll. 201–208)

The thought of Cromwell's narrow escape from death urges Marvell to a reconsideration of the Protector's career, and what he chooses first to comment on is precisely the difficulty and the significance of the choice between retirement and public office that had been so important in 'An Horatian Ode'. In the mode of his earlier metaphysical poems, Marvell analyses Cromwell's decision in a diction made up primarily of paradoxes:

> For all delight of Life thou then didst lose,
> When to Command, thou didst thy self Depose;
> Resigning up thy Privacy so dear,
> To turn the headstrong Peoples Charioteer;
> For to be *Cromwell* was a greater thing,
> Then ought below, or yet above a King:
> Therefore thou rather didst thy Self depress,
> Yielding to Rule, because it made thee Less.
>
> (ll. 221–228)

The elements of opposition between self and nation are clearly outlined, as is the importance of wise obedience as a sign of fitness to command. What is interesting is the suggestion that selflessness is the surest way to greatness, a thought that dominates Marvell's poems on Cromwell and on Fairfax, although the two men chose different ways to achieve the control of self. Cromwell subordinated his desire for solitude (in Marvell's characterization) while Fairfax rejected the public fame that he had earned; and both men were guiding their actions by loyalty to their inmost principles.

Cromwell's choice is confirmed by the forces of Heaven and of Nature; in line 234 he appears upon the horizon as a small cloud, that grows to be a storm that drowns the King in line 238. 'An higher Force' (l. 239) pushes him on to the great work of restoring the collapsed state; yet it is his innate wisdom that guides him in 'Here pulling down, and there erecting New,/Founding a firm State by Proportions true' (ll. 247–248). Creation is always an instance of destroying one thing to find a place for a new and better one; and Cromwell's architecture, we notice, is based on the principles of just measure that were propounded at the beginning of 'Upon Appleton House'.

Then, for seventy lines Marvell pursues a meandering course of biblical allusion, Lucretian similes, and vicious animadversions on religious and secular radicalism (particularly the Fifth Monarchy Men) before he finds an image adequate to the meaning of Cromwell's restoration to health and safety. The long simile that extends from line 325 to line 342 compares the nation's relief to that felt by primitive man when frightened by the inexplicable disappearance of the sun, only to be enlightened the following morning 'When streight the Sun behind him he descry'd,/Smiling serenely from the further side' (ll. 341–342). The situation of what

Miss Bradbrook calls 'the preposterous savage'[37] is implicitly compared to the rudimentary state of the new Republic, and the bewildered ignorance in which Marvell pretends the English people is left by Cromwell's apparent death is a sign of how necessary his rule is, as is the sun to the earth, to the life and prosperity of the nation.[38] Marvell underscores Cromwell's indispensable virtues in the imaginary speech of the 'credulous Ambassador' who represents the nations stricken with awe at Cromwell's invincible power. The speech again reveals a diction which shares equally the manner of Cowley and the manner of Pope. Foreign luxury and idleness is indirectly portrayed: "Yet rig a Navy while we dress us late;/'And ere we Dine, rase and rebuild their State' (ll. 351–352); yet the Ambassador adapts some of Marvell's own ideas, although he phrases them differently:

> 'He seems a King by long Succession born,
> 'And yet the same to be a King does scorn.
> 'Abroad a King he seems, and something more,
> 'At Home a Subject on the equal Floor.
>
> (ll. 387–390)

The tone of English chauvinism is at its best touched with this kind of humour, whether it is directed against the European enemy as in *Henry V*, or whether its target is the excesses of native Englishmen who ape Continental manners, as in *The Rape of the Lock*. And it is curious to see that under the Tudors, the Stuarts, the Protectorate, or the House of Hanover, the basic standards of English 'taste' remain relatively uniform in the minds of the poets— simplicity, utility, native vigour, and directness. As a hero and as the epitome of national strength, Cromwell is not so much a Puritan anomaly as an equal of Henry V, Sir Lucius Cary, and Pope's Burlington.

Marvell ends 'The First Anniversary' on a note of feigned modesty as he pretends to let the startled Ambassador speak more eloquently of Cromwell's excellences than he himself can. But the final simile is audacious in its biblical reference, since he compares Cromwell to the angel who troubled the waters, but also credits him with the power to smooth over the turbulence. The simile is far-fetched, but its purpose is to emphasize once more the absolute necessity of suffering pain and disruption if a new and worthwhile creation is to emerge.

Cromwell died on September 3, 1658, the anniversary of his victories at Dunbar and Worcester. Marvell's 'A Poem upon the Death of O.C.' is, more than 'The First Anniversary', a mixture of his best metaphysical techniques, confused sequences of images and subjects, and hackneyed terms of elegiac praise. In this respect it is a less considerable poem, perhaps, than Dryden's 'Heroique Stanzas' or Waller's 'Upon the Late Storm, and of the Death of His Highness Ensuing the Same'. But what is good in the 'Death of O.C.' is marked not only by Marvell's undiminished ability to perceive and express correspondences between individual events and their abstract meanings, but also by the sincerity and depth of his sense of catastrophe. I do not refer to the famous lines on Cromwell's face in death (ll. 247–253), since it is almost impossible to show *how* Marvell's evident personal grief informs those lines (although I do not doubt that it does). Rather, the attitude Marvell takes toward the implications of Cromwell's death deserves to be compared with Donne's stance in the 'Anniversaries'. Although both poets say much that is not meant to be understood literally, and although much of the diction tends to be hyperbolic because of the decorum of the philosophical elegy, the reach of the hyperboles does not go beyond what each poet saw as the emblematic significance of the death of Elizabeth Drury or Oliver Cromwell. The verses of Dryden and Waller are 'correct', but perfunctory; Waller, indeed, does little more than conjure up flat analogies to Hercules and Romulus, and make reference to the storm that coincided with Cromwell's death. But then, a year later Waller wrote 'To the King: Upon His Majesty's Happy Return', Dryden wrote 'Astraea Redux', and Marvell, completing his first year as M.P. for Hull, had embarked on his long late career of excoriating the court of Charles II in a manner that recalls the venom of Milton's lines in Book VII of *Paradise Lost*. It is useless to speculate on the motives and the thoughts that lay behind the actions of many poets who, in the middle years of the seventeenth century, changed their political allegiance with regularity. Our only explanation for Marvell's own shift in loyalty from the monarchy to Cromwell must be extrapolated from poems that often deal explicitly with quite different matters. And yet we can discern a definite continuity of thought and feeling in poems of the most diverse genres. Marvell's strong attraction for political institutions that respect the values of tradition and inheritance is paralleled by the frequent appearance in his verse of images and concepts that emphasize perfection, purity, stasis, circularity rather than the flux and variousness of the world. The nature of impermanence is not ignored in his poetry; quite to the contrary, it is usually presented in a strenuous dialectical relationship with the opposite values of abstract perfection. But even though Marvell gives the world full value in his poetic universe, it is the white light of the crystalline heavens that illuminates his most important ideas.

'A Poem upon the Death of O.C.' is, in a way, a long farewell to the poems that have been the primary concern of this essay. The remainder of Marvell's poetic corpus was almost entirely satirical, and almost entirely written in closed pentameter couplets crammed with topical allusions and pointed antitheses. His entrance into the House of Commons in 1659 marked the beginning of the last third of his lifetime, nineteen years that would see him involved not only in the minutiae of Parliamentary representation but in the free-for-all slanging-matches that passed for theological debates after the Restoration. In effect, he chose with Cromwell to leave his 'private Gardens' for the exigencies of the great world of affairs. And although the later satires and the prose works as well show the marks of the same intellect that conceived 'The Garden' and 'A Dialogue Between The Resolved Soul, and Created Pleasure', they never again attain the timeless freedom of speculation and image-making that is the essence of those poems.

'The Death of O.C.' begins with one of those wide-ranging allusions that are typical of the early poems:

> That Providence which had so long the care
> Of *Cromwell's* head, and numbered ev'ry hair,
> Now in its self (the Glass where all appears)
> Had seen the period of his golden Years.
>
> (ll. 1–4)

The biblical personification modulates swiftly into a figure of self-contemplation, and then into a reference to the finite limit of an apparently perfect time. The different parts of the trope are not well articulated, so that the idea of Providence reflecting itself does not come naturally from the Scriptural notion of a benevolent and protective spirit. But the lines serve to remind Marvell's audience that in death, as in life, Cromwell's destiny has been in the hands of a supernatural power. And his audience is very much in Marvell's mind, as we see in the following lines that describe the populace as a sensation-seeking mob that admires only what it fears: 'And blame the last *Act*, like *Spectators* vain,/Unless the *Prince* whom they applaud be slain' (ll. 9–10). Any reading of 'The Death of O.C.' gains in depth from the memory of 'An Horatian Ode'. In that poem the 'armed Bands/Did clap their bloody hands' when the '*Royal Actor*' mounted the scaffold; but now the people are scorned for demanding that the death of their Prince be equal to the dramatic traditions of violence and extravagance. The point is, of course, that Charles's execution was just and the King truly an actor because he had forfeited the substance of kingship and retained only its trappings. Marvell introduces the stage-image in order to show the difference between the two central figures, and also to show the eternal incomprehension of the easily swayed mob. He is not really interested in carrying the figure further, since he abandons it at once by explaining that Cromwell has left no living enemies and no one else who is willing to perform the ritual execution. His career is justified once more when Marvell calls him 'he whom Nature all for Peace had made,/But angry Heaven unto War had sway'd' (ll. 15–16), and the direct echo of 'An Horatian Ode' in line 16 must have been intentional. Given a figure who has so skilfully compounded the arts of creative industry and spiritual growth, Marvell can only pretend that '*Love* and *Grief*' are the sole forces in the universe that will consent to mark the 'period of his golden Years'. The personifications are the elements of Cromwell's relationship to his daughter Elizabeth, who died less than a month before her father. The coincidence, and Cromwell's undoubted love for his daughter, give Marvell the occasion for a long digression on the nurture of Elizabeth, the close ties between father and daughter, and their simultaneous decline as they grieved for each other's illnesses. But where Elizabeth is compared to Scylla, or perhaps Atropos, Cromwell is described in diction that again recalls his early career as pictured in 'An Horatian Ode': 'And now his Life, suspended by her breath,/Ran out impetuously to hasting Death' (ll. 71–72). But matched with this energy is Cromwell's compassion, which is compared to the emblematic birds of softness and sacrifice, the swan, the halcyon, and the pelican. These comparisons give way to an extended simile in which Cromwell is likened to a vine that cheers men by giving of its blood (wine), but which, when a branch is cut off prematurely, withers and dies in sympathy. The possibility of Christian allusions in the mentions of the vine and the pelican is subdued, but sufficiently apparent so that it contributes to the sense of Cromwell's selfless, sacrificial spirit.

There is no transition at all to the passage that follows, which deals with the prophetic storm that signalled Cromwell's death. Marvell refers to a venerable tradition, that momentous events are always heralded by unusual occurrences in nature: 'A secret Cause does sure those Signs ordain/Fore boding Princes falls, and seldom vain' (ll. 101–102), a concept that illuminates the irony in lines 4–8 of 'The Mower to the Glo-Worms'. But in Cromwell's death Nature has found a catastrophe worthy of her most extreme upheavals; the aberrations in the natural scene that Marvell recounts are more like those in Calpurnia's speech in *Julius Caesar*, II, ii, than they are like the lines on Cromwell's accidental spill in 'The First Anniversary'. There Marvell had characterized the shock in terms more appropriate to the scene of the Fall in *Paradise Lost*, *IX*; but here the reaction to the death of the Lord Protector is seen in natural phenomena that leave their accustomed courses. And the 'huge Trees, whose growth with his did rise' (l. 119) remind us not only of the groves in 'Upon Appleton House' but of the consistent reference, throughout the three Cromwell poems, to Cromwell as a principle of growth as well as a principle of order.

The dying hero stands, however, outside this wild disorder in nature; he becomes again a celestial body and

> without noise still travell'd to his End,
> As silent Suns to meet the Night descend.
> The *Stars* that for him fought had only pow'r
> Left to determine now his fatal Hour.
>
> (ll. 135–138)

The beauty of line 136 can be accounted for, perhaps, by the fact that in comparison to the image in lines 325–352 of 'The First Anniversary' this descent is to be Cromwell's last. It is much to Marvell's purpose that the day of his death should be the anniversary of two of his most famous victories, since this constitutes almost factual evidence that history means to immortalize Cromwell and his deeds. Marvell adds commemorative praises by mentioning Cromwell's military victories and his success in extending Britain's empire. Yet even these, most memorable in the world's mind, are less important than the religious spirit in which the acts were done.

> He first put Armes into *Religions* hand,
> And tim'rous *Conscience* unto *Courage* man'd:
> The Souldier taught that inward Mail to wear,
> And *fearing God* how they should *nothing fear.*
> Those Strokes he said will pierce through all below
> Where those that strike from Heaven fetch their Blow.
>
> (ll. 179–184)

The language is that of Bunyan and Milton's prose writings, although it is Puritan only in its typical linking of warfare and faith, while its most evident inspiration is Christian, even biblical. The mention of his Christian virtues leads to a discourse on his universal compassion, and on the excessive degree to which he suffered for the ignorant sins of those he governed. The passage reaches its climax in lines that might well have come from one of Donne's 'Anniversaries':

> Valour, religion, friendship, prudence dy'd
> At once with him, and all that's good beside;
> And we death's refuse nature's dregs confin'd
> To loathsome life, alas! are left behind.
>
> (ll. 227–230)

It is typical of the poem's general unevenness that this precedes a dozen couplets of conventional comparisons and awkwardly-phrased lamentation. But these are followed by the well-known lines:

> I saw him dead, a leaden slumber lyes,
> And mortal sleep over those wakefull eyes:
> Those gentle rays under the lids were fled,
> Which through his looks that piercing sweetnesse shed;
> That port which so majestique was and strong,
> Loose and depriv'd of vigour, stretch'd along.
>
> (ll. 247–252)

The melancholy regularity of the verse controls the deliberate antitheses, which serve rather to intensify the sense of living force transmuted into hollow effigy. Nevertheless, Marvell's innate tact seems to have left him momentarily, since he is capable of writing, within three lines, these Shelleyan inanities: 'Oh! humane glory,

vaine, oh! death, oh! wings,/ Oh! worthlesse world! oh transitory
things!' (ll. 255–256). Once he has discharged his grief thus
rhetorically, he returns to the firmer ground (for Marvell) of the
emblematic simile. And, as he has done so often, he chooses the
'sacred oak' as the most expressive symbol for Cromwell, because
it spans the distance between heaven and the earth and because it is
the special tree of heroes. He cannot ignore the fact that even the
oak may be struck down by 'Jove' when its 'period' has come, but
he finds that in that fatal stroke

> (It groanes, and bruises all below that stood
> So many yeares the shelter of the wood.)
> The tree ere while foreshortned to our view,
> When fall'n shews taller yet than as it grew:
> So shall his praise to after times encrease,
> When truth shall be allow'd, and faction cease.
>
> (ll. 267–272)

Marvell reminds his audience that the fall of a tree endangers those
it has sheltered, and then, continuing the metaphor, he converts
an optical paradox into an image of Cromwell's growing fame and
vindication by posterity. The paradox is valid not only in this
particular instance, but it is also related to the many similar paradoxes in the Cromwell and Fairfax poems that insist that abnegation,
humility, and obedience are the keys to supreme power and supreme
achievement.

In lines that recall Henry V's 'St Crispin's Day' speech, Marvell
envisions the future when English soldiers will repeat Cromwell's
name and the stories of his campaigns as encitements to battle.
Meanwhile, Cromwell is enthroned among the great warriors and
leaders of the Old Testament—an idea that was appropriate to the
common rhetoric of Puritan tracts and sermons, suited the picture of
Cromwell as the archetypal English soldier, and avoided the
possibility of offence and blasphemy if the comparisons were to
be made to Christ. In this passage the poem approaches the norm
of the seventeenth-century panegyric style; and as it turns first to the
bereaved state and then to the hopeful reign of Richard Cromwell
it loses vitality and interest with accumulating speed. The praise of
Richard sounds as perfunctory as did Waller's lines on Oliver,
and we have a right to the suspicion that Marvell knew full well
that his optimistic prophecies were doomed to prove untrue. For

even the forced optimism is tempered by the realization that Richard was a lesser creature than his father, that, as compared to the tempest in 'The First Anniversary' (ll. 234–238) that Oliver raised to sweep away the monarchy, Richard 'threats no deluge, yet foretells a showre' (l. 324). Thus Cromwell's unprecedented career ends in the most pathetic anticlimax, and the moment passes when Marvell could write poetry on ostensibly political themes that could yet engage his deepest interests and his most expressive poetic skills. It was undoubtedly the character of Oliver Cromwell that drew from Marvell the imaginative effort that went to create the complex and allusive moral world of these three poems. At least it seems that Marvell could not and would not write as mechanically as a laureate upon passing events. But the public occasion that he could make his own, in which he could perceive the implications he loved to seek out of dialectic intricacy and symbolic weight— this kind of event elicited the slightly marred grandeur of the Cromwell poems. His later satires also respond to occasions, but they deal with them only with the weapons of wit and analytical intellect. In the years before and during the Protectorate Marvell saw in revolutionary politics the opportunity to exercise the full range of his imagination. As the contemplative mind remained the central symbol of the 'garden-State', the heroic figure of Cromwell was the core of the political poems; the two were united always by the image of the green, growing tree, that sacred oak whose roots were deep in the life of earth but whose emblematic crown reached to the heavens.

Notes

1 Margoliouth, op. cit., I, 87–90.
2 See Margoliouth, 1, pp. 236–237; Legouis, *Andrew Marvell*, p. 18.
3 G. Walton, *Metaphysical to Augustan* (Bowes & Bowes, 1955), p. 14.
4 J. F. Carens, 'Andrew Marvell's Cromwell Poems', *Bucknell Review*, VII, 1 (May, 1957), pp. 41–70.
5 G. N. Shuster, *The English Ode from Milton to Keats* (Columbia University Press, 1940), p. 81.
6 The initial statement was made by Cleanth Brooks in 'Literary Criticism', in *English Institute Essays: 1946* (New York, 1947), pp. 127–158. His idea was that Marvell's lines on Cromwell were ironic and disguised a deeper sympathy with the cause of Charles I. Douglas Bush, in 'Marvell's "Horatian Ode"', *Sewanee Review*, LX, 3 (September, 1952), pp. 363–376, answered by showing that a failure to appreciate

historical significances and apparent ignorance of contemporary usages had combined to mislead Brooks into giving a false account of the poem. The debate soon left the specific issues of Marvell's poem and branched out to consider the relative claims of historical and ontological criticism. Unfortunately, the questions raised were never settled decisively, although they continue to assert their importance for literary studies, especially of the English Renaissance.

7 In fact we cannot claim for Marvell even the introduction of this metre into English. Among those who have noticed Sir Richard Fanshawe's translations of Horace into this metre, see W. Simeone, 'A Probable Antecedent of Marvell's Horatian Ode', *NQ*, CXCVII, 14 (July 1952), pp. 316–318; in 'A Study of Marvell's Horatian Ode', an unpublished doctoral dissertation (Syracuse University, 1956), W. R. Orwen points out that Fanshawe's work was finished as early as 1647, although it was not published until 1652.

8 See J. A. Mazzeo, 'Cromwell as Machiavellian Prince in Marvell's "An Horatian Ode"', *JHI*, XXI, 1 (January–March 1960), pp. 1–17.

9 The 'active Star' is of course a reference to the influential planet said to rule a human life in pagan philosophy and in medieval and Renaissance astrology. There are also correspondences between Marvell's lines on the execution of Charles I and Lucan's narration of the death of Pompey. The parallels among Marvell, Lucan, and May's translation have been noted exhaustively in Mr Orwen's dissertation (above, note 7), and I do not intend to rehearse them here. The interesting problem they pose is that both Cromwell and Charles are seen by Marvell as examples of 'Caesarism'. Comparisons between the King and Caesar are a commonplace in the Renaissance. For only one example, see Herrick, 'To the King. Upon his welcome to Hampton-Court': 'Welcome, *Great Cesar*, welcome now you are,/As dearest Peace, after destructive Warre'; *Poetical Works*, p. 300.

10 Cf. 'An Elegy upon King Charles the First, murdered publicly by his Subjects', ll. 69–71: 'And thus his soul, of this her triumph proud,/Broke like a flash of lightning through the cloud/Of flesh and blood'; Saintsbury, II, pp. 92–94. This poem was long thought to be by Cleveland, but the attribution has been rejected by his latest editors; see *Poems*, xxxvii.

11 See Pliny, *Natural History*, XV, xl (Loeb edition, p. 379). In Philemon Holland's translation (1601): 'Of those things which growe out of the Earth,/Lightning blasteth not the Laurell tree'.

12 Cromwell's gardens must be understood to be more symbolic than actual, since his activities as squire and M.P. during his Cambridgeshire days were neither reserved nor austere.

13 See W. R. Orwen, 'Marvell's "Bergamot"', *NQ*, N.S. II, 8 (August

1955), pp. 340–341. Orwen cites John Bodaeus' commentary on Theophrastus' *Historia Plantarum* (1644).

14 See Margoliouth (I, pp. 238–239) for modern opinions that do not accept the story. Robert Paul, *The Lord Protector* (Lutterworth, 1955), pp. 152–153, lists Flecknoe, Carrington, and Henry Fletcher as contemporary authors who believed as Marvell did, however.

15 See S. R. Gardiner, *History of the Great Civil War*. 4 vols. (London, 1894) IV, pp. 91–94. W. R. Orwen, 'Marvell's "Narrow Case" ', *NQ* N.S. II, 5 (May 1955), p. 201, has a note on this passage.

16 It is doubtful that he witnessed the execution, but his description of Charles's demeanour accords with many contemporary accounts. See, for example, *The Trial of Charles I*, ed. R. Lockyer (London, 1959); E. Momigliano, *Cromwell*, trans. L. E. Marshall (Hodder & Stoughton, 1930), p. 282; Sir Philip Warwick, *Memoires of the reigne of King Charles I* (London, 1701), p. 385; E. Warburton, *Memoirs of Prince Rupert and the Cavaliers*. 3 vols. (London, 1849), III, p. 400. However, Marvell's mention of the soldiers applauding, although it adds a grim note to the scene, appears to have no basis in fact.

17 *Studies in Seventeenth-Century Poetic*, p. 179.

18 See 'A Dialogue between the Soul and Body', ll. 43–44.

19 G. M. Trevelyan, *England Under the Stuarts*, 2nd ed. rev. (Methuen, 1949), pp. 244–245.

20 Cf. *The Rehearsal Transpros'd*, Grosart, III, pp. 115–116.

21 There is a similar pun on the derivation of Pict from *pingere* in Cleveland's 'The Rebell Scot', a poem that Marvell certainly knew, as we can see from his 'The Loyall Scot'. Bitter jokes at the expense of Scots treachery and cunning were fashionable in the 1640s and 1650s.

22 'Literary Criticism', in *English Institute Essays: 1946*, p. 149.

23 L. D. Lerner, in an essay on the 'Horatian Ode' included in *Interpretations*, ed. J. Wain (Routledge & Kegan Paul, 1955), pp. 59–74, suggests that Cromwell may be subject to bad dreams. He does not explain how the sword should be handled in this case.

24 See E. E. Duncan-Jones, 'The Erect Sword in Marvell's *Horatian Ode*', *Études Anglaises*, XV, 1 (1962), pp. 172–174.

25 Wallerstein, *Seventeenth-Century Poetic*, p. 156. See also J. S. Coolidge, 'Marvell and Horace', *MP*, LXIII (1965), pp. 111–120.

26 Cf. Horace, *Odes*, I, xiv.

27 Horace, *Odes*, I, xxxv, ll. 33–34.

28 Horace, *Odes*, III, i, ll. 5–8.

29 Cf. ll. 16–20, and 'An Horatian Ode', ll. 47–52, ll. 91–94.

30 Carens, 'Andrew Marvell's Cromwell Poems', p. 53.

31 Margoliouth, I, pp. 103–113.

32 Margoliouth, I, pp. 123–131.

33 There is some question whether 'Tom May's Death' was written in 1650 or in 1661, at the time of the exhumation of May's body. See Margoliouth, I, pp. 239–240.

34 Cf. ll. 111–114. See J. M. Wallace, 'Andrew Marvell and Cromwell's Kingship: "The First Anniversary" ', *ELH*, XXX (1963), pp. 209–235; and J. A. Mazzeo, 'Cromwell as Davidic King', *Reason and the Imagination: Studies in the History of Ideas, 1600–1800* (Routledge, 1962), pp. 29–55.

35 Cf. Marvell: 'and still the Dragons Tail/Swinges the Volumes of its horrid Flail' (ll. 151–152) and Milton: 'th'old Dragon . . . Swinges the scaly Horror of his folded tail' (ll. 168, 172).

36 *Andrew Marvell*, p. 79: 'The repetition [in line 178] is the first break in the rhythmic gravity; but if the last four personifications stand for Cromwell as the Sun does, the verbs are impolite enough, and the last suggests a sousing'.

37 *Andrew Marvell*, p. 80.

38 Cf. ll. 331–332 and 'Upon the Death of Lord Hastings', ll. 41–46.

Index